W9-AYD-969

In Memory of Akram Midani,
Dean, College of Fine Arts,
Carnegie Mellon University

PITTSBURGH FILMMAKERS LIBRARY
10002703

DATE DUE			

PN 1998.A2 M38
ΜEN WHO MADE THE MOVIES, THE
Schickel, Richard
:

THE MEN WHO
MADE THE MOVIES

Books by Richard Schickel

THE MEN WHO MADE THE MOVIES

INTERVIEWS WITH *Frank Capra, George Cukor, Howard Hawks, Alfred Hitchcock, Vincente Minnelli, King Vidor, Raoul Walsh,* AND *William A. Wellman*

BY RICHARD SCHICKEL

NEW YORK 1975 *Atheneum*

COPYRIGHT © 1975 BY THE EDUCATIONAL BROADCASTING CORPORATION
ALL RIGHTS RESERVED
LIBRARY OF CONGRESS CATALOG CARD NUMBER 74-77858
ISBN 0-689-10631-9
PUBLISHED SIMULTANEOUSLY IN CANADA BY MCCLELLAND AND STEWART LTD.
PRINTED BY THE MURRAY PRINTING COMPANY,
FORGE VILLAGE, MASSACHUSETTS
BOUND BY H. WOLFF, NEW YORK
DESIGNED BY KATHLEEN CAREY
FIRST EDITION

For Bob Kotlowitz,

WHO MADE IT ALL POSSIBLE.

And for Billie,

WHO MAKES BOB POSSIBLE.

CREDITS

The Men Who Made the Movies was produced by WNET/13, in New York City, under a grant from Eastman Kodak Company. It premiered on November 4, 1973, on the Public Broadcasting Service.

PRODUCED, WRITTEN AND DIRECTED BY: *Richard Schickel*
NARRATED BY: *Cliff Robertson*
EDITED BY: *Mirra Bank* (Capra, Cukor, Hitchcock and Vidor); *Geof Bartz* (Hawks, Walsh and Wellman); and *Rhetta Barron* (Minnelli).
ASSOCIATE PRODUCER: *Myrna Greenfield*
PHOTOGRAPHED BY: *Erik Daarstad and John A. Morrill*
SOUND BY: *Peter Pilafian*
ASSISTANT EDITOR: *Jill Demby*
ASSISTANT CAMERAMAN: *Paul Deason*
PRODUCTION MANAGER: *Mona Kligman*
STILLS RESEARCH: *Julia Whedon*
TITLE MUSIC BY: *Benjamin Lees*

ASSOCIATE PRODUCER (Hitchcock): *Eugene Stavis*
ASSOCIATE DIRECTOR (Walsh): *Robert Bookman*
ADDITIONAL PHOTOGRAPHY (Capra): *Tony Foresta*
ADDITIONAL SOUND (Capra): *Kay Armstrong*
ASSISTANT CAMERAMAN (Capra): *Peter Blanck*

ACKNOWLEDGMENTS

The credits—and the dedication—cannot adequately express gratitude to the people whose enthusiasm and cheerfulness under inexorable deadline pressure made the production of this series such a happy experience. Moreover, there is never enough space in the credits of a television program to mention—and thank—the other people who contributed to its success. Happily, a book provides that opportunity and it is an enormous pleasure to take advantage of it. The president of WNET/13 is Jay Iselin, and since the place never has enough money I can only assume that it runs a lot of the time on Jay's energy and enthusiasm, from which our program greatly benefited. Among the staff people at the channel who helped in innumerable ways were: Dan Fales, Robert Freedman, Joan Mack, Mike Podell, Angela Solomon and Don Sussman and their assistants. The Eastman Kodak executive whose sympathy and interest generated corporate enthusiasm for the project is Roger Morrison. Without him there might not have been a series at all and we are all greatly in his debt.

There certainly would not have been a series if Philip Gerard and Arnold Shane of MCA had not provided us with the support we needed to make a pilot film. They made a grant to the City Center Cinematheque in New York, which in turn made a grant to me in order to make the film on Alfred Hitchcock, for which they also provided us with film clips. Once this program was a reality, it became possible to proceed with the rest of the series and I cannot thank them enough for their willingness to share a vision that a number of other people could not see at such an early stage. For his unfailing help at this point in the proceedings, Gene Stavis of the Cinematheque deserves more gratitude than a mere mention in the Hitchcock show's credits can convey.

Finally, various corporations made film clips available to us at less than their usual commercial rates. More than that, many of their people went to unusual pains to help us clear obscure rights and lay our hands on rare films, and to supply them to us precisely when our production schedule demanded them. In addition to the aforementioned Universal executives we owe a special debt to the following, who are listed alphabetically by corporation: ABC Circle Entertainment; Columbia Pictures (Robert Ferguson); Janus Films (Sol Turrell); Killiam Shows (Paul Killiam); Metro-Goldwyn-Mayer (Jack Haley, Jr. and Dennis Carlton); National Telefilm Associates (Pete Rogers and Steve Manos); Paramount Pictures (Norman Flicker); Selznick Properties, Inc. (Daniel Selznick); Twentieth Century-Fox (Bill Werneth); United Artists (Bart Farber and Eve Baer); Video Cinema (Larry Stern); Warner Communications (Edward Blier, Leo Greenfield and Irwin Markish). Finally, The Museum of Modern Art film department, headed by Margareta Akermark, was—as it so unfailingly is when you're working on movie history projects—extremely helpful. To all of these people, thanks for services above and beyond the call of contracts.

ILLUSTRATIONS

Unless otherwise cited, all illustrations are courtesy of The Museum of Modern Art/ Film Stills Archive

CONTENTS

THE MEN WHO
MADE THE MOVIES

INTRODUCTION

A F E W years ago, doing research for a book, I got in touch with a number of movie directors—men who had begun their careers in the teens of this century—and interviewed them about the early days of the movies. Some time later I was engaged by WNET, the Public Broadcasting station in New York, to write and help produce a pair of specials about American films and the people who made them (and, inferentially, the people who enjoyed them) in the 1930s and 1940s. In the course of preparing the programs I met more of the older generation of directors. By the time I had finished the second of the shows, in the spring of 1972, I was convinced that someone ought to do a series of television films in which, say, eight older directors were encouraged to reminisce about their lives and their work; their remarks would be illustrated by clips from the movies they had directed, and these two elements united by a minimal voice-over narration to supply historical and perhaps critical perspective. I had also decided that the someone to do the series might as well be me.

I won't rehearse here the difficulties encountered in securing backing for the project, but in the summer of 1972—thanks very largely to the men named in the acknowledgments, executives of MCA, who made a production grant to City Center Cinematheque, a nonprofit institution— we were able to produce a pilot program on Alfred Hitchcock, which in turn secured us grants from the Corporation for Public Broadcasting and from the National Endowment for the Arts, ensuring completion of the series. Later, when Eastman Kodak Co. agreed to underwrite the project, we were able to make a contribution to WNET's burdensome overhead and turn the initial grants back to the corporation and the endowment, where presumably other good works profited from our corporate windfall.

I have, as the length of this introduction testifies, complicated reasons for my interest in *The Men Who Made the Movies*, but these reasons grew and took shape as work on the series took shape. The basic truth is that I had known and admired the work of the men represented here since I was a child and was elated to discover that all of them were as intelligent, engaging, exciting to work with as their movies had been. There was a special quality about them, a healthy-mindedness if you will, that is not encountered often in American life today. They possess something of what I imagined to be the spirit—individualistic, pragmatic, reasonable—of an older America. Whatever one's interest in movie history, I thought, these were men more people ought to meet and perhaps reflect upon, since they had solved two problems that continually baffle us all: they had created a large body of work which sustains the burden of critical analysis without sacrificing general appeal; and they had done so without undue compromise of artistic vision or personal integrity while working right at the center of an industry it has long pleased social analysts to consider a paradigm of American commercial corruption. There was something to be learned from them not merely about movies, but about the conduct of life. And our very simple format—which had our subjects talking directly into the camera, without interruption by an interviewer—might help people to get in touch with the spirit shared by these eight men, and help them to see that if that spirit was capable of sustaining these men at their age, it might still have some general applicability and not be as dead as the pundits and prophets have been claiming it is.

All of that may have been in the forefront of my mind, but we kept it pretty much in the background of the films we made, partly because these men like to talk in specifics—about problems they solved, friends and enemies they made—and resisted, as they did in their films, generalizing from the particulars that absorbed them. Partly we did so because I—and all of my coworkers on the series—have a powerful interest in the history of American film, believe it worthy of study and felt that in making what could turn out to be the only record of these lives that will exist in their own medium, we ought to get in as much as possible of their sense of how things had been when they—and the movies in general—were at the height of their power.

One thing that struck us forcefully was that the careers of some of these men encompassed almost the entire history of an institution some of us care very greatly about and that all the careers of all (excepting Vincente Minnelli, who is younger by a decade or so than his colleagues and came to the movies a little later in his life than most of them did) certainly encompass the most intriguing decades of American film production. We felt, therefore, that there was a responsibility incumbent upon those of us who had taken pleasure in their work to try to convey something of each man's unique character.

What was important in what they had to say was not advice about technique, for questions about why they chose one shot over another, or why they put a camera here instead of there, were generally answered with a snort and a gesture of contempt. They had not merely grown up in the movies, as the rest of us had, they had grown up with them. They had witnessed the birth of the movies' technical conventions and those conventions seemed to these men as natural as the conventions of written discourse seem to a professional writer. There is, simply, a way of doing in the movies which they absorbed almost unconsciously in their youth and saw no reason to analyze. Indeed, it had never occurred to them to try—until these pleasant young men started coming around, interrupting either pleasant retirement or new projects with dumb, if doubtless flattering, questions.

No, what set them apart, and fascinated me, was an attitude. It was composed of a toughness that was never harsh, a pride in achievement that was never boastful, a self-reliance and an acceptance of the difficulties under which they had labored—and of the flops they cheerfully admitted they had made—which contained neither self-pity nor a desire to blame others—producers, the studio system, their actors or writers—for the things that had gone wrong. They would tell funny but affectionate stories about actors, they would generously credit cameramen and writers for their contributions, they would grouse, but never with much bitterness, about the front office. And they left a powerful impression that they were really too busy with the day-to-day demands and pleasures of the set or the location to pay much attention to the inadequacies and inequities of the conditions under which they worked. Most, indeed, seemed to miss what popular mythology has long insisted was a tyrannical, vulgar and humanly destructive method of producing movies. They seemed rather to have enjoyed sneaking stuff past the producers, and most of them recalled old battles, with the likes of Harry Cohn or Jack Warner, affectionately. They may have seemed like bandits to outsiders, but they were honestly what they were, you always knew where they stood, what pressures they were under, what opportunities for the main chance they spied. Moreover, once they accepted a director as a competent craftsman, they tended to leave him alone to do his work—the ins and outs of which were largely mysterious to the producers anyway. Finally, the studio chiefs created a magnificent support system for directors. There is universal agreement among our eight men that they functioned best with a familiar stock company of actors, with crews that worked with them picture after picture. They also derived a tremendous sense of security from the knowledge that when they went to work on a film, it had been well planned in advance by a competent staff, that if anything went wrong there was a powerful backup system that could be counted on to help handle any contingency. They all compared the present system—where a man can spend a year or two packaging and financing a project and then must do it with strangers—most unfavorably with the old way, which permitted a man to do what he did best, and liked best—direct films—efficiently, without fuss. It suited their natures, which tend to be direct, unduplicitous, unpretentious.

It occurred to me that broadcasting the recollections of these men would be a useful corrective to the generally held belief that Hollywood in the old days had been universally ruinous to talent. Their experience simply did not square with the legend, which had been propagated mostly by writers and by actors and directors who had been recruited from the stage and were convinced that the movies were a lesser art than the novel or the drama. The literary gentlemen, in particular, wrote numberless stories, plays and books designed to expose the crassness and insensitivity of the producers and their systems. Even when they did not, they spread tales of an illiterate and brutal industrial leadership, and these found their way into the huge stream of gossip that has always flowed out of the movies and thence into written histories, from which it was but a step toward something like status as *the* history of the medium.

Then, too, in the 1930s and 1940s there was a powerful political substratum in Hollywood in which the most significant forces were also writers (though writers who tended not to have had significant literary or journalistic careers before taking up residence in the writers' buildings at the various studios). They endlessly complained that, in a manic pursuit of profit by offering the public only "escapism," a great medium was being perverted. There was, obviously, some truth in this, but their definition of the alternative to escapism was an extremely limited one, because they did not, I believe, ever see the movies as a great *artistic* medium. Rather, they saw it as a great *propaganda* medium, and were endlessly disappointed that they could not get the Louis B. Mayers and the Jack Warners to see it their way. On the face of it, this was a vain hope—self-made men are rarely very liberal-minded, let alone Stalinist-minded, which is what the most devout of the leftist writers were. More to the point, they never saw that even as they were bitching about executives and joining little "progressive" (as they liked to put it) cells, a set of stylizations and conventions, a group of genres, were being developed that were unique to the movies—that, whatever their sources in literary and theatrical history, were by now completely taken over and transformed to film. Neither the bitterly gossiping literary gentlemen nor the politicized hacks seemed to notice or understand this, and thus they missed—for the most part—the chance to move to the creative center of film-making, which was directing, or the commercial center of it, which was producing. To have passed through Hollywood at that time and not to have perceived this strikes me as amazing.

The directors present in this volume—and a great many more I wish could have been here—were aliterary as well as apolitical. They did not have the time or the temperament to invest in abstract thought about what they were doing and why they were doing it. As much as possible, they stayed the hell out of the front office, jealously guarding the inviolability of their sets, where they took absolute command of shooting the picture and tended to take a rather strong line about visits from the class enemy—namely, executives, people in suits. Even people like Cukor and Minnelli, whose backgrounds were in the theater and who maintained their high regard for the medium that formed them as young men, felt no more need than the action directors (who never worked in any other medium) to exorcise their contempt for Hollywood—principally because they were never threatened by it.

There was nothing neurotic about their habits of independence, as often seems to be the case with their younger successors that I have encountered. They had a natural strength which is apparent even—perhaps especially—in their old age. They seem always to have known who they are, and didn't—and don't—have to prove their strength and integrity on a daily basis. Indeed, it's fair to say that they grew up in and were shaped by an age in which such questions did not arise very often. This was particularly true of the action directors—Walsh, Hawks and Wellman. Walsh had actually been a cowboy before he started making pictures about cowboys, and had come to the movies as a rider. Hawks and Wellman had both been fliers before they started making movies that often dealt with that peculiar breed. They felt in their bones the character and quality of a vanished America which the movies still celebrate and which a younger generation of directors knows about only through their films. And, indeed, all of the men whose words form the substance of this book served long, hard apprenticeships in their art, apprenticeships which taught them something valuable not merely about the art of film, but about ordinary life. At the time these eight men broke into film, the movie world was not as insulated from the rest of life as it was shortly to become, when money and glamour would alienate most movie people from the ordinary concerns of ordinary people.

One does not entirely blame later generations of directors for feeling the need to rebel against the conditions the court life of the moguls and their successors imposed, though there was—and still is—an adolescent quality about their manner of expressing it. One merely notes that for some reason there was not a rebel among the group of directors who are now in their seventies and older. They all knew how to defend their ground, their prerogatives, and they all have long lists of people they tried working for or with, hated and never returned to. But their anger and feuds never turned to thoughts of revolution against the system or into the self-hatred that afflicted many actors and writers. That they maintained this emotional stability, a stability which guaranteed the general quality of their work, seems to me both miraculous and admirable. They would be worth studying if they had been engaged in the manufacture of widgets, let alone something as intrinsically interesting as movies.

Of course, it helped that in the old days a man made so many pictures that the success or failure of each one made a smaller difference in his career than it now does. It helped that films in the 1920s, 1930s and 1940s carried less cultural weight, so that one did not feel that a flop was an affront to all of Western civilization, as Pauline Kael, for example, seems to feel many are today. It helped that the auteur theory has been applied to the work of these men only retroactively. At the time they were making the pictures it occurred to none of them (except, perhaps, Frank Capra and Alfred Hitchcock) that they were the sole authors of the movies which bore their names. Most of them, therefore, were freed of the burden of identification as artists. They were craftsmen, "professionals," proud of their ability, at the very least, to efficiently bring forth—often from unpromising material—solid commercial entertainments, on time, on budget, often with more verve, more sheer fun, than one would have thought could be infused into the banalities they were given to work with. At their best, of course, they created masterpieces, works that created standards by which we judge later movies of the same genres. The weight of the ages, the opinion of future generations did not weigh on them. Not one of them ever indicated to me that he had believed his work would outlast the season of its release. Some said that if they had realized that just a few decades later scholars and graduate students would be running seminars on them and writing books about them, that there would be festivals in their honor, they would have taken more care with their films.

All of this says nothing about the pleasure of restudying the work of these men. In the pages that follow they will be talking about their movies, but you won't be seeing them, and most people will never see them as the cutters and I did—looking closely to find scenes that seemed most characteristic of each film, then running some of those scenes over and over again, trying to discover their essence, trying to make them fit together with our interview material and with each other to make a coherent impression of the director's principal means of expressing himself. We saw some scenes fifty, a hundred times, and the work was never boring.

In every film the director was attempting to communicate to the widest possible audience, to offer something a child could respond to on one level, an adolescent on another, an adult on a third. Moreover, all the directors hoped that people in every region, of every class and every level of intellectual attainment could respond to all their movies. The curse of modernism had not yet been visited on the medium (which is why the literary community generally despised American movies in the 1930s and 1940s) and film-makers were less obsessed with personal expression, ego-tripping, than they are now. When directors considered subject matter and how to handle it, they sought not what was most individual about their sensibilities, but what they shared with their audience. They were content to put a new twist on one of the well-established genres, a new wrinkle on a conventionalized character, a stylized situation. It is important to remember that familiarity with these formalized matters did not breed contempt in creators or audience. It was the business of the director, as George Cukor nicely put it, to help people to penetrate to "the reality beyond convention," by which he meant that these stylizations were not arbitrary but had in the beginning been based on reality as it was commonly perceived, and that in the best movies they served as an efficient way of propelling us to the heart of a dramatic conflict without elaborate detours into matters that were essentially of private concern to a film's creators. It might be added that these conventions also served to remind all of us—movie-makers and audience—that we inhabited the same world, shared values, were at the deepest levels in touch with one another so much that no one worried about that matter.

All of this conspired to create a direct, brisk way of making a movie. The camera in most American films in the 1930s was used objectively, unobtrusively. The ideal, quite the opposite of what it is today, was not to let it (and its master, the director) comment upon the action, or to lead our moral response to it. There really was no need to, anyway, so powerful were our shared opinions as to what constituted right, wrong, truth, beauty, humor.

Many of these directors' films, despite their conventionalized surfaces, despite their routinized stories, were actually more subtle than many of our movies today. There were interesting tensions between directors (and writers and actors) and their material; certainly there was a tension between their ideas about the world and the intentions of producers, which was simply to make a profitable product, except on those rare occasions when they were going after "prestige." These tensions animated the films, enlivening conventions with novelty, inventions, quirks of expression, sometimes sheer pictorial beauty, since a good director can't help but see the world and the people he is photographing in his own way. The men in this book asserted themselves modestly in their work, never boorishly, and were always respectful of the fact that we were more interested in their stories, their people, than we were in the director's opinions of them. They were, in short, like good conversationalists, and in our vulgar age I have come to treasure their good manners, their respect for the differing intelligences of the audience. Their respect for themselves, their confidence in their abilities, and their individuality led them to imagine that the rest of us must have similar qualities. It is good to be treated that way at the movies. It assures, I think, the timeless appeal of the best work of *The Men Who Made the Movies.*

In preparing the text for this book—which contains about ninety percent more material than we were able to use on the air—I have eliminated the kind of irrelevant cross-talk—mostly technical in nature—that goes on when an interview is being filmed as well as recorded. I have also eliminated the normal hesitations and false starts common to interviews, as well as repetitions, a few responses to queries that did not lead to anything significant, and obviously, direct quotations from my questions. Because we did not want to use a Q&A format on the air, all the directors were preinterviewed (with no recording equipment present) so that they could help map out the areas of greatest interest and so that they would be familiar with, and relaxed with, the interviewer. All were asked to respond to questions in the form of statements which, in effect, repeated the question and thus eliminated the need for my voice on the air. In a few cases, where I dropped a line of inquiry at one point in the interview and then picked it up later, I have combined the two responses. I must apologize for the absence of comment on several important films. By the time we conducted these interviews we knew which films would not be made available to us by their distributors for use on the air, so I eliminated them from my list of topics. Still, we were extraordinarily lucky—there were few omissions that I deeply regretted.

Finally, I wish we could have made a longer series. There are several distinguished directors about whom we could not make documentaries—a couple were too ill to be interviewed at the time we were in production, a few more whose work I deeply respect could not be included because the budget could not be stretched to encompass more programs. At this point, obviously, subjective judgment entered the picture and I chose to do films on those men for whose work I had the greatest affection, whose images for some reason had lingered most vividly in my mind. Someone else might well have made some different choices. I have no regrets about that. I only regret that a choice had to be made.

To the right of the tender sentiments—director Raoul Walsh

RAOUL WALSH

I HAVE known Raoul Walsh longer than any of the other directors included here. He was, in fact, among the first of the older generation of directors I met. I had asked to interview him when I was doing research on D. W. Griffith. He invited me out to his ranch in the Simi Valley. His house was a comfortable, rambling affair, nestled beneath a ridge, with a small orange grove surrounding the swimming pool. In a pasture nearby, horses and beef cattle grazed (Raoul was raising quarter horses for fun and profit, but he has since sold most of them). He greeted me on his front lawn, dressed in jeans, western shirt, a Levi jacket and the cowboy boots I have since learned he always wears, no matter what the rest of his costume.

He was leaner than he is now, and still riding his spread regularly, though he was over eighty. In the last couple of years he has lost most of the sight in the one eye that remained to him after an accident in 1930 cost him his right eye. This has slowed him down physically and, from time to time, makes him feel quite depressed. A few years ago, however, his vigor was astonishing. He conducted me through the house to pool-side chairs, plucked some oranges from his trees and had his wife, Mary, convert them into the best orange juice I've ever tasted. He talked acutely of Griffith, and amusingly about the life around Griffith's studio in the period before, during and just after the making of *The Birth of a Nation*. Then we drifted into more general reminiscences and he asked me to stay to lunch, which I did. I lingered too long, and that forced me to undertake a lunatic race across the valley and most of Los Angeles in order to catch a plane for New York. But I scarcely noticed the drive, so strangely moved was I by our conversation, which had followed similar talks with John Ford and Allan Dwan, who also had worked for Griffith.

What they had to say about the early history of the movies was interesting, but what fascinated me was that Raoul and his contemporaries had so obviously *lived*—in the richest sense—before they came to the movies. I believe they would have lived adventurous lives, even if the movies had not been invented and they had been forced to employ their toughness, energy and humor elsewhere. Raoul, for instance, might well have been a full-time rancher instead of a director—and no loss to him or to the annals of anecdote, since I can't imagine Raoul not turning any experience into a yarn of some sort. Moreover, the fact that Raoul and his contemporaries had done something other than movie-making, had lived hand-to-mouth doing rather humble work, gave them an edge in their work. For one thing, it was impossible for a mogul to frighten them. Since they had survived and apparently even relished living on the margins of society, they could always turn away from the big dough and the glamorous life of Hollywood and go back to the life they had known before. More important, they had a direct connection with the way of life that formed the content of many of their pictures. Raoul, who was raised on a ranch and worked as a cowboy and came into the movies because he was an expert rider, knew something about the West that a later generation of directors could not know. That authenticity distinguishes his films, just as it did those of John Ford, who had also done his first movie work as a rider. In Raoul's case, there is a special feeling for lower-class Irish life (*The Bowery, The Strawberry Blonde, Gentleman Jim*) that is a product of the drifting days of his youth, when he gravitated toward this group. The rough humor and sentimentality, the sheer vitality of it, he was able to translate to the screen with a vigor and liveliness that I find more engaging most of the time than Ford's treatment of the same material, which is often softer, verging occasionally on the bathetic.

If Raoul had any hopes for his movies, they were that each film would tell a good story briskly and would entertain the largest possible audience. He did not make them in order to define himself. He already knew who he was. Maybe he hoped that he could, with his enormous technical skill and his amazing working speed, help the writers and actors to define more clearly whatever it was that they thought they were doing. But that was the end of the matter.

In the seminar that we photographed for our documentary, one of the students asked, "Mr. Walsh, where did you get most of your ideas?" "From the script," he replied briefly, and he wasn't being funny or evasive. Raoul never found it necessary to inquire what he was doing or why he was doing it. He did whatever came naturally to him, and it was sufficient for him that his actors do the same. He says in this interview that he didn't like actresses who came in and "posed" for the camera. Robert Mitchum remembers Raoul directing him in a picture neither of them much cared for. Raoul set up the camera for one scene, said "Turn 'em" and walked away, listening to the dialogue but not watching it. When the scene was finished, he yelled, "Cut" and then inquired of Mitchum how it had gone. "Well, I knocked over the lamp," the actor said, trying to get a rise out of him. "You pick it up? Did it look natural? Fine. Print it."

Two years ago Raoul came to a seminar in film history that I was conducting at Yale. As usual, he told long, hilarious stories about the good old days. Toward the end, one of the girls said, "Mr. Walsh, you've told us a lot about the details of making movies, but I was wondering, did you love movies?" There was a long, puzzled pause. "What's that again, sweetheart?" he asked.

That question I believe he did think was stupid. And I don't think he'd ever asked himself anything so abstract. Obviously, he'd loved doing what he did. If he hadn't, he would have quit and done something different, because that's the kind of man he's always been.

The material which follows differs somewhat from the rest of this volume because less of it was gathered in a single interview. Raoul was the guest of honor at the U.S.A. film festival, held at Southern Methodist University in the spring of 1973, and we decided to shoot most of our footage on him at the festival. Therefore the remarks that follow were made in a variety of contexts—as he responded to questions after a screening of one of his films, as he participated in a seminar with SMU students, even as he engaged in a dialogue with a local television interviewer. This material was supplemented by a more formal interview conducted at his ranch. A brief illness forced Raoul to cancel an interview I had scheduled with him, and a tight budget prevented my remaining on the coast until he was well or making a separate later trip. This interview was done by Robert Bookman, a mutual friend, whose contribution both to the program and to this book I herewith gratefully acknowledge. Because Raoul's words were drawn from diverse occasions, I have arranged them here in an order that seems to me coherent; I have not wished to impede the flow of the text by indicating in precisely which context he took up the many themes he dealt with while we were filming.

''THOSE WERE THE DAYS . . .''

(*Raoul Walsh was born in New York City, but as a young man he sailed for Cuba as a hand on a ship captained by his uncle. From there he went to Mexico, then worked his way to Texas. He began his reminiscences for us there.*)

Things were pretty rough in those days. We had a low, rambling ranch house, weatherbeaten, roof leaked. We had a couple of houses outside for the cowboys, corrals for the horses and cattle, no hot or cold running water. And it was a rough life compared to where I am now, [but] I'd like to go back. Men were men in those days. [When I was a young man,] I drifted up into Montana, a place called Butte. That was a wild town. There was plenty of shootings, plenty of hangings. I went to work for a doctor up there, Dr. Raoul Ansenell. He was a Frenchman.

He had lung trouble. He thought the nice clear air up in Montana would kind of cure him up. I used to drive him out to the mines when there'd be shootings out there, explosions, people were hurt. And then finally I used to work with him in his office. I remember one time he was operating on a fellow there and he kept telling me to give him more chloroform. He'd say "Encore, Monsieur Raoul, encore." I'd pour the chloroform into the cone. He'd start working and say, "Encore, Monsieur Raoul, encore, encore." This happened three or four times and then he stopped and looked at me and said, "Monsieur Raoul, you have killed him." I said, "Killed him, hell! You told me 'Encore, encore, encore!' " "Shhhh! He had no chance anyhow."

DISCOVERING THE MOVIES

So I went with a theatrical company, *The Clansmen.** I joined them in San Antonio. They had a scene of a man on a horse being taken across stage on a treadmill. He had disappeared and they needed somebody, and I was sitting on the porch there. I had my knee badly damaged and this fellow said, "Cowboy, do you want a job?" I said, "I sure do." And he says, "Come down to the theater at seven o'clock." So I went down to the theater at seven o'clock and he said, "You'll have to get on a horse and you'll get on that treadmill and they'll pull you across." And he said the pay is $30 a week. I said, "Sign me up." So I watched the first act that night. I heard the musicians and stuff and the applause and the hissing and the people emoting. I said, "Oh, gee, this is great. This is great. No more cowboys for me."

[In time] this fellow asked me to go to New York and he introduced me to some agents. One agent by the name of Bill Gregory wasn't there that day, but his secretary said, "Mr. Walsh, do you ride a horse?" I said, "That's the only thing I can do." But this fellow who was with me, he said, "This is an actor of no mean ability. This fellow played such-

---

* This was an adaptation by Thomas Dixon of his popular—and racist—novel about the evils of Reconstruction in the South after the Civil War. It formed the basis of D. W. Griffith's historic film *The Birth of a Nation*, on which, coincidentally, Raoul Walsh would later work.

and-such a part in *The Clansmen*"—and he named all the parts that I played and I never played any of them. Girl was there with her eyes open, and she kind of looked at me and then she said, "Would you object to working in moving pictures?" I said, "No, I'd love it. Where are they?" See, the Broadway actors didn't want to go into motion pictures at all. So she sent me across on the ferry to Pathe Brothers in Union City, New Jersey.

I met the two Pathe brothers, and they had an interpreter, and the first thing they say, "You ride the horse?" I said, "Yes, I ride the horse." And the two of them started talking in French. "Come, we find a horse." All right. We walked up to a livery stable. The brothers wanted to see if I could ride because in those days nobody could ride. Well, I rode the horse down to these two brothers, spun him around, got off and then made a flying mount and took him off again. "Ah, bravo, bravo, bravo . . . magnifique . . . magnifique . . . Come sign the contract, three pictures."

Well, the first picture they gave me a call and I went down there and I didn't see any horses. Saw this stage and stuff. So they gave me a part to read—"This is what you do, you come in here . . ." It was a thing called *The Banker's Daughter* and I was a young clerk in the bank and I was in love with the banker's daughter, big ex-burlesque dame; and the banker, who was a big guy, he was loaded all the time, acting. We had a big scene in the bank. The police come. The girl protests my innocence. The banker said, "He's a crook." All that kind of stuff. All kinds of titles on the damned thing, you know. And I stood there like a wooden Indian. I figure, What the hell, this is the end of my acting career 'cause he's throwing things and acting all over, you know what I mean. And finally the end—the French director [said], "Dolly, run over there, kiss, kiss, kiss . . . good kiss for the man." Girl came tearing over, threw her arms around me and put her tongue down my throat about a mile. I said, "Jesus, this is acting technique."

The second one, I was a prisoner in jail, waiting for a horse. I was in there I don't know for how long. But I finally dug my way out and the cops chased me. And a peculiar thing happened. They were taking a scene at the big meadow in Fort Lee and the Frenchman told me, "You run across that field like a devil after you. And then these fellows come up there, the guards will shoot. When you hear the shoot, you fall." All right. So I got up there in the fields, up in the woods there, and ran across this big field and guards came running after me and shot and I fell down. All of a sudden, somebody was turning me over and saying prayers. It was a priest. He was sitting on his church steps and he thought it was real. I didn't remember that [there was anything like that in] the scene, you know, this guy talking. The Frenchman came tearing. "It's magnifique—Father, you stay there, we take shot of you." So I remind them. I said, "Give the guy some money." He gave him five dollars.

Then came the big opportunity. "Tomorrow you ride the horse. We have story for you . . . great story . . . you will play great, famous American jockey, Paul Revere." I never knew Paul Revere was a jockey. So they dressed me up as Paul Revere. I picked a good horse that could jump and stuff. They ran me over hill and dale, up and down roads, past old houses, past old cannons that were used in the early days, over stone walls. I took them over picket fences and then, finally, he says, "We have good shot for last scene in picture." There was a big cemetery there and he says, "You will come from over there and jump over every stone, jump over every stone fast as you go. We take." All right. I went up there with the horse, through the cemetery, over the stones. And we were arrested. It cost them $25 to restore some of the stones and this, that and the other thing, you know.

But some of Griffith's people were up there and they saw me ride the horse and I got the job with Griffith. I played in about five or six or seven one- and two-reelers they were making at Biograph. I played in two with Mary Pickford. And talking about stage actors not wanting to work in movies, I remember Lionel Barrymore coming down the alley to the studio and coming in the back way. He didn't want anybody to see him. Then Mr. Griffith decided to make his move to California and he left Biograph, and he had a habit of calling people by their last name. "Mr. Walsh, would you like to go to California?" I said, "When do we start?" So he took me to California with him.

We came to Hollywood at its birth. We had a rough time getting any fellows that could ride in those days. The fellows that applied for jobs were mostly drugstore cowboys. They'd fall off horses and get hurt, and finally Mr. Griffith said, "Mr. Walsh, you've had experience with cowboys. Would you try and find some for me?" About the only place to go would be the stockyards. There were lots of cattle being shipped in from Arizona and New Mexico and Utah, and the cowboys that would bring them in would loll around for a day or two and get drunk and stuff. Then I'd round them up, got them in, gave them a speech about getting into motion pictures and finally got them all settled at a place called Edendale.* They all lived in a big barn there. That's how we got the good riders into the motion-picture business then.

WORKING WITH GRIFFITH

Mr. Griffith was a fine man to work for. I learned all my trade from him. He was a great master of pantomime; he was a gentle man, a kind man, but he was a lonesome man. Mr. Griffith would like to play a pantomime scene and then cut to something with some action, keep it moving, keep the picture moving. In most of his pictures he used the run to the rescue, which was very, very commercial in those days—and still is today. That was his technique and I followed it. Griffith very seldom used notes. He knew what the story was and he would invent things on the set and sometimes he would have a little rehearsal the day before he was going to shoot. And he would watch the people and just tell them what to do and how to look and little pieces of business. Very quiet, calm man.

(*In California, Raoul virtually ceased acting and served as an assistant director almost exclusively. Some years ago he told me that among other duties he had to round up the cowboys in Edendale at two or three in the morning after a night of revelry, and somehow get them atop their horses and heading over the mountains into the San Fernando Valley, where Griffith shot most of his action sequences. Of a Sunday, he recalled, Griffith, who never learned to drive, would ask Raoul to chauffeur him around Los Angeles, looking for new and interesting faces which he might be able to use in his films. Finally, in 1914, when his generally acknowledged position as the nation's great director was challenged by the arrival of feature-length spectacles from abroad, Griffith turned to the huge project he had been nurturing for some time, the adaptation of* The Clansmen, *released the following year as* The Birth of a Nation.

---

* Edendale was also the site of the Mack Sennett studio.

Raoul was among the several assistant directors who worked with Griffith on it—but he also had a more public role to play.)

They'd been looking for a John Wilkes Booth for a couple of weeks; casting director brought at least twenty to thirty men in for Mr. Griffith and Mr. Woods* to see, but they weren't pleased with any of them. And Mr. Woods told me later on that Mr. Griffith [looked out his window one day and] said, "We don't need to look any further. There's John Wilkes Booth over there talking to those pretty girls." That's how I got the part. They built a huge replica of Ford's Theatre, a very expensive set. And I think he filled the orchestra and the balcony with about four hundred, five hundred extras. Then came the time for me to walk into the theater, cross over to the stairway that led to President Lincoln's box. And he would call—in those days there was no sound, so he'd yell at me. He said, "All right. Go up the stairs, take it slowly . . . All right . . . Work your way up there now. Now you've come to the door of the President. Take your derringer out . . . open the door . . . go in . . . and shoot! Now jump!" And I jumped about eighteen to twenty feet to the stage, banged my knee up pretty bad, hobbled to the center of the stage and yelled out, "Sic semper tyrannis," and then I hobbled off the stage. Mr. Griffith came back and found out that I had hurt my knee and he insisted that I go to the hospital to have it taken care of. I said, "No, it's all right. Have you got to retake?" He said, "No, that was perfect." So they insisted; they took me down to St. Vincent's Hospital and they kept me there a day. I remember that night I was in bed there. I [had] picked up an Apache Indian called Crazy Wolf. I let him camp out in back of my house. He was the first one to do the fall off a horse and I brought him out to the studio and he showed Mr. Griffith what he could do and they signed him up. He was very grateful to me, this Indian. So I was in the hospital bed there that night and all of a sudden I saw his face come up to the window there. There was a fire escape outside the old-fashioned hospital. He had a huge armful of flowers. And I waved him in, he came in, and I said, "Crazy Wolf, you didn't need to spend a lot of money on those flowers." He said, "Me like, me like." I said, "All right, put them down there." He

* Frank Woods was Griffith's story editor and, in effect, his associate producer.

put the flowers on the table, sat down and talked a little while, then he left and I went to sleep. In the morning a big fat nurse came in, she saw the flowers. She said, "Ahhh, now we know where the flowers on the lawn have gone." The Indian had picked the flowers down on the lawn. She called me to the window to look down. There were just two or three flowers stuck around this whole lawn.

VILLA RIDES, RAOUL RIDES

(*Not long after* Birth *was completed, Griffith offered Raoul another sort of opportunity.*)

Griffith said, "Raoul, we're going to let you direct." I said, "Fair enough." So he gave me a piece of paper that was the script: Joe meets Jenny, Jenny's mother don't like 'im, the father is a drunk, you know what I mean—and they gave me $75 to go out and shoot it. Go out to the park, you know. If you needed a baby in a carriage, you saw somebody there and you say, "Would you like to make two dollars and be in pictures? You can be a big star someday." "Yes." The woman with the baby would see somebody else. The policeman was always glad to get a fiver. And different types, you know, you'd pick up and go through with the thing. And you'd see a house and you'd go give somebody two dollars to use the front of their house and the side of the house.

In Mr. Griffith's company there were three units—the Majestic, the Reliance and the Mutual. And most of the Reliance and Majestic pictures were what we made at the Fine Arts studio.* If the picture was good, it was released on Majestic. If it wasn't any good, it was a Reliance, and the Mutual was the weekly. The weekly made a deal with Pancho Villa to go through his revolution and photograph the battles and photograph him—$500 a month. They sent a fellow down there and a cameraman with the check for $500 and they never saw them again—the cameraman, the $500 or the guide. So they hired some detective agents to find out what the hell happened and they found out that [Villa's people would

* It was located at the corner of Sunset Boulevard and Vine Street.

only accept gold]. Griffith called me in and he said, "You've been in Mexico, you understand a little bit the customs of these people, would you like to go down and photograph the General?" I said, "I sure would." I took off that night, and he said, "By the way, we're going to make a story [using your footage], so you'd better think of some story to tell him when you get down there." I took the Southern Pacific train, got off at El Paso, the Mutual representative met me, took me to the hotel and told me the setup. And they had $500 in gold this time. Ortega, that was Villa's contact man, was there. A very nice fellow. I made great friends with him, Ortega.

So then I took the bag of gold that night and we started to cross the bridge with Ortega. And when we got on the other side, Ortega put a bandage around my eyes and stuff. And we got in the car and wandered around. I know that he was circling because Juárez wasn't that big. And we finally pulled up to a place and stopped. And then he led me out and took the bandage off and it was a kind of a broken-down headquarters where Villa was. We went in and he had me stay in a room there for a minute. And he went in and saw Villa and came back and then took me in too and introduced me to the General. I knew some Spanish that I learned from an Apache Indian, but it was all wrong. Ortega said, "Tell the General what you want to do, see?" I thought to myself, I'd better start off good with this bum. I said, "Tell the General that the press in America say he is a bandit. I'm going to make a picture of the General to show that he is a great hero and the savior of the Mexican people." Well, that went over and I knew I was in, but I still was watching where that window was that I was going to get out of. Then they started more talking and stuff about what kind of picture I make of the General. "Well," I said, "as I told you, I was going to show that he was a great hero of all time and eighty million people would see the picture of the General. And the story that I'm going to tell of the General . . ." And now I'm thinking like hell—what the hell story was it? I had thought of three of them on the way out on the train. He said, "The General would like to hear story you tell of him to make him great man with eighty million people." Kept doing that eighty million. So I said, "The General is a young boy; he's sixteen or seventeen and he lives with his mother, who he loves dearly, and he has a baby sister that's pretty as a rainbow. Times were getting tough where he lived, money was scarce, jobs were scarce, and he traveled off to Chihuahua to work at a big ranch so that he could get some big money and come back and build his mother a very pretty rancho." I ended up by telling him that while he was away working at Chihuahua at the big rancho there, the Federales came and burnt down his town and killed his mother and sister. Now, he didn't know that and it was coming Christmas and he bought a nice dress for his mother and a nice dress for his sister, and when he comes back the house is in ashes and he sees an old priest over in the yard there and he says, "What happened?" The priest tells him the Federales came and killed everybody. Then I started thinking, How can I convince this bum that he's going to be good?—'cause he was going to work in the picture, although I was going to play him as a young man eventually. So I told Ortega to tell him, "Then the General got down on his knees and he told God above he would kill every Federale I meet. I will raise an army and I will march on to Mexico and save Mexico for the people." I was in.

I went all the way with them down in Mexico and had lots of battles and stuff going. I had a terrible time photographing the battles because they were [always] miles away. So I called Ortega one day and I said, "Look, Ortega, I want you to get me about seventy-five soldades and these dead Federales, take off their uniforms and put the uniforms on our men, see?" "Hey . . . no, no, no . . . we get shot!" We finally had to calm them down, get the uniforms off the dead guys and put it on these seventy-five. Then I had a trench for them and had them firing back, you know. And some of them getting killed. So we had some sort of battle.

One time Villa came down to watch, and to please the guy, I told Ortega to tell these fellows, after they fired two shots, show that they're cowards, throw down their guns and run across that field. Well, he did that and they ran. Villa was watching and he thought it was good. I had a terrible time getting a shot of him on a horse at a little gallop. We'd come to a town sometime, a picturesque place, and I'd ask Ortega, I'd say, "Ask the General if he'll come down on a slow trot." Oh, Jesus, he went by like that! And you had that camera in those days you couldn't turn. Today you could have gone with him, you know.

We came into Durango and I wanted to get a shot of him, but the Federales had all gone. I couldn't get anything. I don't know if you've ever been to Durango, but in the center of Durango there's the largest prison you ever saw in your life, with a wall twice as high as this ceiling. I got a hold of Ortega and I said, "It might be a good thing for the General if he'll open those gates and turn the prisoners loose." And he went and told Villa that, and Villa says, "All right. Do it." Then he told him to open the gates. Now, the guys that were in there, they were political prisoners, they were afraid to come out because they were afraid they would be shot when they saw Villa and his men there. So they stayed in the prison. I wanted to get a release, you know. Well, I finally told Ortega, "Get some of our men, take the banderillas and the guns and everything and their hats and fix them up. Get about a hundred of them," I said, "and put them in the prison. And when the gates open, let them come out and stand around Villa and cheer him, you know." So he says, "All right. I do." They took off all their army equipment and then, I figured, Well, God, with these prisoners turned loose, somebody should greet them. Now it happened that among his three thousand followers, Villa had about two hundred, three hundred ladies of the night following the outfit. It was a real carnival. So I told Ortega to go and tell these prostitutes when the men come out to run because they're supposed to be their husbands that are released. I had them all standing there and I told them, "All right, open the gates, out you come." And then I told Ortega, "Send them out." Well, these dames ran in there, threw their arms around these fellows, knocked them to the ground and started to hugging and kissing them. I tell you, I never saw such a scene in my life.

A MEMORY OF CHAPLIN

I knew Charlie when he first came to Hollywood and he first got a five-dollar-a-day job with Mack Sennett.* He was a comical little fellow right from the very beginning. He'd make you laugh. We used to go to a restaurant called Al Levy's, down on Spring Street. That's where all the Keystone bunch went, and the personnel from the Griffith studio. We all sort of mingled there. The fellow Levy eventually went broke giving credit to actors. I spent Saturday nights there, Sunday afternoons, and Sunday nights with Gene Pallette and Wally Reid, Henry Walthall

* Chaplin's salary was actually $150. a week.

and people like that. Chaplin was then a great jokester. He would take off his coat and get a napkin and put it over his arm and if he saw some tourist or something, nobody in the picture business, he'd get a pad and he'd go over and take their order. While these people were ordering a New England dinner or cabbage or something, he'd tell them some dish that was the specialty of the house and they'd tell him [to bring] that and so forth. And he'd hide and then leave the place.

I was one of the few actors that had a car. I won't tell you how I got the car because there might be a policeman in the house. And Charlie used to admire the Stutz Bearcat and I'd take him on rides and he used to say, "I've got to have a car. I've got to have a car. Where I live, it's too bloody far to walk, you know what I mean?" He says, "How much does a car cost?" I said, "Well, what kind of a car do you want?" He said, "I saved up sixty dollars." I said, "Well, you ought to buy a sewing machine. The hell with it." But Levy told him about a place on Santa Barbara Avenue, a friend of his that had used cars and he'd sell Charlie a car for sixty dollars. So I said, "Charlie, are you working Saturday?" He said, "No, I won't be working this Saturday." I said, "Neither will I. I'll pick you up and take you down to the secondhand guy for the car." And he says, "Oh, great-o, great-o, great-o, great-o," you know. Saturday morning I went down to the Sennett Keystone studio and the big iron gates were closed and the Irish gateman—Paddy Collins—was sitting there reading a paper. I knew him because he used to work as an actor at the Griffith studio, so I said, "Paddy, what's happening? Isn't nobody working today?" He says, "I'll tell you. There was a lady came in here about a week ago, two weeks ago, and she brought her daughter with her and they made some pictures of her. She was a beautiful child. And then the mother went to the District Attorney and said that she was going to have a child." So he says, "We have Pat Malloy that works in the District Attorney's office and he's a good friend of ours. Well, he phoned out and he said if anybody had anything to do with this girl, leave town for two days." And he said, "They all took off." I said, "I had a date with Chaplin. Did he go?" He said, "Sure, he was the first."

FROM GRIFFITH TO FOX

(*Not long after completing* Pancho Villa *for Griffith, Raoul transferred his allegiance to William Fox, and he would stay with Fox's company until 1935, after which he free-lanced for a while before signing with Warner Brothers. Fox had begun his career as one of the most cheerfully piratical of the independent producers, fighting the combine of producers known as "The Trust" because, through their control of the basic patents on cameras and projectors, they sought to restrain the growth of the independent-production motion-picture industry. With his imaginative flair for colorful publicity, Fox became one of the leaders of the fight for economic freedom in the fledgling industry. He would lose control of his studio during the Depression of the 1930s. He died in 1952.*

Well, he was just starting in those days. He had seen a two-reel picture that I made and he sent Winfield Sheehan out and Sheehan signed me up and took me back to New York. And there I met William Fox. He was a dynamic character. He was the first one to really set the big salaries for directors, actors and actresses. He believed in getting the best of everything for a picture.

One day he called me and he says, "Raoul, I've just bought a great story for you. It's called *The Honor System.* I've been in touch with Governor Hunt of Arizona and he wants the picture made and will give us all the assistance that we need." I jumped on a train and took off for Arizona and met the Governor, read the script to him and he said, "That is just what I'm after, *The Honor System.* I believe in turning prisoners loose in the daytime so they can go to various towns and return at night on their honor. This picture is just what I want." So we made the picture. I got Milton Sills, who was a very prominent actor in those days, and Gladys Brockwell, a very prominent actress, and the story concerned turning a life prisoner loose to go and testify at his second trial. He was to return on his honor in three days, which Milton Sills did. The rival politicians tried to prevent him from going back, but the script had him elude them and he returned to the prison about four minutes before his time was up.

We ran the picture for the Governor, and he was so elated, he said, "If the Fox Company will pay the man's expenses, I will turn a life prisoner loose to go back to New York for the opening of *The Honor System*." I called Mr. Fox on the phone and he said, "Raoul, that's great. Tell him to put him on the train. We'll pay for his expenses." So they did and the lifer arrived in New York for the opening of the picture, and during the intermission he appeared on the stage, made a dramatic plea about the picture and about life prisoners and about the honor system. And he said he would be on his way back to prison tomorrow morning. The Fox Company took him to the train, put him on the Twentieth Century, sent him on his way back to Arizona. The life prisoner arrived in Chicago and hasn't been seen since. Bill Fox called me up and said, "Raoul, who picked that life prisoner?" I said, "I think the Governor did." He said, "Well, tell him the bum left the train in Chicago and headed for Canada." I asked Mr. Fox, "Will this hurt the picture?" He said, "Hell, no. It'll help the picture." And it did. The picture did a good gross.

(*Much of William Fox's early prosperity was based on productions starring Theda Bara, for whom he concocted an extraordinarily exotic screen personality. Though she was in fact the daughter of a tailor in Cincinnati, Fox let it be thought that she was half Arabian and in the habit of leading innocent youths to doom through her irresistible sexuality. Raoul, like most Fox employees in the teens of this century, took his turn working with her.*)

I was making a picture for the Fox Company over in a place called Fort Lee. I think *The Siren of Hell* was the name of it and Theda Bara, who was the great vamp of the time, was the Siren. They built a Mexican town. And two days before we started the picture, after all the costumes and everything had been ordered, we had a snowstorm and it ended up six feet deep, the worst snowstorm that had hit the East in many, many years. And my Mexican set was all buried in snow—snow covered the church steeples and all that sort of stuff. Well, money was scarce in those days and Fox had built this set, had ordered the costumes, and the poor old guy was on the spot. So I got an idea and I went down and I said, "Mr. Fox, they can take this story, this *Siren of Hell*, and lay it in Russia and use the snow." He said, "Boy, you're a genius." So we got the Russian costumes. Now he says, "You will have to go and tell Miss Bara the change." Those fellows always stayed away, you know—those money men. I said, "You're the money man, why don't *you* go up and see her?" He said, "I'm afraid she'd hit me."

So I went up and saw Theda, she was a nice sort of girl, she was a wild vamp and lured men to their death on the screen, but she was a great girl off. So I gave her a pitch, you know. And she agreed to it, so they sent the costumes up there and took her Spanish costumes away and fitted everybody with Russian . . . and I had a good break. There was a Russian troupe, not a ballet troupe but performing on horses and stuff, had come to America and they were in Jersey City. They were holed up there because they had finished their tour. So I hired that whole group of about forty with their horses, with all their instruments, and I used them in the picture. And the picture turned out pretty good as a Russian picture.

Then when spring came and the snow melted, I went to Fox and I said, "How about doing *Carmen* [using the same set]?" He kissed me again and raised my salary. So we did *Carmen*. As a young director, I tried to invent new setups, you know, like every young director. And there was a bullfight in *Carmen*, and they built half an arena there and stands. And they sent to Tiajuana to get a bullfighter and he brought his entourage, you know. They came up with all their costumes and everything. And we got ready for the day of the bullfight—and we had this bull brought from Mexico and I had some fellows rope him and bring him in the arena and then I tied his feet down in the ground, drove a peg in there and tied his feet. In those days the French invented a little bit of a camera called a De Brie. I decided to strap the camera on the bull's back, so that the camera, when we turned it on the matador, was coming towards him. The horns would be there, you know, to show how real it was. Well, we got ready to take it. We had the bull staked, and they put the belt around him and put the camera on, and I told the matador to come on. Well, they got pretty close to the camera. That was the last we saw of the bull. He took off, I'm telling you, but not as fast as the toreador did. Two days later they found the bull in a meadow somewhere. The camera was all crushed and that was the last of my artistic shots.

WHAT PRICE GLORY?

(It is impossible to calculate the number of movies Raoul made, since so many in the early days with Fox were short films. However, from 1921 —the year in which the authoritative American Film Institute Index *starts counting—through 1928, when sound came in, he is credited with sixteen feature-length productions. Probably the most notable of them was his adaptation of the hit Broadway play by Maxwell Anderson and Laurence Stallings. Curiously, it was remade, and not improved upon, by Raoul's old friend and contemporary John Ford in 1952.)*

[Victor] McLaglen I figured was ideal for the part and so was Eddie Lowe. They were a wonderful combination, the big dumb captain and the cagey Lowe, the sergeant. And the pretty girl, Charmaine—Dolores Del Rio—between them. It was a great setup and it went on and on. We made many pictures with them [Lowe and McLaglen]. They were good box office. *What Price Glory?* was made where Twentieth Century-Fox now stands. And the Century Plaza with its huge buildings and hotel is where I photographed the battle. It was mostly done at night and the police were ordered to stop the bombarding and the setting-off of the explosions. I was tipped off that I was going to be arrested, and I got the company to give me four or five assistants. After we had taken a series of explosions, the police showed up and wanted to know who was in charge here and one of my assistants said, "I am." And they put him in the car and took him away. When they got out of the gate, we started again. Back they came, another crew—asked who was in charge here. The second man said, "I am." So we went through the battle like that, and one night I remember a fellow came running in through the gates and up towards where the camera was, in his bathrobe. He was an Italian, a big heavy-set fellow. He said, "What's a-going on here? Bomb. A-boom, a-boom . . . all a-night long. I'm taking a bath, the ceiling come down on-a me. What's a-going to happen here? Who's a-going to pay?" So they called the unit manager. They took him aside and told him he'd be paid. It ended up, I think the Fox Company paid $70,000 in damages to homes—broken windows, ceilings caving in, people couldn't sleep and stuff. But that was life in those days.

Everybody had battles with the censors. They went out of their way sometimes to make it pretty tough for us. A kiss could only last three seconds. You weren't allowed to take any love scene if there was a bed visible, even if it was a mile away down the road. Every state had their own censors and Pennsylvania was the toughest. Whenever anybody took a scene that was the least bit off, everybody would yell, "It won't be shown in Pennsylvania." But we battled on and battled on. Sometimes we'd take maybe six or seven risqué scenes, a-bit-off scenes, hoping they'd leave two. That's how we worked. I remember an instance in a picture I made, *The Cock-Eyed World*,* with Lowe and McLaglen and El Brendel. And McLaglen as captain was standing outside his tent in Nicaragua and Brendel went by with a very pretty Nicaraguan girl and McLaglen yelled, "Hey, where are you going?" Brendel gathered himself together and said, "Captain, I'm bringing you the lay of the land." He took out a card from his pocket and said, "Here is where all the enemy is for you." Well, when the picture opened and Brendel told the captain, "I'm bringing you the lay of the land," the audience nearly laughed the roof off the theater. They didn't wait to have him take out the card and show this was where the enemy was. That got by the censors because in the projection room when the censors ran it [they heard] that "I'm bringing you the lay of the land and here is the map to show you everything . . ." but they never heard that in the theater.

On *What Price Glory?* I had about a hundred Marines that I got at the Marine base down at El Toro or someplace. And of course McLaglen and Lowe, when they got talking to each other, they'd say "You dirty son-of-a-bitch, you lousy bastard, you prick"—and then, of course, we'd put on the title: "I don't want nothing more to do with you. You're not a pal of mine." Well, after the picture ran two or three weeks at the Roxy Theatre, they got thousands and thousands of letters from lip-readers that said that it was the most disgusting picture they ever saw, and the most terrible language that these men were talking. Now, that also sent people back who saw it. They became lip-readers. So the picture grossed over $700,000 in four weeks and it cost $360,000.

* A sound sequel to *What Price Glory?* made in 1929.

THE COMING OF SOUND

Sound didn't affect me at all. I don't know why. But it affected a great many directors, and I remember they had a meeting and they got up—you know how directors will talk sometimes—and said: "We have established a medium; now the medium is about to be destroyed" and so and so and so. I was the first one to get up and say, "I'm going for sound." They booed me and I walked out.

The only problem I got into with sound, I lost my eye. I'll tell you what happened. I was with Fox at the time. Warner Brothers had all the patents for sound, but they could only produce sound pictures indoors. They had no outdoor equipment, so all the sound pictures with Jolson and those were made indoors. I went to a theater one night in Beverly Hills and saw some picture, I forget what it was, and all of a sudden on comes a Fox Movietone News wagon and I saw a fellow interviewing a longshoreman there with all his gorillas and stuff. So I said, "There's a guy talking outdoors." I left the theater fast, I called up Winnie Sheehan* at his house. I said, "I want to make a sound picture." He said, "Are you drunk?" I said, "No. Get me a Movietone News wagon." He told me, "Why in the hell didn't I think of that? C'mon up to the house." So I went up to the house about twelve o'clock. He phoned to New York and found out that there was a Movietone News wagon in San Francisco and he ordered it brought down and they put it on the back lot and Sheehan said, "Don't let anybody know about this." He said, "You used to be an actor." And I said, "Yes, a lousy one." He said, "Get some sort of a story and do a two-reeler. Don't let anybody know about it." I went out and took a few tests. I knew a short story called "The Cisco Kid," and I jotted that thing down and got myself a Mexican outfit and took the wagon and started off for Utah. I worked about ten days with the stuff and they started to see the rushes back there. And they phoned me and said these rushes look great, stay up there and make it a five-reeler. I figured how could I make it a five-reeler? I've done most of the story. So then I figured, Well, I could get some chases in. I told them to get a hold of Pat Jones, who was the fellow that rented all the horses,

---

* Sheehan by this time was the executive in charge of production at the Fox West Coast studio.

stagecoaches to the studios, and I said, "Get him to put the stagecoach in a big truck, and send him up here right away." Two days later they arrived up there and I started some chases with the stagecoach and stuff and then the bloody wagon broke down, the sound thing broke down, the sound man came to me and he said, "Going over these rough roads and stuff, it's all gone haywire." I called the studio and told them the bad news and they said, "Well, come on home, we'll finish it inside." So I jumped in a car with a cowboy and we headed off through the desert to get the train to Salt Lake City and then to Los Angeles. And on the way to this thing we went through all sorts of country. And a big jackrabbit jumped up in front of the car, through the windshield and cut my eye out and damned near cut my nose off—had me all scarred up. They took me to a hospital in Cedar City and the guy, I don't know, put eight or ten stitches in my eye. I said, "Have you got a shot of whiskey? This is starting to hurt me." He said, "We don't have any liquor in Utah." I said, "Remind me to never come back." So they patched me up and sent me to Hollywood. The doctor worked on me and said, "The eye should come out." I said, "What are you waiting for? Take it out." "Oh," he said, "it might be good to give it a little time." So I went to New York and saw a doctor there and he said it should come out. And I said, "Take it out. You've got a table there and you've got a lot of knives in that cabinet. Take it out." He said, "Oh, no, you have to go to the hospital." And I knew that meant three days. So I went there and had the bloody thing out. He said, "You want me to fix it up so you can wear a glass eye?" I said, "No, I'd get drunk and lose it." Irving Cummings finished the picture. They left a lot of me in it, the long shots, the rides and different things. And they gave me equal credit with Cummings as the director, which was all right with me because he did a good job and he got a fellow named Warner Baxter to play my part and he won an Oscar.*

But talking about glass eyes, I'll tell you a funny story. I used to go visit at the Hearst ranch up at San Simeon for many years and met all sorts of people up there. Met Winston Churchill up there and he wanted to go to the races and I took him to Santa Anita—charming old fellow. And Marion Davies threw a party that night at the beach house and I

* The picture, when it was released, was called *In Old Arizona*.

sat over at a side table with Sir Winston, who was a great bottle man, you know, and they brought him an imported bottle of very fine brandy and a box of cigars and he watched all these people that Marion had invited to come in. Every pretty girl that'd come in, "Who's that, Walshie? Walshie, who's that?" And they were just young girls—no stars. But he was a fine old man.

But to get back to the story, there was a young fellow called Lloyd Pantages. He was the son of Alexander Pantages, who owned a terrific group of theaters all up and down the coast. His father was a Greek and his fortune was estimated at about $20,000,000 and he couldn't read or write. And he used to call me Ralph—he couldn't say Raoul. Now, in the early days Lloyd was an immaculate dresser, he was a sort of a dandy, you know what I mean, who was a great wit—full of sarcasm and full of booze. So Marion used to like to have him up there because he was witty, and everybody liked Lloydie. And Mr. Hearst used to run a picture, start about eleven o'clock and it would be over at about one, and we'd gather in the big room and Mr. Hearst would go up and work and then we'd have some drinks and talk and stuff. And this one night Lloydie-Poo got pretty noisy.

Before then I meant to tell you that Mr. Pantages said to me, "Ralph, that boy of mine he costs me a lot of money. I had to pay $20,000 to bring German man over here to make him eye. He make him one eye for nice, he make him another eye for not so nice day, he make him an eye for when the clouds come, then he make him an eye for night. And he make an eye for when moon shine, make an eye for this." And I said, "Why in the hell didn't he make him a bloodshot eye, he's drunk all the time?"

Well, anyhow, Lloydie got pretty noisy that night up there and Marion came to me. She said, "Raoul, better get him to bed. If Popsie hears this noise, yelling and screaming down there, he's going to cut off the liquor for a week," which he used to do. So I went over and I said, "Lloydie, I think it's time to go to bed." Well, he called me a lot of names—about wearing a patch, a bloody bandit bastard and all that stuff. And I said, "Look, you're going to go to bed or I'm going to pull that marble out of your eye." Well, he started to yell at me again and I put my foot under and I put him down on the floor and I said, "Are you going to go to bed?" He started yelling. And I said, "Well, out it comes." And I started to dig into his eye, and you never heard such screaming in your life. Marion came over and touched me on the shoulder and said, "Raoul, you're taking out his *good* eye."

Those were the days, my good friends, those were the days, as Barrymore would say.

JOHN WAYNE ON *THE BIG TRAIL*

(*The first film Raoul made after he had recovered from his eye operation was also an outdoor western, this one making use of a pioneering attempt at wide-screen projection. It is remembered, however, not for its introduction of a new technology, but for its introduction—in his first long role—of an actor.*)

I was getting ready to start a picture called *The Big Trail*, and we were looking high and low for a young fellow to play the lead. We took many tests, and I was strolling out around the Fox lot one day, and as I walked by the property department, I saw this young fellow come out, about six feet four in height. He walked over to a truck and picked up a big stuffed armchair and lifted it up over his head and carried it into the property department. So I went over and waited until he came out and I asked him what he was doing, and he said, "I work here in the property department." I said, "Have you ever been in a picture?" He said, "No, sir." I said, "How would you like to be in a picture?" He said, "Oh, I'd like it right well." I said, "All right, you let your hair grow for about two weeks"—his hair was cropped short because he just came from the USC football team—and in about two weeks he showed up and he had a fair length of hair, and I got him into a good buckskin suit and took a good test of him—a silent test—and the company ran it. Winnie Sheehan was the studio executive then. He said, "That's a hell of a good-looking boy. Can he speak?" And I said, "Sure he can speak. He's a college boy." So he said, "All right. We'll sign him up if you want to take a chance with him, a newcomer." I said, "All right, I will."

They didn't like his name—Morrison—and got changing it around, and called him Joe Doakes and Sidney Carton and all those sort of names —and I remembered I had read a book that I liked one time about Mad Anthony Wayne. I thought this Wayne was a great character. So I said, "Let's call him Anthony Wayne or Mad Wayne or whatever the hell you want to call him—call him Wayne." Well, they called him John Wayne. That's how he got his name.

So we went to make the picture. Now, while I was out looking for locations, the Fox Company got together—Sheehan and Sol Wurtzel—and figured this boy should have some help. They sent back to New York and they engaged five prominent character actors, the most prominent actors of the day, and brought them out and surprised me with these fellows. Well, they certainly did surprise me because when I got a look at them, I knew none of these fellows had ever seen the sun rise or the sun set—I knew I was going to have a hell of a time with them on location. We got out on location, got started and I called John and said, "John, sit down beside me when I'm directing these character actors, because they're the best and you'll learn something from them." Well, the night before, a bootlegger got in to them and they were pretty well oiled up for this scene. Not only did they scare the Indians that were sitting around, they scared the hawks and the crows that were in the trees, and I said, "John, go over there and mingle with the Indians. Pay no attention to them." The great character men stayed loaded all through the picture, and finally got so bad we nicknamed them Johnnie Walker, Gordon Gin, several names of whiskey. We finally struggled through the picture. John was very attentive, very good. He's a nice boy to work with. And I feel pleased that I discovered what is probably the world's greatest box-office [star]. I also discovered a great American.

THE BOWERY

(*In the 1930s, Raoul made many films which Andrew Sarris, the critic, has correctly characterized as "maddeningly routine." The first film made by the newly merged Twentieth Century-Fox,* The Bowery, *was an exception, a rich, nostalgic, roughneck comedy, full of period flavor and broad Irish humor.*)

Of course, in the early days, when I made *The Regeneration* for Fox, the locale was the Bowery, so I used to wander up and down that street sometimes at night, see these derelicts lying in the gutter, see the fights and look at all the brawlers in the saloons, and I became quite familiar with the type of people when it came to make *The Bowery* with Wally Beery and George Raft and Fay Wray. Famous McGurk's Tavern, I had been in that as a young fellow, so it was easy for me to re-create what I knew and what I had seen. These were rough characters. The Bowery was no place to stroll on a Sunday afternoon. In fact, I had to stop drinking because in my early days I got into a barroom fight and I was arrested and taken before the judge in night court and I was a bit off. And the judge looked at me and he said, "Are you drunk?" And I said, "I'm as sober as a judge." He said, "That'll cost you thirty days." I said, "I can do that standing on my hands." He said, "I'll make it sixty, that'll put you back on your feet. Get him out of here."

George Raft was playing the part of Steve Brodie. Steve Brodie in the early days was supposed to be the only man that jumped off the Brooklyn Bridge and lived to tell it. That was our story. So the final scene we were taking on the Brooklyn Bridge. I had the cameraman set up at a spot where the jump was supposed to have taken place. George Raft was sitting in his limousine with his friend Mack Gray, and I thought I'd play a little gag on George, and I walked down to the limousine and I said, "George, we're in trouble—the stunt man who was going to take the jump quit, so it looks like you're going to have to do it." He looked at me for a moment, then he turned as pale as a ghost. I said, "Don't worry, everything'll be all right, George," and I went back to the camera. Mack Gray, his friend, came up and said, "Raoul, George can't swim." I said, "That don't make any difference. I've taken care of that." I walked back to the limousine; I said, "Don't worry about anything, George. I have three boats there to pick you up. He said you can't swim, but they'll pick you up. Don't worry." I walked away again. Mack came back again. He said, "Raoul, the chauffeur driving George said that three hundred people have jumped and none of them lived." I went back to the limousine and said, "George, these people wanted to die. You don't want to die. You're doing this to become a big hero. Just think, when it's on the [front] pages—George Raft jumps off Brooklyn Bridge." "Yes," he said, "but what if I don't make it?" I said, "What the hell—the company will bury you and give you a hell of a funeral." He looked at me and shook his head. And he said, "Can I call my agent?" I said, "What? Do you want *him* to do it?" And I said, "Don't worry, George. I'll see that you make it all right." And I went back to the camera. And Mack Gray came up and said, "Raoul," he said, "I don't know whether George can do it or not. I told you he couldn't swim." I said, "Get him up here. I'll show him how to do it." So he brought George up. I said, "All right, George, stand there. All right, turn the camera." I said, "All right, throw the dummy over." They threw the dummy over, and George shook hands with me.

WARNER BROTHERS

I was fifteen to sixteen years with the Fox Company.* Then I went to Europe and then Jack Warner knew that my contract was up and he signed me for seven years. He always wanted to get me in his organization since he saw *What Price Glory?* Jack and I became very good friends because I always brought [pictures in on budget]. We had a budget meeting. They'd say this picture is going to cost so much—$200,-000, $500,000 or a million. And, of course, then it would be sent up to Jack and he'd read it over. "Hell," he'd say, "cut $100,000 out of it and let them shoot it." I'd go up to him and say, "You can't cut it out, Jack. You need this scene . . . you need this." He'd say, "All right, go and shoot it." And I'd try to stick to that money and to the eighteen or twenty days I had, you know.

Now, a lot of actors didn't want to work with me because I worked too fast. I believed it was a motion picture, so I moved it. And Jack and I became very good friends. He has very few friends. He was sort of like Griffith, he sort of stayed away. I had an arrangement with Jack Warner about schedules. He gave me three huge bonuses for bringing in the pictures under budget.

Lots of pictures I made because Warner would weep on my shoulder. "Look, Raoul, we've missed two releases. These bums, we can't get any pictures out of them. Will you make this one? We need it. We need it." You know. I'd say, "Well, all right, Jack, I'll make it. Who's in it?" He said, "I don't know. A lot of people have turned it down." I said, "That's

---

* Actually, Raoul had been with Fox for two decades.

a hell of a thing to tell me. Suppose *I* turn it down." He said, "I know you won't. You're my pal."

I would work sometimes until one o'clock in the morning to finish a picture down on what we called the New York street—and finish at one o'clock in the morning and go home. And at eight o'clock the [next] script was thrown on my lawn like the Los Angeles *Times*. Go to the studio and meet these people that were in it. "What part are you playing? You'll be all right. You've got a good face."

Whenever I made a picture, Warner turned me loose with it. I never had any trouble at all. I went around making my type of pictures, you know, and they'd buy those stories for me, and at one time there was a very, very sedate sort of fellow, good writer and a producer on the lot—I won't mention his name—and he buttonholed me one day and he said, "Raoul, I have the most tender love story, and I think it would be a great change of pace for you to do it. I'm going to ask Jack Warner if you can do it. Do you mind?" I said, "No, a change of pace is good. Who's the girl?" He said, "I don't know yet, but it's a very tender love story." So he went in to see Jack Warner and he told Warner about this tender love story and he'd like to have Raoul Walsh do it. And Warner said, "Look, a tender love story to Raoul Walsh is to burn down a whorehouse."

THE ROARING TWENTIES

(*Raoul's first film for Warner Brothers was* The Roaring Twenties, *a stark tragedy about a couple of Irish gangsters clawing their way out of the slums by establishing themselves as bootleggers during Prohibition. One, played by James Cagney, was not immune to sentiment or a code of personal morality, and he lost control of his mob, becoming eventually a near-derelict. The other, played by Humphrey Bogart, stopped at nothing and attained, by the end of the picture, wealth and power. They were both killed in their final confrontation.*)

Of course, in the picture I probably had two of the finest actors that have ever appeared on the screen, Jimmy Cagney and Humphrey Bogart. They weren't gangsters at heart, they were fine men, very fine men. But they played these parts to perfection. They loved their work, they were great people. They were kind of opposite. Jimmy Cagney was a quiet sort of fellow who studied the script, studied the part, watched the wardrobe he was going to wear. He was very meticulous about it. He would come on the set in the morning, would say, "Good morning, Raoul," and he'd always be ready at nine o'clock to shoot, ready . . . ready. He knew the whole script. Bogey'd come on and he'd say, "What the hell are we going to do today?" He disliked motion pictures; he disliked the hours. He didn't like to get up at seven in the morning and come to the studio and hang around till six. Because he had come from the stage, where he worked in the theater at eight o'clock at night and at eleven he was through so that he could go out and continue his drinking. So he was always beefing. And I'd always quiet him down. I'd say, "Bogey, how about that salary at the end of the week?" He says, "That's the only thrill I get out of the damned business." [Cagney] had that quality of commanding sympathy and, at times, great love from the audience: will he make it? He will give it an approach that nobody else can handle. And your audience is arrested, their attention is to him from beginning to end. They follow every little thing he does. Now, the same thing is [true of] Humphrey Bogart. He was another powerful character, and if you had the two of them in the same picture, you knew that you had a good audience interest in the conclusion of this picture—if one of them was going to be killed, and possibly two—and they were sitting on the edge of their seats to know and find out when it happened. Now, a peculiar thing—you could kill a Cagney or a Bogart and have a very successful picture, but you could never kill a Gable or Cooper or Peck—the audience wouldn't go for it at all. In fact, in the early days, if you had those fellows in a picture where they were killed, the theater owner wouldn't play it because he knew the audience wouldn't stand for it. But with Cagney and Bogart they accepted it. Even though they were tough gangsters and stuff, there was always a bit of sorrow in their death. In *The Roaring Twenties* when Cagney finally caught up with Bogart and killed him, and then he left the house and ran down the street—one of Bogart's henchmen shot him and it was a great death scene that Jimmy played, running down the street. He fell and knocked over a trash can, picked himself up and crossed the street, ran onto the church steps, up the church steps, staggered, fell, rolled down—and died in the gutter. Funny thing, one of the festivals I was at, somebody said, "Why did it take so long for Cagney to die?" I said, "It's always hard to kill an actor."

[Cagney] was a great man and a great actor and he was interested only in his picture. He would sit back and look at the scenes that I'd take with other people and he'd say, "That's great, Skipper, that's all right." We became very warm friends during all the years. And we'd meet at his house several times for dinner. He'd come to my house for dinner. We'd go maybe to Chasen's restaurant or something and talk about old times and old pictures.

BOGART AND *HIGH SIERRA*

High Sierra was originally written for George Raft. They sent it to him, he read it and turned it down. Warner, who calls all actors bums, said, "Go over and see the bum and see if you can talk him into playing it." So I went over to see George and he said, "I read the script and stuff, but I'm not going to die in the end." I said, "You have to. You killed a couple of people, the censors are going to demand that you pay the penalty." He said, "I don't give a damn about the censors, I'm not going to die." I said, "Well, then you're not going to play the picture."

I told Warner and he said, "Who the hell can we get?" I said, "You've got a fellow on the lot here that's coming up like wildfire, Humphrey Bogart." He says, "Well, well, he's a tough guy to handle, this fellow. He's grumbling all the time and, in fact, he's going around town telling people I'm a fairy." So Warner said, "Go and see the bum, read the script to him. I don't think he can read." I went over and saw Humphrey and sat down and talked to him and he said, "It's great. I'll do it. It's right up my alley. When do we start?"

We started with the picture. Suddenly he started with his grumbling, but I found a good spot where I could really hear him grumble. In *High Sierra* the chase scene starts in the desert with about eight motorcycle cops chasing Bogart up the mountain, through the passes—a real sensational chase, it was, through curves, around eleven thousand feet and the road ends. Then I had Bogart get out of the car and I said, "Bogey, run up and get your back against that canyon wall and hide behind those big boulders." And he took off, you know what I mean. And then I said, "Bogey, stay up there, we'll start there after lunch." He said, "You bet your A I'll stay up here." I got a hold of the property man and I said, "Eddie, when the lunches come, have the truck hidden over behind the trees there and when I take my hat off, you holler up, 'They forgot to send the lunches.'" So I walked up there and joined Bogart and he was beefing about the sun. It was about a hundred and ten or a hundred and twelve and up that high there are no trees. There was no shade and he wondered who the hell picked this location, you know, beefing about the sun—"nothing but a lot of lousy rattlesnakes around. Christ, I'm afraid I'm going to get bitten," you know. He's beefing and beefing and I just let him beef for a while and said, "Yes, look at all the beautiful scenery, look at this snow-capped mountain in the background here. You should have been a painter, Bogey." He said, "Ah, I don't want any part of this. Give me the parlor—give me the parlor, bedroom and bath. To hell with this." I took my hat off. "They forgot to send the lunches, Mr. Walsh!" Bogey said, "What? Jeez, here I am up in the mountains and no lunch." I said, "Well, those things happen in the picture business, Bogey." And then he went off on a tirade—oh, gee, he raved and screamed, and he said, "That bastard Jack Warner, eating in his private dining room, sinking his puss into a filet mignon with asparagus and trimmings and such and I'm up here starving to death. What a lousy business." So then I gave the fellow the signal, he said, "The lunches are here." I said, "All right, bring up a couple." Now this was the first location that Bogey had been on. Eddie came up with the two box lunches. I sat next to Bogey and watched to see the expression on his face when he opened his lunch. Well, he opened it up. He saw a dried-up ham sandwich, he saw a pickle, he saw an olive, he saw a banana and a cookie. He said, "They feed the convicts in San Quentin better than this!" I said, "Eat it, Bogey, you can't eat too much when you're up this high anyway." But he was a great guy to handle, nice fellow, and we became the warmest of friends.

One close shave after another—James Cagney in
The Strawberry Blonde (*1941*)

A desperately tired Cagney faces down Bogart
moments before the big fight in Roaring Twenties
(*1939*).

Ida Lupino and Humphrey Bogart in High Sierra
(*1941*)

THE STRAWBERRY BLONDE

(Raoul's next film was one of his—and Cagney's—tenderest movies, a wonderfully touching and funny evocation of turn-of-the-century life in New York, featuring in the romance between James Cagney and Olivia de Havilland one of the most memorably sweet, yet never cloying, love stories I know of in American movies. Characteristically, Raoul mainly remembers from the filming a curious incident.)

I was in New York at the time of the Gay Nineties. I knew all the songs of the period. I knew the people, knew their mannerisms, and it came in as a great help in directing *Strawberry Blonde*. Of course, I had a great man playing the lead in it—Jimmy Cagney. Another Irishman and an actor of no mean ability.

When I was doing *Strawberry Blonde* with Jimmy, Rita Hayworth, Olivia de Havilland, Jack Carson, we had a tragedy on the New York street. It was a hot summer day and we'd just finished lunch and clouds came up and we had to stop shooting. We had about a hundred-and-some-odd extras dressed in Gay Nineties costumes, you know. And in those pictures about New York they always had an Italian with his organ and a monkey. So people were lolling about. It was a hot day and they were lolling. And the girls all wore those long skirts of the time. And there was a girl asleep on one of the porches there. The organ-grinder was asleep, but the monkey wasn't. He got away, and he started running in the back of the set. And the organ-grinder missed him and started yelling, "Joey!" The monkey's name was Joey, I remember. "Joey, Joey, Joey, Joey, Joe . . ." chasing him up and down on buildings and down and round. And then Joey worked his way through one of the buildings and came to the place where the girl was sleeping on the porch. He lifted up her dress and went in there to hide. The girl started screaming, she jumped up and ran down the street and I remember I thought she was sun-struck or something. I didn't know what the hell was . . . And this guy yelling and screaming for Joey in back of the set. Now, when he heard the girl screaming, he knew Joey was somewhere where he shouldn't be, you know. So he came tearing around and ran up and caught the girl. She was still screaming. He lifted up the dress and got the monkey. Joey was holding on to her garter belt and the man took him away.

The girl sued the studio for $20,000, said the monkey bit her on the navel. They settled for $2000 and she had a new navel.

THEY DIED WITH THEIR BOOTS ON

(Shortly after this, Raoul made his first film with Errol Flynn. Their association began with tragedy, but it included what seems to have been the closest relationship Raoul ever had with an actor, since he was the one director Warners could count on to handle their difficult, profitable star.)

Those scenes were very, very difficult, and we ran into a lot of trouble. In the first place, in those days a director could request the riders he wanted and usually he used all the old cowboys that had been in all the westerns, but the Screen Extras' Guild passed a ruling—no more requests. They would furnish the riders out of their ranks. Well, the first day about eighty of them fell off their horses, were kicked and hurt. Sometimes I watched these riders get on their horses and they mounted from the wrong side. And it became a very gloomy prospect to get any kind of a decent charge. Next day we took a scene of a Union cavalry coming across a bridge. Explosions on either side of the bridge. A young fellow—I can't remember his name now—was the lieutenant that was leading the charge, and as they got to the bridge, the powder man turned off the explosions. The young lieutenant was thrown up in the air—he let go of his sword, the sword came down and stood upright on the bridge and he tumbled right on top of it. Usually in the long shots we give them fake swords, not the real blades—but the property man told me that this lieutenant refused to give up his real sword and take the phony one, and the property man said he argued with him for quite some time and then he saw it was to no avail, and we took the scene and the fellow was killed. We took him to the hospital and his folks wouldn't allow the doctors to open him up and see what the damages were, and he passed on. There were two other accidents: one of the riders fell off, broke his neck; and another fellow, while he was riding, died of a heart attack and fell off. It was a rough, tough picture to do, and the outside interference caused most of these casualties. I remember when we'd be leaving the studio with the four busses full of these riders, an ambulance would follow up. And in the last days we were going out, Tony Quinn, who played Crazy Horse in the picture, thought of a joke. He put a hearse following us. When the extras in the busses saw this hearse, they all left the busses and ran back to the studio.

Errol Flynn was a terrific guy until they told him he was going to die and then he wanted to die . . . he wanted to die. He was a good actor, a much better actor than the people realized. The Custer picture, *They Died with Their Boots On*—he got great writeups on that. And he also got terrific writeups in *Gentleman Jim*, when he played the prizefighter Jim Corbett. He liked those two pictures very much and he really worked—really worked. And down toward the end Warners was getting ready to break his contract, you know. I found out through the grapevine that Warner had phoned down to the police at the gate and said, "I want to know what time this Flynn gets in." I heard about that. My house wasn't very far from his house up on Mulholland Drive, so I went up and told him and I says, "Look, you're in trouble and I know you need the money. You bought this $100,000 yacht and you've got a crew on it. I'm going to pick you up at seven thirty every morning and take you through the gates so that you can register in and you go to your dressing room and I'll have some coffee sent to you. Take a nap for about an hour or a half an hour, and I'll work with somebody until you are on your feet." He put his arms around me and kissed me and said, "You're my only friend." Then I'd go up there at seven o'clock, and I knew he always had some girl or somebody there, and I didn't want to go in and embarrass anybody. He had a Russian butler, so I'd say, "Alex, is anybody in there?" "Oh, no, Miss So-and-so just leave." And some of the names he told me would astound you.

IN WITH FLYNN

(At some time in their association Raoul accompanied Flynn to New York to help promote one of their pictures. As we fade in, Flynn is on the phone, placing an order with room service.)

He ordered ten bottles of Johnnie Walker, he ordered eight bottles of Gordon's. He ordered five or six bottles of vodka, six bottles of champagne, two of them to be on the ice right away, and several other things. Then he ordered a lot of caviar and Guinness' stout and three dozen oysters. He was there on a Roman holiday. And he said, "By the way," before he hung up, "if there are any pretty girls in the lobby, send *them* up." So he called a friend of his, a very famous stockbroker in New York, and the stockbroker told him he was giving a party that night at his house and wanted Errol to come, and Errol said, "I have a one-eyed bandit with me," and he said, "Bring him along." So we went to the party and Errol spotted a beautiful society girl and he went right after her like Don Juan. And this romance lasted for about five or six days.

Now, as long as everything was charged to his room, he ordered six dozen roses to be sent to her in the morning and six dozen in the afternoon all the time we were there. Then he ordered I don't know how many dollars' worth of bonbons and chocolates to be sent there. And he eventually ended up sending her two French poodles that cost $500 apiece. And he just signed for them, you know.

After about five days I came back from visiting some friends, and he was in the dumps. He was drinking and drinking. And I said, "What's the matter?" He said, "Uncle, she walked out on me." Well, this was the first girl that had ever walked out on him. *He* generally did the walking. It shocked him, you know? So I said, "Forget it, what the heck?" He said, "Uncle, she won't talk to me on the phone or see me, I'm going to jump out that window." I said, "Errol, let's talk it over, you're not going to jump tonight." He said, "Yes, I am, Uncle." Another drink. Then we got to talking a bit and he said, "Uncle, you're my closest friend, will you please go and see her and ask her if I can call on her?" I said, "All right, I'll go." I put my hat on and went downstairs and walked up Madison Avenue—went into a little bar on the corner and sat down for about three quarters of an hour and had a drink. And I came back in the room and he was still down and he saw me. "Did you see her?" I said, "Yes." He said, "Did you tell her what I was going to do? Jump out the window?" I said, "Yes, I did." "What did she say?" "She wanted to know what time you were going to jump. She wanted to come over and see it."

FLYNN AND BARRYMORE

(Through Raoul, Flynn became a friend of another legendary bottle man—John Barrymore. The news of the great old actor's death struck the younger man with great force. Ironically, when Flynn made his brief but strong comeback in the 1950s as a character man, one of his best roles was as Jack Barrymore in Diana Barrymore's autobiography, Too Much, Too Soon.*)*

I was up at Errol's house and he'd been drinking quite heavily. We'd heard that Jack Barrymore died that day. There was a couch there where Barrymore used to sit. Jack would tell us his wild stories about his travels. I don't think he'd even been to Tiajuana. But he amused Flynn and later Flynn sort of started copying Barrymore. And down on the set I'd say, "Look, forget Barrymore, you're Flynn. C'mon." So he was all saddened by the death of Barrymore, and he said, "Uncle, I can see the old fellow sitting there now telling us his most marvelous tales, like the great story he told when somebody asked him if Hamlet had had an affair with Ophelia. And he said, 'Only in the Chicago company.' " And Flynn said, "How I miss the old fellow." Finally the phone rang and Alex came and told him something. And Errol came back to me and he said, "Uncle, I've got to go over and see my lawyer. I'll only be over there a short time. I'll come back and we'll have dinner. Will you wait?" I said, "Yes, I'll wait." I poured myself a shot, got in my station wagon. I called up a friend of mine. I said, "Where they got this body of Jack?" He said, "It's temporarily at Malloy Brothers on Temple Street." So I jumped in my station wagon and headed for Malloy Brothers. I went in there and, lo and behold, one of the brothers used to be an actor, a character actor, worked in my pictures. He wanted to know what he could do for me. I said, "I'd like to borrow Barrymore's body for about two hours." Well, he was a bottle man, he was loaded, and I said, "I want to take him somewhere to surprise somebody." He said, "All right, for you I'll do it." Both of us got a hold of Barrymore, stiff as a board, put him in the back of the station wagon, and I drove carefully to Errol's house, 'cause I didn't want the cops to pick me up with the guy in the back dead, you know. So I pulled into the yard there and I went in to Alex and I said, "Alex, Mr. Barrymore didn't die, he's drunk. Help me carry him in the house." Hell, the dumb Russian helped me carry him in and we sat him on the couch there. And he said, "He's terrible, isn't he?" "You bet your ass he's terrible." Sat him on the couch and we had a hard time putting his legs down. I said, "Alex, push harder!" We finally propped Barrymore up. Alex said, "I never see so drunk a man." A little while Flynn comes in, walked up . . . EHHHH!!! And he dashed out of the house and went and hid in the brush. I went out and called him and said, "Come on in." He said, "No, what the hell have you done?" I said, "Well, you missed the old boy and I brought him up here. At least come in and say hello to him." "No, I'm not going in there." I said, "All right. C'mon, Alex, let's get him back before he falls asleep." Got Alex to put the guy back in the station wagon and back to Malloy Brothers, and the guy was waiting. He said, "Where the hell did you take him, Mr. Walsh?" I said, "I took him up to Errol Flynn's." He said, "Why the hell didn't you tell me? I'd a put a better suit on him."

GENTLEMAN JIM

In the early days I spent some time up in San Francisco with Jack London—I met him when I was working for Griffith. He came to the studio and asked me what kind of a fellow Pancho Villa was, whom I had made a picture with, as he was thinking of writing a book about him. So Jack and I became pretty warm friends, and he invited me up to visit him. And we sailed around the bay there and he took me to all the famous haunts that he wrote of in his books, so I had a good inkling of what to do with *Gentleman Jim,* which was in the period of the Mother Lode episode. And all the great multimillionaires of that time.

In my companies we had great camaraderie because we used the same people all the time—the same cameramen, the same electricians, the same carpenters and grips, the same sound crew. I always demanded that, so I had a good organization. We all were great friends.

I remember when I was doing *Gentleman Jim* with Ward Bond playing John L. Sullivan. After Flynn defeated him in New Orleans and became the world's champion, Flynn's manager threw a big party at the hotel and Ward Bond came and played a magnificent scene where he handed Flynn the World's Championship belt and there's some marvelous dialogue between the two of them and finally some tears came to Ward's eye and he walked out. And when the scene was over, the whole cast, the electricians, the crew and everybody applauded. That was the kind of camaraderie they had. They were all marvelous people. The sad part about it, I lost four of them—Bogey, Flynn, Gable and Cooper, all within four years. Bogart in '57, Flynn in '59, Gable in '60, Cooper in '61. One right after another—all great friends of mine. Between pictures we used to pal around. I used to go fishing and hunting with Cooper and I used to go hunting down in Utah and Arizona with Gable. And I used to go out drinking with Flynn.

I was at my house one afternoon about three o'clock and the phone rang and a fellow introduced himself. He said, "I'm Mr. So-and-so. I'm a reporter for *Life* magazine." He said he was just up there interviewing Errol Flynn, and he said, "The reason I'm calling is he just passed away." And he said, "He was talking about you when he lay down on the couch and . . ." That's what the reporter told me. Errol kind of liked me, so I guess he gave me a good writeup.

ON DIRECTION

(Over the years I've talked many times with Raoul about his life and his movies, and though I can recall dozens of anecdotes from it and about them, I can't remember any long statement about the director's craft, about how he accomplished what he accomplished—namely, the creation of at least a dozen completely memorable films, hundreds of unforgettable scenes. The questions are answered by implication in his anecdotes;

he used the screen as he used words, to tell stories simply, clearly, humorously, sometimes poignantly, always with plenty of movement which never seemed forced, which seemed to flow naturally out of all sorts of material, some of which must have seemed to him, at first glance, ill-matched to his essential spirit. So there isn't much for earnest film students to learn from him about how to work, though they can learn everything from him about how to think. Still, he did give offhand a few generalizations and abstractions, and I've gathered them—from the several occasions at which our cameras were present—and grouped them here.)

A TOUGH JOB: You're always a bit disappointed after. You see, it's a tough job to go down on a cold set in a room and bring two people in to play a scene and that's sent to the lab and printed and stuff and that's it. Then, when you think of it, you think, "Oh, gee, I could have done this or that"—if you'd had more time. In a stage play you've got a month to fool around and manipulate the scenes and play them. But with the picture thing it's hit or miss. So lots of times when I see a picture of mine, I see a scene and I say, "Ah, why didn't I do this . . . ?"

WRITERS: The director seldom pays much attention to the script. After he knows the script, he throws it away. I've known a new writer to come into the studio, never been in the studio, but yet he will give you the camera setups. Now, how does he know anything about the camera setups? The director sets up the camera shots: he wants a closeup there. You don't need a closeup over here. He needs a two-shot there for that dialogue. He needs something over here. But they will waste time and write closeup, closeup, dolly shot. That's all got to come out of the scene as you see it, to keep it moving and stuff.

ON ACTORS: Actors are very particular about hats. I've seen fellows, some of the best of them, stand in front of a mirror: "Give me another one . . . ah, this is the one." I'd let them play around with it. They knew what their face needed, don't you know? I never insisted you've got to wear a sombrero or you've got to wear a jockey strap or anything—put something on for that period. And they'd run up to the wardrobe department and they'd bring down a big box of all kinds of hats, different sizes and everything. Some of them were full of fleas.

[But] plenty of times, when an actor would come and say, "Look, can I transpose this . . . can I cut this word out . . . this reads a little better," I'd agree. Sometimes, though, we'd have battles, but they'd be minor; they make too much of it. I'd just say, "Look, get the writer on the phone; let him tell you what he meant by that line."

ON ACTRESSES: Some are finicky and some are not. The greatest thing was arranging the hair. It generally took about two days to get their hair set. And it's a terrible thing, you know, to be out on the desert and the wind blowing. The hairdresser trying to fix their hair, you know, and the rest of the cast drinking Coca-Cola with a little shot in it.

I liked Virginia Mayo, Marlene Dietrich, liked Marion Davies, Ida Lupino, Mae West. They sort of fitted in with the people I knew and grew up with, you know, and they were sincere. They never came in and posed, you know.

FAVORITE THINGS: Some scenes I put in for my own gratification, but I generally decided to play for the public, because that's what kept us alive. In the early days we referred to the public as "the inch-and-a-quarter brows." I made some hits, I made some near-hits and I made a lot of turkeys. You make a lot of pictures. It's like raising children. Some go out and make good, and some don't. And you don't want to play any favorite. Let it go, you know.

Right to left: Frank Capra leans on Clark Gable who leans on Claudette Colbert on the set of It Happened One Night, *for which all of them won Oscars in 1934.*

FRANK CAPRA

F RANK CAPRA is a brave man. He might be called a premature auteurist, since long before that critical theory was enunciated he believed that the director was the logical person to be the author of a movie. "One man, one film" was his credo and he was not modest about taking credit for his work. To borrow the title of his autobiography, he believed his deserved to be "the name above the title" on his films and he fought for and won that prominent position when few others were able to do so. A little later Alfred Hitchcock would gain a similar position, but back in the 1930s Capra's was—excepting perhaps DeMille's—the most famous directorial name in the country. People responded to his skill, of course, but, more important, they responded to his populist beliefs. It was the decade of the little man, and Frank's little men—Deeds, Doe, Smith—became archetypes which reflected back to us our best qualities—common sense, down-to-earthness, idealism, patriotism, fidelity to family values. We understood that the "little men" were fictions, but we felt that we were all capable of at least a few moments as fine as their finest. We also understood that there was nothing cynical in Frank's presentation of them. True, they uncannily suited the spirit of the time, but neither then nor now—as we see the films anew—can we imagine that their creator made them up merely to cater to a mood, exploit our feelings. The integrity of the work was visible in every frame of Frank's films. You could sense that feelings animating his films were authentic, highly personal. We now know that Frank was of humble origins, that he had reason to be grateful to the country that had given him, a poor immigrant kid, a chance to educate himself, a chance to gain fame, wealth and (most important) the power to express his strongest feelings in what was then the most powerful medium available to an artist.

But times change. The Second World War came along, and Frank went off to serve in it with great distinction as chief of the unit that made the *Why We Fight* series. He returned to (again somewhat prematurely) pioneer the age of independent production with Liberty Pictures, cofounded with other prominent directors, but then in the late 1940s and early 1950s found that his optimistic spirit was no longer in tune with the confused and groping spirit of a new time. Oddly, he found that he had had more independence as an employee on a contract at a studio than he did in the new independent era. Now enormous concessions were being made to stars, and Frank found himself at the mercy of a not very good actor who has long since faded into B westerns, Disney films and unsuccessful television series, but who was then riding high. Frank hated it, and if the name was still above the title, it no longer reflected, he felt, the true order of things. And so he quit.

But he is a proud and even egocentric man. He had liked standing above the crowd, and relished the fame that he had certainly not tried to avoid in the old days. To be visibly groping for a way to be true to himself and yet stay active in the business must have hurt him. To quit, to be in the cruel judgment of the industry a has-been, must have been brutal. I can't pretend to know all his feelings in the matter. He is very guarded about them in his book and I never had the nerve to ask him. Once at a film seminar we both attended, I joined him at a lunch during which he was interviewed and the reporter asked him if he ever went back to the studios. He said sometimes, but that he didn't dare enter a sound stage. They have, he said, a special odor, the residue of a chemical reaction set off when the arc lamps are fired up, and that odor is an intolerable assault on his emotions. He spoke briskly, eager to get on to another subject.

But it is precisely here that his bravery becomes manifest. Frank says he always knew that if you were willing to take a lot of credit for your successes, it was inevitable that you would receive perhaps more than your share of the blame for your flops. And he took it quietly, without public expressions of bitterness, without changing his fundamentally optimistic view of existence. He moved out of Los Angeles into a house hard by the golf course in La Quinta, California, a new and prosperous settlement not far from Palm Springs. And though he makes good use of the golf course, it is not his major preoccupation. Instead, he sat down and wrote his excellent autobiography. It was a book-club choice and a strong seller in hardcover and paperback. Better still, it opened up a new career for him as a lecturer on films, mostly at colleges, but wherever people want to hear about the movies. As you will read in this interview, he takes great pride in the response he gets from young people, with whose specific political and social beliefs I suspect he frequently disagrees, but whose idealism he finds very familiar and similar to that which he expressed in his films and has felt all his life. He seems to me a very happy man, full of a restless energy, a bristling intellectual curiosity that I imagine to be unchanged from that which people must have felt on his sets thirty or forty years ago. He speaks rapidly, almost stammering, so quickly do ideas flood his tongue, and he is fun to talk to because, like King Vidor (whom he is unlike in most other ways), Capra is one of the few directors who have a conscious sense of what they were trying to do, and why, and can articulate it.

Nor does there appear to be any end in sight for his activities. The last time I talked to him he was passing through New York on his way from one lecture to another. He told me that he had just finished a magazine piece and that he was still struggling with a book, the subject of which he doesn't want to talk about. All he will say is that it's hard work. But of course he's used to that.

When you are driving to his house, incidentally, you never have to ask directions. It's the one underneath a giant American flag which once flew over the Capitol in Washington. The flag is a challenge to the sky and a fine thing to see out there in the desert oasis where Frank lives. It marks the home of a self-made man who late in life made himself all over again. Frank still has energy to spare, and it animates wisdom, pride and great sweetness of spirit.

FALLING IN LOVE WITH AMERICA

I fell in love with Americans when I was a young kid. None of my family, not one, could read or write—my mother and father or brothers and sisters. And this struck me as just something that I couldn't [stand]. I wanted to get an education more than anything in the world. I was going to learn how to read and write. Regardless of what they did. I was born a peasant, but I wasn't going to die one. That's all. Now, that's [why] this thrust toward getting an education, toward getting ahead. And then how easy it was for me to get ahead—just because I had this ambition. How easy it was for me to find things to do. I worked my way through grammar school, through high school, through college. I did all kinds of things. I made money enough to, finally, in my last two years of college send my mother $90 a month. And yet I was okay on grades. Actually, I won the freshman scholarship prize at Cal Tech. I had this mania for education, for books, for learning. And I suppose [because of] the ease with which I got that and the opportunities that were given me to rise above my family so quickly and so well, I just forever admired this country and will forever love this country for giving me that opportunity.

FIRST DISILLUSIONMENTS

My first big disillusionment came when I got out of uniform after World War I. I didn't go anyplace, I just stayed in San Francisco all that time, teaching mathematics to artillerymen. [But] I couldn't find a job afterwards. Here I was a chemical engineer, a diploma and all kinds of education behind me, I couldn't find a job. Of any kind. I had to leave home.

I couldn't let my mother constantly keep me. One of the first jobs I got was to sell photographs house to house for the Heartset people. They had various photographic centers throughout the West Coast and you rang doorbells and asked if anyone wanted their children photographed or anything else and collected a dollar. And you gave them a little contract that would be good for twelve big pictures. And naturally I kept the dollar. The dollar was mine. So if I rang enough doorbells, this was good for three or four dollars a day. This was a fine little way to make a living whenever you wanted to work. Well, that took me from town to town, all over California, Nevada, Utah, Oregon, Arizona. I fell in love with Nevada. I stayed there a great deal of the time. I learned how to play poker. I could play a guitar very well as a kid. And I got a little job playing the guitar with small combos. . . . I lived freely. And I met the American people, day to day—farmer, gambler, saloonkeeper, doctor, dentist. And got to know them very well, got to like them.

FIRST FILM

"Fuller Fisher's Boarding House" is a poem by Rudyard Kipling and it all takes place in a Calcutta barroom. It's a very, very dramatic poem. Two men fighting for a girl and one of them killing the other one and then the other one suddenly kissing his cross and all this kind of stuff— very, very heavy. All in one reel. Everything happened fast. The man Montague, who had promoted this thing, was a vaudevillean. He was a Shakespearean actor. His act in vaudeville was doing little bits from great plays. So he translated this to the screen. He wanted to do these little poems, little gems as short subjects. And he had himself an idea—he used the stanzas as titles. You'd see the stanza right over the scene and then the scene would be played and then the next stanza would come and the scene would be played. So I went out just to see him [in San Francisco]. I was broke, absolutely broke. And I introduced myself as Frank Capra from Hollywood, which was true, but not in the sense that he thought. I wasn't from the studio Hollywood. Our home was in Los Angeles. But the doors fell apart when I said "from Hollywood" and I was welcomed—asked to come and help them make this film. And being young and ambitious and broke, I said okay. But I didn't want real actors because they'd know right away I hadn't been near a camera or a studio. And that was my first film.

I was not aware of [the movies]. I'd go once in a while to see one of them, but they didn't give me any great kick. No, it came on suddenly when I peeked through the camera, through the eyepiece of the camera, on a job I conned myself into with this man who didn't know anything about films and I didn't either but I was younger than he was. And I looked through the eyepiece of this camera and saw this little set and this stage—"Fuller Fisher's Boarding House" and the bums in there and the sawdust and this bar. And I got a terrific thrill, goose pimples ran up and down my back. And I kept my eye glued to that camera. My, didn't that look great! I'd move the camera a little bit. And I still get the same kick. If I go and look through the eyepiece of that camera, I still get the magic kick of seeing into a magic square. There's life in this magic square that seems to be somehow unreal.

MACK SENNETT

(*Fascinated by this first experience of the craft that would become his life's work, Capra, after a few minor detours, made his way back to Los Angeles and got a job at the Mack Sennett studio as a gag writer. He takes up his story there.*)

Mack Sennett was one of the most interesting characters. You can understand this character when you understand he didn't like books. If you came in the studio with a book under your arm, he'd pull it right out and throw it in the wastebasket. Didn't want any books. He kept saying, "No gags in books." So if you read or in a sense were literate, he didn't want you around because he distrusted people who read. Now, gag men to him were something he didn't quite understand but were absolutely necessary. So he kept them caged up on the top of a tower, a four-story tower. The bottom was administrative, the second was administrative, the third was administrative, and the top [was where] the prisoners of Edendale, as they called themselves—the gag men—worked. And they had to punch a clock at nine o'clock in the morning, twelve, one and six. Like the janitors and everyone else—no freedom for creativity at all. And there were these benches, depot benches they were, with armrests in the middle to keep you from lying down. So, if we had to sleep, we had to sleep on the floor.

Now, there was a little closed-in stairway from the third floor up to the tower. And Mack Sennett would take his shoes off and sneak up there and see if anybody was asleep. He caught a couple of people like this and he fired them quickly. You didn't have to think of anything [right away]. You were good for six weeks if you didn't open your mouth. But if you did open your mouth and you didn't make him laugh, out you went. Anyhow, it was good for six weeks for anybody to get a job; they just went into thinking poses and that was okay [too]. But he didn't want you to sleep. When I was there we got the head carpenter to raise the riser on one of the steps by about three eighths of an inch. So when he'd creep up there, he'd hit the high riser and stumble, and the noise, of course, would wake the dead and everybody would jump into thinking pose the minute he came up. He never did get on to it. It was there for years and years and years, that high riser, and he never got on to it; he always stumbled. He had it coming anyhow for sneaking up on us.

Now, Mack Sennett himself was not funny. He was not a jokester. He couldn't tell jokes, but he could laugh. He had a laugh that rolled, a big basso laugh—it shook the windows when he laughed. I think if he laughed, the audience was pretty sure to laugh. What was funny to him would be funny to the audience. This was, of course, a great advantage in a producer. And we knew this and we used to try things on him. If he didn't laugh, we threw it away. All except one gag that I had about a wheel coming off that I thought was funny. And I told it to him and he said, "No, it isn't funny." Ben Turpin was making violent love to Madeline Hurlock in a buggy and she was very cool to him and he was very ardent in his way. And every time he'd grab her to kiss her, this wheel would almost come off on this cliff, you see. And every time he'd cool off, the wheel came back. And finally the wheel fell off and he fell off and he rolled down the [cliff]. Sennett said, "It isn't funny. Don't tell it to the director." By the way, the only way that the writers could communicate with the directors was to tell them the story in front of

Mack Sennett himself; nothing was written and nobody was allowed on the sets. But I told it to an actor who was working with Lloyd Bacon, who was the director. The actor told Bacon, Bacon shot the scene. They loved it. We [always saw] the rushes with Sennett, and that's when he'd say, "We need another gag. . . . That's no good there. . . . Somebody's got to think up another gag. . . ." Anyway, he saw it coming and he said, "I thought I told you not to tell that to—" I said, "I didn't tell him." He said, "Well, somebody did, now get that crap off." And I begged him to show it at a preview and he said, "No, no, no." And finally he said, "Oh, I'll teach you a lesson. I'll take you to a preview. You come with me." We went to the preview and the gag was very funny. And I thought, My goodness, this is really good. As we come out of the theater, he came over and he said, "Whose name is above that gate?" I said, "Yours, Mr. Sennett." He said, "You're god-damned right. You're fired." So that was the end of that gag. And I was fired. Being fired by Sennett didn't mean much, really. If you stayed outside the gate and and walked up and down like a penitent [looking] hungry and certainly respectful and everything else, he'd see you from the tower. You'd do that for a couple of days. Everybody had to do it. It was called walking the gate. You'd be fired, you'd walk the gate two days, then you could come back in. This was Mack Sennett.

HARRY LANGDON, THE STAR

I did have a great ambition to direct at all times. I wanted to be a director. I kept bugging Mack Sennett to give me a job as a director and he said, "What, and lose a good gag man?" To him directors didn't mean much. So I'm signed up to write for Harry Langdon. I've never met him, but Harry Langdon had been around the studio there for about a year and they had put him with various comics—these fast-moving comics—and he was nothing. But Mack Sennett said, "There's something to that man and I want you guys to find out what it is." So it became my turn, and my partner, whose name was Arthur Ripley, and I had to look at this film of an act that Harry Langdon had done with his wife. He was the little hen-pecked husband. And we look at it and it wasn't much. And somebody made the remark: "Only God can help that guy." And that started me off. I said, "Yeah, that's an idea. That's Soldier Schweik, he sees no evil, hears no evil, bears no evil to anybody. He's Mr. Good—he's this good little elf. And only his goodness wins out." Well, this got us started and we concocted a new story for him and a new star was born with this character—overnight. Funny—funny because he was so innocent. In a year or two he went out and they gave him a big contract to make features at First National, which is now Warner Brothers. And he took his team. He took the director he had, Harry Edwards, and he took me and he took Arthur Ripley as writers. We made one picture with him, *Tramp, Tramp, Tramp*, which was very successful. Then he began to get the swell-head. The director couldn't take it any more and he quit. So [Langdon] advanced me up to directing. I would do anything to direct him, of course, and the first film I directed was *The Strong Man*, which I think was one of the ten best pictures of 1926. He was a great star, a new star. But you'd have to keep him from trying to emulate Chaplin. His great ambition was he wanted to do what Chaplin did. Chaplin wrote, acted and directed his own material. But Chaplin had invented his own character. He knew his character better than anybody. Langdon did not know his character, did not know why he was funny, did not know that his goodness was his power. But he wanted to be smart. He wanted to be Jack the Giant-Killer, like Chaplin was. And furthermore, he insisted on it, and when I argued with him about these things, he finally fired me. Then he began to direct himself. Now he was Chaplin. He wrote and directed himself, and his downfall was faster than his rise. It's a great tragedy of a man not knowing what made him funny, not wanting anybody to help him, so jealous of Chaplin, so wanting to surpass Chaplin that he just flopped miserably. And he never did know why. That was the tragedy.

He spread rumors [that Capra had not directed Langdon] and thereafter I had a very difficult time getting a job again. I didn't get a job for quite a while. Eddie Mannix of M-G-M said, "Oh, I'd like to give you a job, but you didn't make those pictures. Langdon says he made them." And I said, "Well, all I can tell you . . ." And he said, "But I gotta believe him." I said, "Okay." So—I had my sabbatical year.

HAIL, COLUMBIA

The way back in for me was Columbia Studios, through "Poverty Row." I had an agent and he said, "Go over there and see if they want to talk to you about directing." So I went over there and the place stunk to me. It was a riff-raff of a place, it was really Poverty Row. True, the only place I'd been to was Mack Sennett, but Mack Sennett was heaven compared to this thing on Gower Street they called a studio. And that was my introduction to a very, very strange, odd, powerful, forceful and controversial man by the name of Harry Cohn. Later I asked why they wanted me, and Sam Briskin* said, "He didn't want you, I didn't want you. But we looked through a list of unemployed directors and your name was at the top of the list. So he said, 'Get me Capra. He's on the top of the list.' And I said"—this is Briskin talking—" 'But, Harry, what about the others?' He said, 'If Abraham was good enough for the Lord, Capra's good enough for me.' He said, 'I want the top of the list— Abraham, Capra.' " That's how I got in there.

When I found this out, I said, well, he's a hunch player anyhow. And I began to perk up a bit. Of course, all kinds of stories have been told about Harry Cohn. They're all true, but for a man who wanted to make pictures, he was ideal. He ran his own place. He didn't have a committee running it. Not even the people from New York would tell him what to do, and so he made his own decisions and it's wonderful to be working for a man who can give you a yes or no right now, and mean it, and not go back on it. And that's the way he worked. And he wanted his employees to be the same. He wanted his employees to be cocky, to think they knew what they were doing, and to know what they were doing. And then he could sleep well. Then he'd let them spend his money. But if the employee—the writer or director or an actor—was unsure what he was doing, and was asking him for advice—out. And that way, many a sensitive artist went through that studio quite chewed up, but Cohn didn't care. If you had guts, he'd give you an opportunity. If you didn't, he didn't want you around, no matter what your reputation was.

* Briskin was Harry Cohn's executive assistant. For many years he played "good cop" to Cohn's "bad cop."

ONE MAN, ONE FILM

I made my first picture with Cohn for $1000—write it, produce it, direct
it. If I couldn't write it, produce it and direct it, I didn't want it. And I
worked twelve weeks on it. It turned out to be pretty good, according
to their standards, and it was called *That Certain Thing*, so I got a contract for three more at the same price. Now I insisted, of course, that I
get my complete freedom on free choice of material, complete freedom
to cast the actors—I mean, not the stars, but the actors—complete freedom to edit the film any way I wanted to, and that's the way it should be.

As long as I got small money, it didn't matter to Cohn, really, because
he could fire me any time he wanted to and replace me any time he
wanted to, but he didn't. So I learned. He and I got along together from
the very beginning. I would have complete freedom, complete control
of my own films. Now, he wasn't paying me what other people would
pay me, but that was okay, I traded money for power. I wanted to make
my own films—"one man, one film" was for me a fetish. I wanted to
show that it could be done. And I made about six or seven small pictures
for him—$20,000-budget pictures—less than Sennett spent on a two-
reeler, actually. But we made them in two weeks and then in two more
weeks we edited them. Then I got my chance to replace a man by the
name of Irvin Willat, who was making the big splash picture Columbia
was making for that year, big headliner, *Submarine*, $150,000 budget. In
the middle of it, Harry Cohn got a little worried about Willat. He
didn't like the rushes, he didn't like the fact the Irvin was saying, "Well,
how do you think it should be done?" So he said he wanted me. He
called for me, his cockiest employee, to go down and replace—not because I was a better director than Irvin Willat, but because he thought
he knew I had more guts, I could handle the situation better. And it took
a lot of guts to handle it, really, because Irvin Willat and one of the
stars, Jack Holt, were very dear friends. They were gentlemen of the
old school and ramrod stiff. To have Irvin Willat replaced by a foreigner
and a comedy director was ridiculous. So I had my problems in getting
Jack Holt to [cooperate]. I finally got him to agree to it by picking on
one thing: makeup. I said, "I want the makeup off you two guys.* You

* The other star was Ralph Graves.

look like bandbox sailors to me, you don't look like United States sailors. You look like musical-comedy people and I want that toupee and all that stuff you're wearing all off. Now, if you want to do it, fine. If you don't want it, I'll leave." On the basis of that kind of attack, I stole their thunder. And I said, "Now, if you want to work with me for one day and see the rushes and then decide, I'll leave it up to you." We left it on the one-day basis and they were very, very satisfied with what happened, so they went on and I finished the film. It was quite a film, *Submarine*. The first really big hit that I had.

FROM SILENCE TO SOUND

The biggest trouble we had was from the silent actors who were asked to read lines all of a sudden and memorize lines. And the biggest hangup was the silence. I mean the actual silence because everybody had to be still. The silent actors used to work with people hammering things, and directors shouting at them all the time, and cameramen yelling. There was always a lot of noise around a silent movie. And then everything was quiet, a thousand people yelling quiet at one time: "Quiet, quiet, quiet, quiet . . ." And suddenly the stillness would settle over you and the actors would shake. They weren't used to the silence and this got them. The silent actors I'm talking about had the most difficult time of all. Those that came from the stage were used to it, but it was a big change, a big mutation from a silent actor to a talkie actor. And a lot of them didn't make it—couldn't make it.

AMERICAN MADNESS

There was a character in California by the name of Giannini. He started the Bank of America. It was called Bank of Italy at the time and changed to the Bank of America. Now it's the biggest bank in the world. He started by financing the pushcart people—it was the kind of bank that made you think if you came in with an idea, they'd finance [it]. As a matter of fact, they were the first to finance motion pictures. If you had a story and a script and a star, you could go there and get part of the financing, which was a very big step [for] the motion-picture world.

At the time of the Depression, of course, everybody was talking about banks. Prior to that I'd been making films that sort of were escape films, entertainment, comedies. But this time I thought, Well, why don't we make a picture about the contemporary hangups—you know, bank runs and things? So we concocted this story about a banker [like Giannini] who trusted the people. He loaned the money more on character than he did on collateral, much to the disgust of his board of directors and other bankers all around. Finally, he got into a jam, [through] this trust of the people, and there was a run on his bank. But he was saved by the same people that he trusted, who came to his help in whatever little way they could, and that made everything okay for him. So his trust was repaid and that was the idea.

Another thing about *American Madness* is interesting to me technically. I used to go to see my films in the theater and kept wanting to urge them on. I felt that the audience was way ahead of the film itself. They knew what was coming, they could anticipate what was coming. And this always worried me. Everything moved slower and I didn't know whether it was the fact that the heads of the actors were so big or because the audience—perhaps a thousand pairs of eyes and ears—would accept stimuli faster than one pair of eyes and ears. I didn't know which. I tried talking it around, but I couldn't get any answers from anybody. But I knew that in the movieola and in a small projection room, films that I had made looked all right. But I got them in the big theater and they slowed down. So I said I've got to do something about this. In *American Madness* a scene that would rehearse in one minute I'd [force the actors to] cut it down to forty seconds. It did look faster when we photographed it, but when we finally got it on the screen there was an urgency about it, and I saw that the audience couldn't take their eyes off the screen. They were afraid of missing something . . . and I've used that accelerated pace in all the rest of the films I've made, except in mood scenes where pace is not a problem.

THE BITTER TEA OF FRANK CAPRA

I wanted an Academy Award very badly. I thought I was as good or better than the other guys. I had never had any worries about thinking I was good at all. This cockiness I had as a kid just stuck with me and I'm still cocky. And anyhow, coming in second is no better than coming in last, as far as I'm concerned. I wanted to get out there in front. I wanted to win one of those Academy Awards for directing. It became an obsession; all ambitious people, all nutty people think that way. I'd seen how the Academy voted—they voted for art; they didn't vote for comedy. They didn't vote for this kind of junk I'm making. So I thought, What the hell, I'll give them art. And I took on *The Bitter Tea of General Yen*, which is a story about miscegenation between a Chinese warlord and an American missionary. But I fell in love with the story, too. And I think I made a very fine picture out of it. I loved the film myself. It had a quality of honesty between these people.

This warlord said all the things that needed to be said about miscegenation, about racism. And I felt that this woman had depth enough to understand. She was so bigoted [at first]. And this reformation of this character from a bigot to one who could love anybody—why, this was an honest story to me.

But no Academy Award. As a matter of fact, it was one of the few pictures that lost money for Columbia, because it was barred from the English empire. And the English empire then *was* an empire. It meant Australia, Canada, Africa. And if you lost that British market, that was almost half of our market. So, when that lost money, that is when I took on *Lady for a Day*. I went back to comedy.

LADY FOR A DAY

Lady for a Day was [an even bigger] hit. The others [had been] minor hits. It came from a Damon Runyon short story. It was a fairy tale.*

* About a streetcorner apple vendor who is briefly projected into high society.

The only star I could think of was Marie Dressler, and Louis Mayer wouldn't let Marie Dressler go for anybody. And Harry Cohn had nothing to trade, so we couldn't get her. But we finally got a seventy-year-old lady of the stage called May Robson and we used her. And she was wonderful in it.

May Robson had fifty years on the stage and she had an enormous voice that carried right to the top of the second-floor or the *fifty*-floor balcony. Now, you don't need that kind of a voice for movies. In the motion picture, you only talk loud enough for the person you're talking to to hear. You don't have to reach an audience with it. That is done mechanically through the microphones. This she didn't understand, [and] I took a test as she began reading these lines, and I said, Oh my, how do I tell this dear old lady we can't use this voice? I thought she didn't have any other kind of a voice but that. So I said to her, "I haven't told you this, it's not in the script, but there are two detectives that don't think you're quite on the level with this whole thing—you being a grande dame. They kind of know you're Apple Annie and they are constantly following you around, so that you must speak so that you don't let them overhear what you are saying because if you do, you'll queer it." She said, "Oh, I understand. I understand, yeah. I see. I see." And she began to talk in a hushed voice that still carried. You could hear it all over the world practically, but it had this urgency and this excitement about it, this toned-down repression, and she was just wonderful. Sometimes a little lie helps things immensely.

IT—FINALLY— HAPPENED ONE NIGHT

The Oscar shower [finally] came when I was doing what I knew best—comedy. And besides that, timing and luck are involved—it's not such a great deal. But it was unexpected because Columbia had no votes in the Academy. I doubt that there were more than four or five Academy members in the whole studio. Mostly, Academy members were people who worked at M-G-M, Paramount, Fox, Warner Brothers, Universal. Something from Poverty Row would never win an Academy Award. But it did. *It Happened One Night* won all five major awards, the only picture so far to have done so.

I was at a Palm Springs barber shop when I picked up a copy of *Cosmopolitan*, flipped through while I was getting a haircut and read a story called "Night Bus." It sounded kind of interesting because it was about motels, busses, and I'd always wanted to make an exterior picture— to get out of the Poverty Row studio and make a film around the country. And this kind of hit me and so I asked the studio to buy it and they bought it for $5000. We laid it aside because I had some things to do. Finally we got around to it—Bob Riskin, the screenplay writer,* and I. A director directs a writer by falling in love with him and becoming friendly with him, and the two of them then collaborate and the man becomes part of a team, though it is still the director who's got to make the decision. And this was the case with Bob Riskin and I. We were great friends and we loved each other. We were great audiences for each other. And we collaborated on all those stories we did with each other, but in the end I had to have final yes or no on everything because that was my province. That was why I was a director. I can't say too much for Bob Riskin. He was the greatest screenplay artist that I've ever known—great ear for dialogue, and a great person to be around. And we had a symbiotic thing going between us. We created together. When that happens between a director and a writer, it is a wonderful thing for both.

But we couldn't cast *It Happened One Night*. No girl wanted to play the part. Five girls turned it down, *five* girls. And finally we got Claudette Colbert to agree to play the part if we doubled her salary and could get through with her in four weeks' time. She had a vacation [she wanted to take]. But then we couldn't get a leading man. We wanted Bob Montgomery. He turned it down. Well, the perils of *It Happened One Night* just grew and I finally got pretty sick of it and said, "Let's call it off, Harry, everybody says that bus pictures won't go, so the heck with it." And Cohn says, "No, no, we have to make it, Louis B. Mayer wants to punish an actor and he's told me I could have Clark Gable." That was an order from Louis Mayer. Every time Mayer got a cold, Cohn did the sneezing. And so we had to make the picture because

---

* Riskin had credit on a number of Capra's films, including *Mr. Deeds Goes to Town, Lost Horizon, You Can't Take It with You, Meet John Doe.*

Louis Mayer had to punish Clark Gable. This is not a pretty way to start a film, so I asked Clark Gable to come over. He was absolutely roaring drunk when he came over to see me. I won't tell you about that whole *magilla,* but we made the picture really quickly—four weeks. We stumbled through it, we laughed our way through it. And this goes to show you how much luck and timing and being in the right place at the right time means in show business: how sometimes no preparation at all is better than all the preparation in the world; and sometimes you need great preparation, but you can never outguess this thing called creativity. It happens in the strangest places and under the strangest of circumstances. I didn't much care for the picture, [yet] it turned out to be *It Happened One Night.*

It opened in New York at the Music Hall and the reviews were very mediocre—two and a half stars for it in the *Daily News.* Other reviewers called it adequate. Some, entertaining. And the people didn't come. The picture took in only $80,000 the first week, which was not enough to keep it as a holdover for a second week. And that boded ill for its future box-office return because the way it played at the Music Hall was considered a bell-wether of what it would do throughout the rest of the country. But when it got to the various cities—Salt Lake, Kansas City, places like that—it began to build. People would come to see it again and bring their friends, and instead of one week in Salt Lake, it would stay six weeks. It built right from the bottom. And after the first month, it became an avalanche. Critics went back to see it a second time to see what all the shouting was about. And they still couldn't see it. They went back again later on—six months later—and then, you know, some began to read some things in it, but most did not. [It succeeded because it was] pure entertainment, well-done entertainment, believable entertainment, and unfettered with any ideas, any big moral precepts or anything else. Just sheer entertainment, fun.

GOOD DEEDS, IDEALISTIC SMITH

Mr. Deeds Goes to Town was the first film that I made in which I consciously tried to make a social statement. I wanted to see what an honest small-town man would do with $20,000,000—how he would handle it, and how he could handle all the predators that would surround him, and what good would come out of that thing, what statements you could make about a man being his brother's keeper. But I didn't forget [entertainment], of course, and I think if I have any strength at all in the films that I make, it's that I don't forget the entertainment. I use comedy to, in a sense, warm people to my subject. I don't say, "Now I'm going to tell you a moral tale and you'd better like it." No, first I entertain them. I get them in the spirit of laughter and then, perhaps, they might be softened up to accept some kind of a moral precept. But entertainment comes first. Without it, it's very heavy, and without it, you can't sell the American people anything.

Mr. Deeds was really a man of the people. I mean, he was people himself. He was a small-town man. Mr. Smith [in *Mr. Smith Goes to Washington*] was also small-town people, but he was an educated man, an idealist on a higher level. Mr. Deeds was honest, but not necessarily an idealist. He didn't go out and really think up this thing to do with the money; it was forced on him. But Mr. Smith was a young Ivy League idealist who gets put into the Senate, a dewy-eyed freshman—always speaks of Jefferson and Lincoln and Washington, is full of the ideals that started this country. And he gets into the Senate and sees it work— how it works. The pragmatic work of politics [reveals itself and we see] how disillusioned he becomes and his reaching down for something strong within him and his determination to fight it.

[Official Washington] turned against the film. Hollywood has always been a dirty word in Washington anyhow. And the fact that somebody had nerve enough to make a film about the Senate—this real aristocratic club, private club, private preserve—have this snotty-nosed thing called films get in there—was a revelation to them of the power of film, the power of film to do what they hadn't been able to do, which was expose the workings of something and really tell people all about it visually.

The Washington premiere was under the auspices of the National Press Club at Constitution Hall. All the elite of Washington was there, four thousand of them, to see this *Mr. Smith Goes to Washington*. Two thirds of the way through the picture, they started walking out, booing, disgusted. About the time of the filibuster [in the movie] they really began to walk out in droves. And the newspapermen were just vicious about it and the Senators were all vicious about it. The next day they voted against it ninety-six to nothing. And it was a great surprise because we had previewed the picture with various audiences and they loved it. And critics all over the country loved it. But this group in Washington really lambasted it. There was so much hue-and-cry about it that producers and studios in Hollywood began to fear that some punitive legislation would be passed against motion pictures, such as a bill, then being discussed, proposing to break up the combines of production and distribution and exhibition. So [the other studios] offered Columbia $2,000,000 if Columbia would shelve the film. Now, that was much more than the picture cost, it cost about $1,500,000, so it would have been a fine profit for Columbia. Of course, I objected violently. And I had many a talk with Mr. Harry Cohn and said, "No, this is the wrong thing to do. We've made this film. We have to show it. That's just a few people. Don't let them run this country. The people like the picture, the people like it. And that's our money, not the Senators'. The hell with them; let them do what they want." The big pressure [finally] was a cablegram that came from London. Now, you must realize that *Mr. Smith* came out in October 1939 and Hitler had just invaded Poland. The whole world was going up in flames. The cable was from Joseph P. Kennedy, Ambassador to the Court of St. James at the time, saying [in effect], "For God's sake, don't show that picture in Europe. It'll be taken as Nazi propaganda. It'll put us all in such a bad light that it'll destroy the morale of the Allies. Please don't show the film." Well, this coming from a source like that really made us stop and think: Have we got something here that is anti-American? That's exactly what the problem was. I pleaded with them not to listen to politicians, but to release it and show it and send it to Europe. And, thank God, we did. Thank goodness, Columbia Pictures had enough guts to show the picture.

Three years later, I think it was, when I was in the Army, the Germans had overrun France. The Vichy government was in power. They told all the movie theaters they had one more month to run Western films, and that's all. From that time on, only German films would be run. The theater managers went around to their various customers and said, "Well, now look, we've got thirty days. What do you want to see?" And they selected the pictures they wanted to see. Invariably, *Mr. Smith Goes to Washington* was one of them. And not only that, but one of the theaters ran it every day the last thirty days. People came from all around to see this film, and to cheer when the man made his speech about liberty. They refreshed themselves. It was like Antaeus touching the ground every time he needed to refresh his strength. This was a marvelous example of the power of the film. A marvelous demonstration that it's never untimely to ring freedom's bell.

JIMMY STEWART AND JEAN ARTHUR

Jean Arthur was an enigmatic figure because she doesn't do very well in crowds, and she doesn't do very well with people, and she doesn't do very well with life, but she does very well as an actress. She's afraid. She'd stand in her dressing room and practically vomit every time she had to do a scene. And she'd drum up all kinds of excuses for not being ready. Well, I finally got to know her. All I had to do was push her out in the lights, turn the camera on, and she'd blossom out into just something wonderful, very positive, certain. An assured, poised, lovely woman. And she could do anything, could express love or hate or anything else. And when the scene was over, she'd go back into that dressing room and cry. She certainly had two sides to her: the actress, this wonderful actress, and this person, this shy personality that she was in reality. She's quite a study.

Jimmy Stewart first of all is a very, very fine actor. He's a fine man. He can project whatever his thoughts are. He can project what he's dreaming, what's in his heart, what's in his soul. He can let you see that. He's a very humble man. And at the same time he's very educated and a very knowledgeable sort of a guy. But he's got this wonderful quality —all the women want to mother him, that's his great quality. Now, they don't want to jump in bed with him, perhaps, but they certainly want to mother him. When he's in trouble, they're for him. They want to help him.

To act hoarse for the filibuster scene [in *Mr. Smith*] would be an additional hurdle that he would have to go through in doing this part. So I thought I'd like to relieve that [burden] from his mind. I asked a doctor, "Look, you can cure a sore throat, can you produce one?" And he says, "Oh, sure." So about three times a day he'd swab Stewart's throat with a vile mercury liquid of some kind that would swell his vocal chords and make him hoarse. He'd have to fight to get that voice out. That, of course, was a great, great help in playing that part.

YOU CAN'T TAKE IT WITH YOU

You Can't Take it with You I usually refer to as the first hippie picture —thirty years ago. A group of people who were tired of the whole rat race, you know, want to do their own thing and they get together in the house and do it. This just follows along with my feeling that the individual should be an individual, no matter what other people think of him. The individual is divine, he's worthy, he's unique and he's the most important thing there is. So this, in a sense, was individualism gone mad, this *You Can't Take It with You*. This family of individuals got together and lived their own lives and did a pretty good job of it. It won the Best Picture of the Year at the time it was made, and it was a very big popular success too, which was a pretty good combination—if you could get an Academy Award and get people to the box office at the same time.

LOST HORIZON

Harry Cohn was taking a gang of us to the Stanford-USC football game up at Palo Alto on the train. I went into the station to pick up something to read and I picked up this book called *Lost Horizon*. I had heard [Alexander] Woollcott say something about it on the radio. I read it that night before going to bed, but I couldn't really go to sleep. This book, I kept thinking about it. I kept thinking about it all night long, and in the morning when I got up for breakfast with Harry Cohn, I said, "Harry, that's my next picture. Buy it for me." And he said, "What is it about?" I said, "Well, never mind reading it. It's going to cost an awful lot of money, I can tell you." And he said, "Well, we can't spend a lot of money." I said, "Well, that's it. That's the next picture." He said, "How much do you think it's going to cost?" "I think it's going to cost about $2,000,000." He said, "What!" But he bought it and we made it. I thought it had an enormous statement to make, this *Lost Horizon*. I thought, first of all, it's a good tale, it's a mystery story, hijacking of a plane, people brought in against their wishes from a lot of far-off places and being forced to live there in Shangri-La and then loving it finally. I mean, it's not only about an idea, but it's great theater, great melodrama, great suspense. Plus the idea of Shangri-La—that they are collecting all of the good things of the world in case things are destroyed by war and here we will still be when the strong have eaten each other, here we will be. Now, I think that's one of my great films.

MEET JOHN DOE

[In making *Meet John Doe*] we did have great difficulty with the ending. I think for seven eighths of the film it's a great, great film, with great power, great emotion, and then the ending, of course, to me has always been weak. And we didn't have one at the beginning. I thought it would come during the making of the show. It didn't. And at one time we had three different endings playing at various places. In Washington we had one ending, in New York one ending, in San Francisco another ending—trying to see if the audience would tell us which they preferred. None of those three was satisfactory, either to the audience or to me. When, all of a sudden, here comes a letter from the outside, signed "John Doe." And it said, "The only way you can keep that man from jumping off that City Hall on Christmas Eve is if the John Does themselves come and tell him he'd be much more use walking around than dead." And my gosh, this was the best ending we could [come up with]. I'm surprised we didn't think of it. But it came from the outside, so we brought the whole cast back in. We went up to the set and shot that ending. And that ending is the ending that is now on the film. And yes, it's perhaps the best of the lot. And probably because it came from the outside rather than from within us. I don't think it's as good an ending as the audiences say, but it is the best ending we had.

Walter Brennan and Gary Cooper sample the good life in
Meet John Doe (*1941*).

*Gary Cooper and Lionel Stander recruit a
worker for their agricultural recovery scheme in*
Mr. Deeds Goes to Town (*1936*).

*Left to right: Isabel Jewell, Ronald Colman,
Edward Everett Horton, Thomas Mitchell and
John Howard contemplate a gloomy future
before discovering Shangri-La in* Lost Horizon
(*1937*).

John Doe was to me an important film because it did dig pretty deeply into the tempo and the mood of our times, which was fear of military aggression, fear of losing our sense of well-being and our sense of satisfaction, and fear that we might lose everything that we ever stood for. Hitler was a real, real problem. When he came, his stuff was real poison. I'll tell you how poisonous it was. In the films, we were not allowed to use Jewish comedians any more because they put the Jews in a bad light with their dialect and their long noses and things like that. That was how frightening this thing was. It poisoned the minds of men like Louis B. Mayer and Harry Cohn into saying, "No more Jewish comics in our films. We don't want to give Hitler any ammunition." This is how deep it went. And I remember having to give Benny Rubin little odd jobs—inserts of his feet and his hands—to keep him going. How terrible this bigotry is, this poison. There were fascist groups and there were people who were developing paramilitary organizations, usually very rich people, very powerful people, in order to take over—when it happened [when war came]. This was what *John Doe* was about: a man who was just a drifter—just a man. A baseball pitcher with a bad arm, not even the bush leagues would have him any more, and he was a bum who was taken up by a newspaper person who made him into a cause, made him say that he was so disappointed with the way world conditions were that he was going to jump off the City Hall building at Christmas Eve as a protest against all the evils of man's inhumanities to man. And this got a lot of attention in the press and so forth. Now, he was paid to say that, but he finally began to believe in it. He got caught up in the idea when he saw how it affected people. John Doe Clubs began to form. People would form anything to sort of herd together in little groups so they could trust their neighbors. They formed these clubs and talked to each other, helped each other. They didn't feel so much alone. They felt maybe they could stave off these coming things that Hitler was talking about.

Naturally, as these clubs were being formed, somebody said, "We're going to take advantage of these clubs." The newspaper owner decided to take advantage of them, to finance them and help them, that way getting them to vote a third ticket [on which he would be] made President of the United States. But when John Doe finds out about it at a big convention of the John Does, he [decides to tell the truth]—to spill the beans. Whereupon the newspaperman beats him to it and gets up and says, "This man's a fake. Been a fake all his life. He's fooled me as well as he has you. I've put up a lot of money for this thing. He has no idea of jumping off anything. He's a pure fake." And now the people turn on him as well. Up to then we have a real fine story, lots of conflict, lots of decisions. Now what? It was as if St. Patrick slew the dragon and then got killed himself. I mean, there were no answers if this man jumped off the roof. So, when the people turned on him, [you see that] your neighbors can turn on you and can turn on each other and can turn on somebody if they are disillusioned. If you get their hopes up and they open their hearts to you and then they find out you are a fake, well, you'd better watch out for those people. They don't like to be disturbed and opened up like that and then be double-crossed. And this is what made *John Doe* such an interesting picture, showing that people can become mobs, and one of the occasions they can become mobs is when they become disillusioned, when somebody has tricked them.

ARSENIC AND OLD LACE

I knew I was going into the Army. I had volunteered the year before, and the way things were happening, it was only a matter of time before we were in war—it seemed imminent. And I thought, Well, if I go into the Army, I'd like to have something going for my family while I'm there. Perhaps I can find a picture that I can make fast and get a percentage of the profits. Then that will keep them going, it'll be something for them. So I saw *Arsenic and Old Lace* on the stage in New York, fell in love with it, and I said, Here's the thing I can do fast, quickly, I can do it in one set. Then I found out that Warner Brothers had already bought it. But they couldn't make the film for another three or four years because that's how long the play would run and they couldn't make the film out of it until the play stopped running, which might be three years from then, which would spoil my plans. But anyhow I didn't give up. I said, "Could I make that film for you now? I got the two little leading ladies, little women in the show. I got the guy that runs up stairs and says, 'Charge!' and I got Cary Grant for your lead." Warner said,

"But I can't release it now." I said, "Well, I know, but you can release it later. I'll make it now." I talked him into it and we made it in about four weeks, as a matter of fact, and that truly was a fun show, as far as I was concerned. I had everybody going—the actors were crazy about it. Peter Lorre and Cary Grant had a ball with the whole thing. Grant is a great comedian, a great light comedian. He's very good-looking, but he's also very funny. That makes a devastating combination, and that's why he's been a star so long. I think he's been a star for forty years, and is still a star today because he is a great entertainer. And fun to work with, lots of fun to work with.

MAJOR CAPRA

Leni Riefenstahl made what I think is the powerhouse propaganda film for all time, a film called *Triumph of the Will*, which glorified the Nazi Party and, in a sense, deified Hitler. She scared the hell out of me. The first time I saw that picture, I said, "We're dead, we're gone, we can't win this war." [I responded] just exactly as the Austrians did and the Czechoslovakians did and the Channel countries did. That picture just won them over. They were frightened. That shows you the power of that film, or any film if you make the right film. When I saw it, I just thought, How can we possibly cope with this enormous machine and enormous will to fight? "Surrender or you're dead"—that's what the film was saying to you. And how do we counter that? It took us quite a little while. There was a lot of worry before I got an idea that might work. And the idea was to just fight back with their own words. I thought if our young soldiers could just hear what the enemy had to say, they would know why we were fighting without being told. That was the premise of *Why We Fight* films. We didn't produce anything, we didn't shoot anything except headlines and maps. The rest was all taken from German films. We just showed our soldiers a piece from *Triumph of the Will* and other films and they seemed to get the idea better that way than if we tried to tell them what bastards the Nazis were.

It was General Marshall's idea to produce these shows, not mine. He's the one that got me to come into the Army. He's the one that asked them to get me. I didn't know why I was asked to join the Army until he told me, and he said, "This is what we've got to do. We've got to tell our young men why they're in uniform. They're going to fight seasoned soldiers who've got a thing going for them, a superman thing, and the soldiers believe it. And we haven't got that. But," he said, "I think free men will prove themselves stronger. And I think if they're informed completely, we will have no trouble with Americans holding their own against this military machine. If you shoot at Americans, they're going to shoot back. That's axiomatic. But what are they going to do when they're stuck on these islands, they're stuck in these bases, and waiting here and waiting there when homesickness comes in? And all the nice things they had at home, they can't have them, what about the morale then? This is what we've got to worry about. Why are they in uniform? Why are they in deserts and in these jungles and these places like this?" And this is the job he gave me, and I thought it was great, only a great man could think in those terms [about informing] the common soldier.

We did have a lot of problems breaking away from the Signal Corps and getting a separate unit to make these *Why We Fight* things. But we did it, just strictly by going out and doing it. This is exactly what General Marshall wanted somebody to do. He wanted them done, no matter what. So we got them done. And I say God bless the Army; we did it anyhow. It's possible to do things in the Army if you work hard enough.

When we were making the *Why We Fight* series—which was a big enough job and we had our hands full—Secretary of War Stimson sent word to me that he wanted me to make a film showing what the blacks had at stake in this country, what they had done, how they had helped develop this country, because the morale of the blacks in the Army was very, very low. The amount of discrimination was just terrible. Well, I didn't want to take the job on. I tried to get out of it, but couldn't. He said, "Would you please come up here and read something?" So I went into his office and he handed me a sheaf of papers and these were reports of cases of discrimination that had taken place in various parts of the country, various parts of the Army. Some of them were truly unbelievable—that man could degrade his fellow human beings in so many ways. I could see what was in Secretary Stimson's mind. So I said,

"Okay—I don't know what it'll be like, but we'll work on it." We went to work on it and I found out things that I didn't know about the blacks. I found out that the first man to be killed at Bunker Hill was a black, that there was a black kid in the boat with Washington crossing the Delaware, there were blacks that played a very important part in our history here and there. I didn't know these things. So we made a film in which our primary interest was to show the blacks in the Army that they had a stake in the United States that they wouldn't have if Hitler and Japan took over. In other words, it was to their advantage, in spite of all the discrimination, that Hitler should not win the war, nor should the Japanese win the war, because then they would really be [sent] back to slavery. The other purpose of the film was to show the whites what the blacks had done in our history for our country.

When we finished it, we called in about two or three hundred leaders —especially editors and writers of black newspapers. And we brought them all into the Pentagon, seated them all in one big projection room. They were sure they were going to get some kind of a snow job and I had to tell them what the film was about and I had to tell them how it was made and I had to tell them that if they didn't like it, we wouldn't show it. They were the first ones to see it. If they had any objections to it, it would not go out. Those were my orders from General Marshall. So we ran it for them. The film ran about forty minutes. There was complete silence after the film. They were kind of stunned. This was the first time any documentary film had been made about the black race in America. Finally, one man spoke: "Mr. Capra, we know about the kind of films you made in Hollywood. But how come the Army brass let you make this kind of a film? How do you get away with it?" I said, "The Army brass is not letting me get away with anything. I was *ordered* to make this film because there are people at the top here who care about these things, they care about them, probably, more than I do, because they ordered me to make it. And this is a training film to be shown to all soldiers, black and white, and we won't show it unless you say the word." Well, they were unanimous in praise of the film, and we showed it. But the point is that for the first time I was able to say there are people at the top in this Army who care about these things. And I'm sure it has something to do with alleviating the morale problem of the blacks. It didn't cure it, but it did alleviate it, because many of the white soldiers hadn't known these things about blacks. This is again the power of film.

LIBERTY FILMS

That idea [for an independent production company owned by directors] came into being while we were in uniform. George Stevens was in uniform, Willie Wyler was in uniform, John Huston was in uniform, Sam Briskin was in uniform. There were quite a few of us in uniform who thought perhaps we should come back and make films as individual director/producers, form a unit [owned by] director/producers, not a studio. But we wanted film-makers, not stars. So we formed Liberty Films—George Stevens, William Wyler, Frank Capra, Sam Briskin. And the first film we made was *It's a Wonderful Life*. And by the time we got through with *It's a Wonderful Life*, it was 1947 and it was right after the war and the boom was over. We found that theaters which were filled throughout the war were not filled any more. Great, great drop in box-office attendance. And it evidently was not the time when we could make a go of it with an independent unit, because there was no way to finance it. We had to draw salaries from the money we put in the company and we kept paying income tax on the salaries. It was the most gentlemanly way of going broke, and the fastest way, anybody ever thought of. We didn't have enough capital, so we decided to sell Liberty Films, which was a very, very hopeless thing to do. My partners did not want to sell. But I got cold feet, and I'm the one who insisted that we sell. And I think that probably affected my picture-making forever afterward. Once you get cold feet, once your daring stops, then you worry a little bit. And when you worry about a decision, then you're not going to make the proper films any more. That is, *I* couldn't. And I think that was the start. When I sold out for money, which is something that I had always been against anyhow, and security, I think my conscience told me that I had had it. Really. There wasn't any more of that Paladin out there in front fighting for lost causes. I dragged my partners into it [selling out]. We shouldn't have sold it. We could have made it go. And it was a thing in my life I've regretted ever since, having sold Liberty Films.

IT'S A WONDERFUL LIFE

Wonderful Life was the first picture we made with Liberty Films and it was my production. And to me, that's a great film. I love that film. It's my favorite film, and in a sense it epitomizes everything I'd been trying to do and trying to say in the other films. Only it does it very dramatically with a very unique story. The importance of the individual is the theme—and no man is a failure. If he's born, he's born to do something, he's not born to fail. And this idea is carried out in a unique way because a man who thought he was a failure, and thought everybody around him would have been better off had he never been born, was given a chance to see how the world around him would have been, his own small little world, had he not been born.* And he suddenly saw that it would have been a much worse place, much worse world, had he not been born. And he realized that life was a wonderful, tremendous thing to have, a great enormous gift, and that everybody must do something with it. And that he was not a failure at all, he was actually a pretty successful man. And, as his own brother says, "He's the richest man in town," really, because he has the most friends. The uniqueness of the plot is what prompted me to make the film and why I loved the film so much.

STATE OF THE UNION

State of the Union was a Pulitzer Prize play and quite an important property. We had to make it at M-G-M because I wanted Spencer Tracy in it, and Spencer Tracy wanted to play the part very badly, and the only way we could get Spencer Tracy in the part was to make it at M-G-M and have the picture released through M-G-M even though it would be owned by Liberty Films. So that's the way I finally got to M-G-M after, I think, the fourth attempt to make a picture there. I found it a very pleasant place to make a film—on my own terms. But the Un-American Activities Committee had gotten into the act about "reds" in

* In a remarkable dream sequence.

Hollywood at that time. We had in the cast Adolphe Menjou, who was quite a right-winger, and then we had a left-winger in Katharine Hepburn. Now the whole press flocked onto this set, hoping to start some controversy, and everything was controversial at the time. The Un-American Activities Committee was meeting in Hollywood and calling people in as "reds" and trying, you know, to ferret out the Communists they said had infiltrated films during wartime. But I must say that those two people, Menjou and Hepburn, they might have talked privately, but they never on the set showed one bit of animosity toward each other. They were professional people doing their parts. They were wonderful to work with as actor and actress.

It was a very, very bad time in Hollywood. People didn't trust each other any more. And the Writers' Guild had great problems internally between the lefts and the rights, and in the Directors' Guild we had our problems. My attitude toward Communism was that I could never understand a great deal of it. There are two things that I can't understand, really. I couldn't understand M-G-M directors who said they didn't mind other directors finishing their pictures. Why should anybody want somebody else to finish his picture? The other thing I couldn't understand was why writers became Communists. Writers! The free-spirited, freewheeling thinkers of all time are writers. Writers, who should be free to write against and for anything! How could they put their heads in a block of cement, a dictatorship like Communism? And yet many writers became Communists. I just couldn't understand it. There were many things I couldn't understand, but there was one thing I tried to understand all the time, and that is the dignity and the importance of the individual. I tried to hang on to that. And that I tried to hang on to all the way throughout my films.

COMEDY AND TRAGEDY

I don't believe in tragedies. I'm not interested in them. I'm an optimist, and comedy to me is victory. Victory over anything. Tragedy is failure. I just don't believe in failures. And it's a strange thing about comedy. I think that the gospels are a comedy—good news. I think that the greatest comedy of all is the Divine Comedy—the Resurrection, victory over death. Every Sunday the Catholics celebrate the mass, celebrate a victory over death. That's what comedy means to me. Victory over your environment. When you think about it in those terms, you probably know a little bit more why I use so much comedy in my films and what comedy means to me. And happy endings mean the same thing to me. I'm not interested in defeat; we have too much going around already. And I think what is going on all over the United States is lack of morals, lack of ideals. I think it's up to you young guys to get yourself some ideals and stick to them and to hell with this nonsense that there is nothing but greed and power and gain out there. Sure, the good people—good hasn't taken over the earth. But neither has evil taken over the earth. And you shouldn't let it. Think in terms of ideals—in terms of self-commitment to ideals that are positive. Boy, we confuse them today. We can use a Mr. Deeds, we can use a Mr. Smith today in our country—in our highest places. We lack morality, we lack ideals.

DREAM FILMS

Everybody has those kinds of dreams. I wanted to make *Cyrano* very much throughout my whole life, but I had no chance to. I wanted to make *Don Quixote*, Cervantes' show. I never got an opportunity to make that. I've always wanted to make those two. I read them over and over at times. I also wanted to make the story of Saul who later became Paul, which to me is one of the greatest stories ever told: a man, a Hitler-type guy, suddenly becomes converted and becomes the thirteenth apostle— great story of an individual, great story of clashes of ideas. I wanted to make the story of Luke, a Greek, a born slave of the Romans, who worked his way up and becomes a great physician—doesn't believe all that mystical nonsense about religions—he's a complete scientist—how he gets converted and becomes an apostle—what happens to him.

These are enormous tales about individuals who've got to make choices. Drama is choices, drama is a man having to choose this or that— the more difficult the choice, the more intense the drama. And when he makes one choice, it's failure, it's tragedy; you make another choice, it's victory. Now, it's that choice, that's what drama is. And that's why when you've got to tell an idea, you tell it through people actually acting out the idea, not through rhetoric, or not through preachment, or not through talking like you would in a tract. You tell drama through people. If your film is dubbed message, you haven't got anything. First you've got to entertain; first you've got to get the people to like the people on the screen, to make the audience forget they are actors and think they are living human beings. When you can involve the audience that much, this grand illusion takes place. These shadows become real and you become hooked with a human being. You pull for them, you pull against them, you become involved with them. Then you are able to get across some message, some piece of morality. And that's the way to sell messages, that's the way to sell anything. That's the way to make the whole thing believable.

CHANGING TIMES

In 1951, '52, '53, television aerials began sprouting all over the tops of houses, and the studio executives, picture executives, were quite sure that the film business was over with, that television was going to bring the theater to the home and that nobody would go to theaters any more. So they sold out. They canceled their contracts with their stars, canceled their contracts with directors and writers and just abdicated. And left a vacuum in Hollywood. All kinds of people out of work. And there were two talent agencies that felt the unemployment greatly. The William Morris office and MCA. They were out of money because their clients weren't working. So they decided to package their own clients in the independent production companies and borrow money from banks and make independent productions with their own clients. And independent production was born in Hollywood. It is still there now. Eighty percent of it is done independently.

Well, the film business was not dead. These independent companies went out and made pictures that made money and, lo and behold, everything was okay. But in order to borrow money for individual films, bankers (or bankers' wives, I don't know which one, I have a hunch it is the wives more or less) said they had to have stars in the pictures before they would lend money to any producer. They wouldn't lend money to an independent director or producer unless he had two stars. Or one great big star. There were only a few stars around that they [the bankers] could accept. [Now] because these stars were not dumb, because they were used not only for their performances, but as collateral, their salaries went up. They used to get $50,000 a picture, which was big, but they went for $100,000, $200,000, $300,000, $400,000, $500,000, $1,000,000 a picture, finally. And with them they drew up all the other satellites. But [the trouble was] not so much that the salaries went up, but that when a star gets ten times as much as the director, he has to feel somehow that he is ten times as important to the film. Therefore he wants a piece of the film now. And when he gets a cut of the film, then he becomes an owner. He made the decisions. And he became the actual producer because you couldn't do without the acting. People like me couldn't possibly make pictures under those circumstances. I tried it. I tried it in *Hole in the Head*; it worked in *Hole in the Head* because Sinatra is a very smart man. If somebody is around that knows his business, he lets them operate. But it didn't work in *Pocketful of Miracles*. For me. And so I was really forced out of the business because I wouldn't yield to supervision by stars. I wouldn't let stars tell me how to make a picture. It was just that simple. And then I liked being out of work. I started doing other things, and here I am talking about film again.

RETIREMENT

So I retired. I made four educational films for the Bell Telephone System and I loved making those because they were a subject that was very dear to my heart: education. Then I thought I'd write a book and I did write my autobiography [and] that proved to be very successful and that was very gratifying. And then what? Should I go back to making pictures when I just couldn't see myself making films again? It's a personal thing with me. I know what it takes to make a motion picture, it takes a tremendous amount of physical energy, a tremendous amount of mental energy, nervous energy. It's like fighting a war, the logistics of making a film are a terrific burden on you. The hours and the responsibility and the suspense—you never know what you have until you finally see the picture with a thousand people. You've got to be young to take all that. You take it better when you're young. And as you get older, you worry more, because you know more. And this knowledge is no good for show business at all. The less you know, the better off you are. You've got to trust your instincts, you've got to gamble, you've got to trust your hunches. A hunch is the only thing that really counts. If you get a big hunch, that's better than adding up all the figures and coming up with the right answer, because it's a creative business, an intuitive business. It is not just a skill. You've got to make your decisions, and they are gut decisions when you make them, mostly.

If you make a decision on trends or on past performances, if you try to treat motion pictures like you do horses, you handicap them and you make book or you go on past performances, you're doing the wrong thing. You've got to go on your own judgment entirely. That's the safest. You've got to make your decisions fast, then you mustn't worry about them after you make them, right or wrong. You're going to make a lot of wrong ones. As you get older, what happens to you, you take a little longer to make the decisions and you worry about some of them. You worry about whether you've made the right ones or not and that's fatal in the creative business. It really is a young man's game. Not that I couldn't make a good picture today, probably make as good a picture as I ever made, but I'd feel better if I were younger. And I knew, too, that I couldn't make the kind of pictures that I wanted. I couldn't make them again.

So what else is there for me? Well, I've always been interested in the young people and in the schools, so at the moment I'm going around doing lectures and holding seminars for students at various universities. I've done a great deal of that and I find that very rewarding and profitable as an individual. As a matter of fact, I feel as useful today as I did at any time in my life. And talking to the young people certainly is a revitalizing thing. This is the film generation. These young kids, even in the elementary grades, go around filming each other, little scenes with each other. They will create directly for the film rather than translate from another medium. And I think it's their art, it's their art form. They are finding that out. And the great films are yet to come and they're going to come from the students.

In these seminars and lectures that I do, they actually love my films.

They love them because in some ways there is some kinship. They are moved by these films the same way [audiences] were moved thirty years ago, thirty-five years ago. All young people are idealistic. Therefore this idealism that comes forth in some of these films that I made, that's their meat. And so they're very strong for them, and I'm some kind of minor-league folk hero with some of the students that I've seen, and it just pleases me no end. And at the same time I can tell them some of the positive things about life. That not all people go around kicking each other in the teeth or in the groin. That love is still the most moving force in the world. And that honor and honesty and a few things like that, they're things to hang on to, and to make pictures about. And not to have all our heroes creep heroes, to have some other heroes, moral heroes who give their life for a cause, for an ideal, for something. And this interests them, and it interests me, of course. And if I can be useful in this way, that's the way I'd like to spend the rest of my life.

Director Howard Hawks wearing the Red River D brand on his belt buckle, a gift from John Wayne—a twin of a buckle that Hawks himself originally made for Wayne after the completion of Red River

HOWARD HAWKS

THE first half of the interview with Howard Hawks was shot on a Sunday morning somewhere in the Mojave Desert, in a beautiful and desolate location where he and his son Greg, then sixteen, had gone to try Greg's new motorcycle in a cross-country race—eighty miles over a figure-eight course, only the beginning, middle (where the riders refuel) and end of which were visible to spectators. Greg is one of the leading riders of his region and nearly every Sunday finds the Hawkses in such spots. We had brought our cameras here before going to Howard's home in Palm Springs, where we completed the interview, not merely to get a striking outdoor background—appropriate for a director of action films— but because I had once previously interviewed Howard on camera and thought he was rather stiff and uncomfortable pinned to a chair in his living room. At seventy-seven (when we shot) he was (as he remains) a man who likes to keep moving and a man who resists such formalities as interviews. I thought it would be better if his mind was only half on the business I had with him, if there was something going on around him that distracted him somewhat from a process I suspect he dislikes and distrusts.

This strategy worked out better than I dared hope. We arranged to meet the night before the race at a singularly dismal TraveLodge in a town whose name escapes me; it was just a crossroads, really, with a lot of gas stations, a few small stores, a couple of bars and a restaurant—no amenities, just essentials, like a lot of Howard's movie sets. He and Greg arrived late because they had been out scouting the racecourse. Howard invited us to his room, poured drinks into bathroom glasses and began sketching out the possibilities for the next day's shooting, his finger tracing quickly disappearing patterns on the motel's chenille bedspread. He had very strong notions about what our camera positions should be at various points around the racecourse. I thought of the critic Manny Farber's discussion of Hawks' "mother hen" instinct, worrying and nudging the groups of men in his films into effective action and correct modes of behavior.

Practical considerations taken care of, we repaired to the restaurant nearby. It was a typical example of small-town Americana—formica tables, plastic flowers, a jukebox, offering beverages ranging from milkshakes to booze, main courses prominently featuring steaks—thin, stringy, fried. Now, Howard is a man of courtly reserve and I had never talked informally with him and I didn't know quite what to expect when my crew and I sat down with him and his son. I had reckoned without the pleasure he takes in masculine company, especially if that company is engaged in some difficult or at least interesting venture. He set about putting us at ease as if we were grouped around a campfire, yarning about other locations, the trials and tribulations of making movies in awkward places. We lingered long over coffee and by the time we rose to go Howard had converted us into one of those small bands of brothers whose constant presence in his films has so bemused critics.

The next day we worked together smoothly and the footage our cameraman, Erik Daarstadt, shot was brilliant. He camera-cut whole sequences on his feet. And after the race, when Howard sat down to submit to questions, he was easy and relaxed in a way that I had not seen him before. I have since read a piece by Peter Bogdanovich in which he recounts a similar, though more taxing, desert expedition with Howard, and my impression is that Howard sees these little adventures as tests for would-be interrogators, a way of determining that your intellectual understanding of his work is matched by a willingness to put theory into practice.

There is, I should emphasize, nothing mean-spirited about it. He's just curious. And he enlists your curiosity about yourself. For if you have been a red-blooded American boy, the values of masculine comradeship and civility, practiced in isolated places, are bound to have seeped into your system—principally from the movies—and there is an inexplicable thrill in living by them, however briefly, under the eye of someone like Hawks who really represents an old-fashioned way of doing, a way that is not as readily available to us as it once was. You want to be as good as you can be when he's around. And somehow he does make you an edge better than usual—in my case, less angry, less anxious, less cynical than I customarily am on the sidewalks of New York. So it's machismo. So what? Mostly I find it preferable to the neurotic whining that I hear around me most of the time.

Now, I would not say that in cold print, or even on screen, Howard's best self comes through readily. His reserve is not cold, but it is formidable. His humor is so understated that it can slide right past you if you're not looking out for it. And he has a strong desire to make what was obviously difficult seem easy in the retelling. Moreover, the desire he expresses late in the interview not to analyze what he does too closely, lest he become self-conscious about his gift and thus spoil it, is real. All of this adds up to a form of pride, an implication that if you're good—"a professional"—you don't have to sweat at your job, you accomplish it easily, naturally. This accounts for the relatively simple surfaces of his work, its lack of "fuss" (a word he uses to encompass all the obvious forms of directorial self-assertion). On the screen and in person he wants you to come to him, discover the merits in his work and in himself which he knows are there. He will not sue for attention or favor. And if you miss out, that's your tough luck.

It makes, I think, for a rather isolated life. He doesn't seem to have many friends in Palm Springs, to which he has retreated completely, having sold his Los Angeles home some years ago. He works on stories he hopes to turn into movies. He has a workshop where he turns out intricate silver jewelry (you can see some of his handiwork on screen— a belt buckle bearing the Red River D brand, which he gave John Wayne and which the star wears in westerns) and massive oak furniture. He tinkers with the motors on the vehicles he gives Greg. He seemed glad when, after we finished shooting, I called to ask him if he'd make a couple of extra shots we discovered we needed after we started editing. "Glad to do it, Dick; hell, I've been in that spot lots of times." Hardly a week goes by that I don't have an impulse to call him up, but I usually resist it. Maybe I shouldn't. But I always feel that we wouldn't know what to say to each other if we didn't have some practical matter to discuss. Hardly a day goes by, though, that I don't think of him, trying to imagine how he'd solve a problem or cool a hot emotional situation. This is more than a matter of admiration. It is a way of saying that, once exposed to the enigma of his personality, you can't turn away from it. It becomes a part of you and works on you in odd, sudden ways. Just as he means it to.

BORN TO SPEED

So many people ask, "Aren't you afraid to have Greg do this?" And I say, "No, I'm pretty old and lived through it fine. No reason why *he* shouldn't." But speed is rather natural. I started racing because my grand-father gave me a car that was the best car of that era—a little Mercer racer. And having the best car, I was able to win quite a few races. I also met an older man who came up to me and he said, "I can give you some help. You're just beginning." And he taught me a great many things about driving. He was very good. Sometimes cleared the way for me. We weren't very polite about our racing in those days. And it was pretty competitive. I remember tipping over on the first turn of one race and had a leather jacket just about taken off me, they came so close to me, going by. I never tipped over on the first turn of another race after that. We raced from Los Angeles to—oh, let's see—we raced from Los Angeles to San Francisco, we raced on the desert from Los Angeles down into Arizona—really tough, just single-road places. It was fun. [Later] I drove the car that won Indianapolis, I raced for two or three years professionally and had the fastest speedboat. And then when Greg started going he had fast time in the nationals in the quarter midget racing, won a hundred races in a year. Then he started out on the desert here. Riding motorcycles. He started winning when he was about fourteen, about two years ago. And the Checkers* had some bylaw that you had to be eighteen and I had to admit that he was about fourteen then. They changed their bylaws so they'd let him in. But it's a lot of fun. It's also a great sport. Today there are over a thousand people, about twelve hundred, racing, and they bring their wives and their children and spend a whole weekend. And it's nice and clean and the kids learn to ride and it's a cheap way of having a whole weekend.

BREAKING IN

I got into pictures during summer vacation from college. To earn a little money. And I worked one summer and they wanted me to come back the next summer. I went back the next summer and I got a better job, and the next summer I went up to assistant director. Then the war came along, and after the war I was hired to go back and take charge of the story department.

But I started in pictures as a property man. I wasn't even good enough to be assigned [regularly] to a company, I just moved furniture around the sets and moved it away. I became [a regular] property man because they wanted a modern set—Doug Fairbanks did. And I had studied architecture,** so I knew what [was needed and] we made them a modern set. Doug was very pleased, and I met him. We became good friends. And through Doug I [became] an assistant director to Mary Pickford, because they were beginning their romance then. We were working along and I was an assistant director and one day the director suffered from too much of a night before and he didn't show up and she said, "I guess we can't work." I said, "Why don't we make some scenes?" She said, "Can you do it?" And I said, "Sure." So we made a scene, two or three scenes, and—she was playing a dual role—she said,

* The racing club of which Hawks' son is a member.
** Hawks was a graduate of Phillips Exeter and of Cornell.

"I wish I could follow myself into this room." I said, "I think we can do it." And I talked to the cameraman and he said, "You're nuts."* "Well," I said, "let's try it." And we tried it and it worked. He said afterwards I was the luckiest bastard in the world because he said there is one chance in a hundred of doing it. And that was really my first directing.

Then the war came along. And after the war there was a young fellow that used to come up and talk story with me, and he told Mr. Lasky, the head of the Famous Players–Lasky studio, that I knew more about stories than anybody he knew. So Mr. Lasky hired me and put me in charge of the story department. And after he agreed to do it I said, "That's quite a jump. I was getting $50 a week here." "What doing?" And I said, "Assistant director." "Well," he said, "good for you. You're a lot more than an assistant director now." So I learned to direct, but they wouldn't let me direct. They said they could get a lot of directors.

I read everything that was written. And they were making pictures [based] on original stories, written by screen authors. And when he said, "Can you find forty stories in a year?" I said, "Yes." I bought two Jack Londons, two Joseph Conrads, two Zane Greys—got them easy. Didn't take me six weeks to buy forty stories. And they were very successful because they were written by good writers. I titled them all— that was before talk started. I left there and went to Metro-Goldwyn and did the same thing there. Then I just quit one day. I was out playing golf and I ran into the head of Fox. And he said, "What are you doing?" And I said, "Playing golf." "No," he said, "aren't you over at Metro-Goldwyn?" I said, "No, I quit." He said, "Well, you started work at Fox." I said, "I don't want to do that work I was doing." He says, "What do you want to do?" I said, "I want to direct." He said, "You start directing this morning." And the first picture worked out well and I've been a director ever since. I didn't like preparing stories for other directors to do. I thought it would be a whole lot easier to work on one for me to do, rather than twenty for other people to do.

I made a bunch of one-reel pictures [after that] and it was fun making them and we learned how to do comedy. We made one a week. Leading men got $50 a week, the leading lady, $30. And if the leading

---

* The scene required what would now be called a matte shot. In those days it had to be done in the camera—and it called for the careful timing of double exposure on the set.

man got obstreperous, I'd just say, "Go on up that ladder and come down the chimney." He'd say, "What's that for?" I'd say, "You'll come out in blackface and I can put anybody in your part and nobody will know the difference." And he'd get down and say, "I'll behave myself. I'll behave myself." And that always worked.

ON ACTION, EMULATION AND JOHN FORD

You had to have action when you were making a silent picture. And it had to look good in motion. And it was truly a motion picture. When dialogue started, it was easy. I can do three times as much work writing dialogue as I can thinking up things to do in action. Ford, for instance, did fabulous pictures where he used the camera and action. Nobody's equaled the kind of work that he has done. [Other] people depend purely on lines. They have no motion in the thing at all.

A very good man, asked to name the three best directors, said John Ford, John Ford, John Ford. And most of us who have studied that kind of a thing, we agree on that. I have enjoyed very much the [fact] that Ford [said] I made the best westerns. I think he is a lot better than I am, but I like it when people say I'm somewhere near as good as he is.

His work has the quality of silent pictures. If he wants to make a funeral, he doesn't need words. He can make use of bad weather and a grouping of people. . . . Peter Bogdanovich did a very good thing like that in *The Last Picture Show*. He's a student of Ford's—and he did very well with it. I made a very good burial scene once that I told him to look at [in *Red River*]. I saw a cloud coming and I knew it was going to pass over the hill behind and I said to Wayne, "Now get ready and no matter whether you make a muff, just keep on going, we can dub it in easy." And he did, and he went on with some more things, and he said, "What was happening?" I said, "The cloud went right over as you were reading this thing—that made it very good." Ford fills his pictures with stuff like that. He has an amazing eye for what is dramatic, and for the use of bad weather.

I emulate anything that anybody has done that is any good. I love to go to a picture to learn something. Doesn't mean I'm going to try to do it exactly the way they did it, but I learn from it. We have a lot of fun. [Ford's] going to run a new picture and he says, "I stole that thing from you. See how you like it." And I do the same thing. I tell him, "Hey, I was able to steal something from you too."* [Once] I [told] him about a scene that I had made—this man got a badly mangled finger, [it got caught] between a rope and a saddle horn. And they came in and they looked at the finger and said, "That isn't going to be much good to you. Better get him ready, boys." And they got a jug of whiskey and started giving him whiskey, and they got a fire going and put a piece of iron on the fire, and another fellow started honing a knife, and finally when he got kind of tight they said, "Well, I guess he is ready." And they put his finger down and chopped it off and brought in an iron and seared the end of it. And then the man said, "Where is my finger?" "Well, what do you want that for?" And he says, "Well, a man wants to be buried whole. I want my finger." End of the scene they were all hunting around in the ashes of the fire, trying to find the finger. And Ford said, "This is going to be a comedy scene?" "Well," I said, "I hope so." And he said, "I want to see it." And it was. It was a very funny scene, they laughed at it all the way through. I [also] told the scene to John Wayne and he said, "I don't think it is funny." And I said, "Oh, all right. You don't have to do it. I'll use it in another picture." So finally when he saw it, he said, "Well, if you tell me a funeral is funny, I'll believe it."

My humor is probably a little different. [Ford's] is kind of raucous—on the Irish side. Mine is a little more tart. But when you put it all together, it ends up about the same. You accomplish what you want to do.

THE DAWN PATROL

When talking pictures came in, they asked all of us, John Ford, me, "What do you know about dialogue?" We said, "Nothing. We just know how people talk." And I was out of work for about a year and a half because they said, "He doesn't know anything about dialogue." So

---

* This interview was conducted before John Ford died, August 31, 1973.

I wrote the story and all the dialogue for *Dawn Patrol** and Richard Barthelmess read it and said, "I want to make it. I want Hawks to make it." I didn't tell them I hadn't ever made a talking picture. They didn't find out until I was about a month into it. And I used to get notes saying that I had a chance to make a good scene and I blew it. Because the dialogue was very understated, very natural—it wasn't stage dialogue. And I think I had forty letters from the front office saying I missed things. Picture came out, made more money than any that year. And made a couple of fellows who were heads of studios very angry with me because they said, "Now people are going to try to do that kind of dialogue and they won't know how to do it." But they began to switch over and then they used the understated dialogue for many years until Kazan made that picture where the people got really emotional and started acting. I've forgotten the name of it. And then people started back getting melodramatic again.

THE CROWD ROARS

I think probably the first picture that I made where I did something that was fun for me was *The Crowd Roars*. I'd been driving races for a little while. I knew all the great drivers. We had about eight Indianapolis drivers working in the picture, and we had fun all the way through it. From that time on, I found out that the public liked those things, so I just made pictures that appealed to me. If I liked them, then the public seemed to like them. We made everything ourselves.** We started on a dirt track and made all the footage on the dirt track and went to the night scenes at a little oval track, which was interesting because fires and things then came into play. I remember making one scene where we let gasoline out behind the camera car and there were flames shooting up and the drivers had to go through that. And very good people helped. One of the Duesenberg brothers, who made one of the famous cars in America, I told him [about a crash scene I wanted to make] and he said, "I'll have

---

* It is a story of a British squadron in World War I, focusing on the anguish of their leader, who must order his comrades into combats he knows will eventually kill all of them.

** In other words, no stock footage was used.

something for you. You can tow a car going a hundred and twenty miles an hour, let it go, the wheel will come off five seconds later and— Lord knows what will happen to it then." All that stuff is kind of fun. It taxes your imagination—to try to do something no one else has done.

DRIVERS AND PILOTS

They find out that they are good at handling a car. And they gradually move on up and they gradually go just as far as their talent will take them. They have great coordination. They haven't any fear. Some time ago in England I saw a little chunky fellow drive a car and I told a friend of mine who made racecars that I saw a great driver. It was Mike Hawthorne. He became one of the world's best. You just see them and you know by what they do that they're good. I have two boys, one of them Greg, and another older, and the older boy would love to do what the younger boy does so easily. But I wouldn't let the older boy drive unless he was in a car where he couldn't hurt himself—because he's not going to do the job on it.

I was in the Air Corps in the First War. And, oh, I really started to fly 'long about '15. And then after the war was over, I owned about twelve, fifteen airplanes, all different kinds. Had about ten thousand hours—a lot of time. Flying isn't much fun any more, you have to make up plans of where you are going to go and what time you are going to leave and it's no fun.

[But, anyway,] I knew all of the pilots. When airlines started I knew everybody, every pilot who flew on the airlines. I knew all the test pilots. You unconsciously begin to find out how they think and what they do, and I made several airplane pictures and I've utilized those things.

ANGELS—AND TRUTH

I made one picture that people criticized. It's called *Only Angels Have Wings*. It was a kind of a flamboyant thing. They said—certain critics said—that's the only picture that Hawks ever made that didn't have any truth in it. I wrote them a letter and said, "Every blooming thing in that is true." I knew the men who were in it and everything about it. But it was just where truth was stranger than fiction. We didn't have to write for it at all. People that I've seen die and how they die and what they said, and you don't have to elaborate on those things. You can take a real scene and make a much better scene than something you dream up. Death scenes are very hard to do because they either get mawkish or sentimental or something like that. It's nice to be able to do them honestly.

We made a scene in *Only Angels Have Wings* where Cary Grant's best friend, Tommy Mitchell, was dying. He said, "I feel kind of funny. My neck is . . ." Cary Grant said, "Your neck's broke." And he said, "Well, I always wondered how it would be when I knew I was going to die. And I don't know how good [I'll be]." He said, "I'd just as soon you'd get out of here."* So Grant went out and stood in the rain and left the boy alone to die. Well, I saw that happen. I didn't see it happen in the rain. We added the rain, but it was that kind of scene. That's exactly the kind of dialogue they used. It's far more effective than some crazy thing.

THREE-CUSHION DIALOGUE

Frank Capra came to me and he said, "What's this kind of dialogue you're doing?" "Well," I said, "Hemingway calls it oblique. And I call it three-cushion." In order to say something, you bounce around from one cushion to another and then you've said it and it doesn't become a rash statement. People rather like it. Noël Coward came over and made a visit on the set and he said, "Where does that kind of dialogue come from?" I told him that Hemingway really started it. And I took it up and Noël started using it. Just an interesting way of saying a thing. Capra did it beautifully. One of the best love scenes that I've ever seen in a picture was Jean Arthur getting tight and trying to get Tommy Mitchell to marry her.** She was in love with another man. So she was trying to get

---

* Hawks, of course, is paraphrasing this dialogue from memory.
** In *Mr. Smith Goes to Washington.*

Tommy Mitchell to marry her. And that was really *four*-cushion. That went all the way around. That was a beautifully done thing.

MOVEMENT

I think that motion is far more interesting than just talking. Anybody can stand still and talk, and even in motion I've tried to make my dialogue go fast, probably twenty percent faster than most pictures. Sometimes we put a few unnecessary words on the front of a sentence and a few on the end, so that people can overlap in their talking and you still get everything they wanted to say. We did that in—oh, several pictures. We did it in a picture called *The Thing*. We did it in a picture called *His Girl Friday*. And if you have actors who are good enough, it's a lot of fun to do. It gives you a sense of speed. I rehearse a scene first to get the action and then the words go in afterwards. People say I change a lot, but I don't. I just don't want them saying a long line while they're running, so I just have them say a short line. If you can get the sensation of speed, people can't just sit back and analyze how bad it is.

ANGLES ON REALISM

I believe they asked me how I liked *The Wild Bunch* and I said I didn't think too much of it. I said, "I can kill three people and get them off to the morgue before he gets one down to the ground." Because he accentuated everything with slow motion, and I think violence is in getting it over so fast you don't know—hardly know—what has happened. And we work to that goal. We don't just use buckets of red paint and a lot of film to slow it up. I think occasionally slow motion is great—in a picture like *On Any Sunday*, a motorcycle picture, where it became lyrical. [But] I think it gets away from reality. I want to see the scene the way it would look if I were looking at it, not the way that somebody, you know, did it in a camera or something. It's always been so. I got away from [the eye-level camera] one time and everybody started writing me about it. It was in *El Dorado*, where a man was shot up in the belfry of a church, fell down, hit the floor. I didn't have enough set, [so] the only way I could get it, I had to put a camera on and let a dummy fall into it. The camera was shooting straight up. I saved myself a day's work in building a set by doing it and that was all. But I believe that you ought to see it from your eyes. See it as it looks to you. I think it is confusing to an audience to have a camera on the floor, you know, or above and everything like that. I made a picture down in Mexico and I was very struck with the shadows and the big hats. And I wanted to get out and get above them and have three people talking and never see their faces, [just] see the shadows and the great big hats. [Then] I saw it on the screen, went back and did it over.*

I think the best cameramen are able to give you your effects by lighting so that, you know, you just get a feeling of the whole scene by what they use for light. I was working with a very fine cameraman, Lee Garmes, and we had a very difficult scene. I didn't realize what was the matter with it. I said, "Something is wrong with this thing." He said, "Give me five minutes." And he sent for some curtains that were all lace. And he cut off all the light in the room and then everything was just the light that came through these lace curtains. You didn't see the faces, you just saw silhouettes. Scene was really a good thing. And it was a scene that shouldn't have been brought out in the full light. He made the scene, I didn't.**

Today they discuss new forms of photography, new forms of camera. Nothing is new. We did it as much as forty-five years ago. We did all of those things. A fella called [F. W.] Murnau came over, was filled with strict camera angles. The camera did trick things. It went up on hoists. It went around on booms. I thought this was marvelous. I went him a few better. They liked the picture so much they held it out for a year. By the time they showed it, everybody had used the same stuff. So I quit. I just wasn't going to do that. I was just going to shoot it as plain as I could shoot it. The only tricks that I've used in the last four or five years is that if John Wayne draws a gun and shoots quickly, I have the cameraman zoom right up there. You're never conscious of that. All of a sudden the gun is in your face, going off. . . . If you can think of things to do with a zoom lens, then I think that's fine, but who [can look] at a picture when the camera goes all around and you're trying to get reality? I'm

* From eye level.
** It is the incest scene in *Scarface*.

very fond of moving shots. But [I use it as if] you're walking alongside [the action], seeing it.

BLACK AND WHITE VS. COLOR

You've got a nostalgic feeling the moment you use black and white. I think Peter Bogdanovich was very smart in making *The Last Picture Show* in black and white. It gives you a dead quality—a wasted quality, you know. For instance, that marvelous picture that Jack Ford made about the Okies—you remember, *The Grapes of Wrath*—I would have hated to see that done in color. That showed up so much better in black and white. It took quite a little time to sell me on color, mostly because the people around the studios wanted to have it so brilliant. They said, "We're paying for color. We want color." Finally we got them tamed down to where they would accept pastels. For instance, the best color picture that I ever saw was *The Quiet Man* that Jack Ford made with John Wayne, made in the fog. Never had a clear day. Just beautiful. They went to foggy Ireland and made this great picture.

[Now], in taking the good painters who painted westerns, you're always conscious of the fact that out of a saloon door came a bright yellow light that hit the streets and it gave a funny quality. So we tried that. If you put yellow light on people, they look like they have yellow jaundice. But if you just use it as a general color scheme, it becomes rich and kind of easy and mellow to look at. So we use amber, yellow, on the back walls, on the streets, wherever we can, and then light the people with white light. It gives you a little of the feeling—it does me, anyway—of a period. Because of the fact that Remington used it more than anyone else.

ON COMEDY AND CARY GRANT

I worked with Cary Grant a lot and he is so easy to work with because you do a scene and [he says,] "How's that?" And I say, "Pretty dull."

"What's wrong with it?" And I say, "Well, the way you get angry. You ought to find some other way of getting mad." And then we talk about one way and another way and another way and I might say to him, "I knew a fella that got so mad he'd whinny like a horse. You know." "Oh," he said, "I'll do that. Let me do that." And we did it and he was very funny.*

We were doing a scene that we both liked in a picture called *I Was a Male War Bride*, where he is a French officer married to an American girl and had to go through the same things that a French girl would if she had married a G.I. And they asked him all kinds of questions: have you ever had any [female] trouble and have you ever been pregnant? It was a very funny scene, but when we did it, it wasn't funny. And we didn't know what was the matter with it. Finally I said, "Cary, you're a pretty sophisticated man. *You* shouldn't be embarrassed. The man asking you the questions should be embarrassed."

LOMBARD AND *TWENTIETH CENTURY*

Twentieth Century was fun right from the beginning, because it was written by Hecht and MacArthur, who I thought handled dialogue better than anybody that I knew. They'd written [the play] for Gregory Ratoff's wife, who was a very stylized Russian actress [Eugenie Leontovich]. And I asked them, "How about writing it for Sophie Glotz of Third Avenue?" And they said, "Oh, that would be fun."

I got [John] Barrymore; I called him and told him I had a story and he said he would be down to talk to me and I said, "I've never seen your house, I'd like to come up there." And so I went up there and he'd read the thing by that time and he said, "Just why do you think I could play this?" And I said, "Well, you're the biggest ham in the world and there is no reason why you can't play this thing because this is the story of the next greatest ham." He said, "All right. When do we start?"

I had an awful lot of trouble getting a girl to live up to who Barry-

* In *His Girl Friday*.

more was. I knew Carole Lombard. She was a second cousin of mine. [Our families] came from the same little town in Wisconsin. And I thought, well, she was a great personality. She couldn't act for a damn. She just became completely phony. I told the head of the studio I'd use her and he said, "Oh, you could do better than that." And I said, "Well, find me somebody, then." In about a week he said, "I've signed Carole Lombard."

We started to work and I said to Barrymore, "Now, no matter what happens, no matter what you think is wrong, I don't want you to say anything until four this afternoon." He said, "All right." We started to rehearse. He was kind of amazed, she was so bad. He held his nose behind her back and I told the cameraman I'd like to have fifteen minutes off—find a reason and dismiss the people for that time. And I took a walk with Carole. Told her she had been working hard. And she said, "I'm glad that it shows." And I said, "Yes, you know your lines perfectly. How much do you get paid for this picture?" She said, "$5000." I said, "That's pretty good. What do you get paid for?" "Well," she said, "why, acting, of course." I said, "Supposing I tell you you earned all the money. You don't owe anything." She just stared at me. Her eyes got awful big and I said, "What would you do if a man said such-and-such a thing to you?" "I'd kick him right in the groin," she said. "Well," I said, "Barrymore said that to you. Why didn't you kick him?" She just stared. And I said, "What would you do if a man said such-and-such a thing?" She made a typical Lombard gesture. And I said, "Well, he said that in the third line. Why didn't you wave your arms? We're going to go back there and if you don't kick him where you said you were going to and wave your arms and do any damn thing you want to do, I'm going to fire you and get another girl." She said, "You're serious, aren't you?" I said, "I'm very serious." "Okay," she says, "that's fine."

So I went back and said, "Let's try a take," and Barrymore said, "We're not ready." I said, "Who's running this thing?" And he said, "You are." So we started the scene. Cameramen had three cameras set up so that we didn't have to rehearse where [they] went. They were just in a little compartment of a train. They could go and do anything they wanted to do. She made a kick at him and he jumped back and started pointing his finger at her and she waved her arms. She got back on the seat in the compartment and was kicking with both feet up at him and he was dancing around and finally he exited out of the scene and I said, "Cut, print it." Barrymore came back and said, "That was magnificent. Were you fooling me all the time?" And she started to cry and ran off the stage. He said, "What the hell goes on, Howard?" And I told him. "Well," he said, "this girl is absolutely marvelous." I said, "She is a star. But I need a lot of help from you." We made the picture in three weeks. I just turned them loose. And she *was* a star after that picture.

If you'll notice, almost all of my comedies have been in restricted areas. It is much easier to keep them going fast, and, actually, scenic shots haven't much place. All you need is some action, limited action, and make it move fast. A picture like *Bringing Up Baby* moved all around and everything. It was quite a problem. If I hadn't had such good people who could talk while they were moving and do everything, it would have been hard to make the picture. But *Twentieth Century* was written for the stage and the dialogue was so really good that you wanted to keep it that way.

HIS GIRL FRIDAY

I'd always liked *Front Page*. And I always thought that Hecht and Mac-Arthur did the finest modern dialogue that there was. One night a bunch of people were up for dinner and I had a couple of copies of the play and so I said to a girl, "You read the part of the reporter, I'll read the part of the editor." We read two or three pages and I said, "It's better with a girl playing the reporter than one of the men." So I called Ben Hecht and said, "What would you think of it?" He said, "I think it is a great idea." And he said, "I'm working on a story, I'm kind of stuck. I'll come up and help you if you will help me." And I said, "Come ahead." And we started in and did the script and made the picture. And it worked out. It was a better picture with the girl doing it—playing the reporter—than a man playing it.

[And] Roz was marvelous. The two of them [Rosalind Russell and Cary Grant] worked so well together. All I had to do was just tell them a little story and say, "Now do this" and they'd do it. And they did it so well. She had fun and they had fun together, you know, and they made a great team. I don't think she had done a comedy up until that time.

In making *His Girl Friday*, one of the problems was the fact that [*The Front Page*] was recognized by all the newspaper people as the fastest picture that had been made because of the dialogue that the boys had written. And when the newspaper boys came out and [asked] "Is it [*His Girl Friday*] as fast as the other picture?" I said, "Well, I'll run one picture on one projection machine and one on another in the projection room," and they said, "My lord, that's half again as fast." And it was.

Naturally, we used [overlapping dialogue] because that's the way we all talk. If we were holding a discussion, you'd talk and I'd butt in on you and you'd butt in on me, but our little trick of adding a few words in front and adding a few at the end of a line makes it come out as clear as it can be. To me it sounds more like reality.

COMEDY IN DRAMA

I've only found about four real comedies that I thought were fun and I've done them. And finding the people getting more and more to like the comedy treatment of things, I started using it in westerns. I used it a little bit in *Rio Bravo*. Used it a good deal more in *El Dorado* and found that the [basic] seriousness of a good western made it so easy to get a laugh. You could give Wayne things to say—he hit a man in *Rio Bravo* across the head with a gun and blood was running down the man's face. Dean Martin said, "Take it easy, Duke." Wayne said, "I'm not going to hurt him." And the audience thought it was very funny. And those things are funny because you are in the middle of violence. I had Jimmy Caan chasing a man and he couldn't shoot a gun and he shot this sawed-off shotgun and he missed the man, but he hit a sign and the sign fell down and knocked the man down. That's really going back to Keystone days. And you have more fun when you are making a picture that way. And I think more and more the audience enjoys humor. It's natural. It's part of things. Even in the middle of trouble. I enjoy a television show called M*A*S*H because they do just that. They treat very serious things so lightly.

STYLE

You ask why did I repeat myself [in] business, characters, plots, things. Probably I could answer it better by [saying] if a man, a good boxer, hits somebody with a left hook, he doesn't stop left-hooking in the rest of his fights. And anybody who is any good—any writer—is always going to repeat himself, so that you're going to know who wrote the thing. And any director that I think is any good puts a stamp on his work. And he naturally will use things again. If it has been good once, it's good another time. That's the only answer that I can give to a thing like that.

I used to think that if anybody is any good, I can go into a theater and recognize [his work]. I can certainly recognize Ford's work or Willie Wyler's or Frank Capra. [Or] Hitchcock. If you don't, then the person isn't much good.

It probably could happen when you run into a little situation and the scene isn't too good. And you realize that such-and-such a thing helped a scene before. So you do a version of that thing. I've made the same death scene twice. I've [used the same type of] meeting between two people many times by realizing that's a good way for people to meet. They use different dialogue, they meet under different circumstances, but that's a good way for them to meet. You get little ways of doing it. You find out that's good and the audience likes it, so you do it again. It isn't actually doing it the same, but . . . I like it when [people] say, "You repeated yourself." Because if they can remember that long, the scene must be pretty good.

FAULKNER, HEMINGWAY AND *TO HAVE AND HAVE NOT*

I read a story of William Faulkner's which I liked—and I was working at the time with Hecht and MacArthur, and they were surrounded in

New York by a group of the intelligentsia, the writers and everything, and I asked if any of these fellows had read William Faulkner. They said no. I said, "I think he's the best writer I've read in a long time," and they bought the book—they probably bought it from Bill without knowing it, because he was a clerk in the bookstore at one of the big department stores—and they began to like him. And I read a short story of his and bought it from him. I asked him, in a telegram, if he'd like to come out and work on it. And he came out, and we became friends. We both liked to hunt, and we did—we hunted together. He bought an airplane with the money he earned. He wrote me a marvelous letter one time, he said, "I am sitting on the porch at my place in Oxford, Mississippi, and," he said, "there's a kind of light rain coming down; it's very comfortable. I got a jug of corn liquor, a pitcher of water. There's a great sound that I can hear; it's the sound of the first toilet we've ever had." Up to now, he had used an outhouse. So he said, "I want to thank you very much, because you paid for that."

He came out here, and we were going down in Imperial Valley and Clark Gable called and said, "What are you doing?" We said, "Going hunting." Clark said he'd like to go. So we met and started off in the station wagon. They somehow started talking literary, and Clark asked Faulkner who the good writers were. He said "Thomas Mann, Willa Cather, John Dos Passos, Ernest Hemingway and myself." Gable said, "You write, Mr. Faulkner?" And he said, "Yes. What do *you* do, Mr. Gable?"

Faulkner and I got along very well. He was amazing. I could get stuck for a scene, call him and have the scene the next morning. We were doing a picture—oh, it was called *Air Force*—during the war, and we needed this death scene for the pilot of the thing. And he wrote a scene—all it was was a takeoff procedure that a crew goes through to get into the air, and the pilot died at the end of it. Faulkner didn't get screen credit. He just wrote the scene. I'd call him about anything like that. I think he enjoyed working on anything that had Hemingway's name on it.* For Faulkner to come in and make it better, you know.

To Have and Have Not was made into a movie because of a rather odd circumstance. I was trying to get Hemingway to write for pictures

---

* Faulkner shared screen credit as a writer on *To Have and Have Not*.

Inside—Cary Grant. Outside—Katharine Hepburn. The subject under discussion— Bringing Up Baby (1938)

Humphrey Bogart with the rod, Lauren Bacall with the belt, in To Have and Have Not (1944)

John Wayne getting his point across to Montgomery Clift in Red River (1948)

and he said, "Howard, I don't want to. I don't know enough about writing for pictures. I'm good at what I'm doing and I don't want to go to Hollywood." I said, "You don't have to come to Hollywood. I'll come to meet you and we'll fish and hunt and work on a story." "Oh . . ." he said. I said, "Ernest, I can make a picture out of your worst book." "What's my worst book?" he said. I said, "*To Have and Have Not* is a bunch of junk." "Well," he said, "I needed money and I had to—" I said, "I don't care what happened." He said, "You can't make a picture out of that." And I said, "Yes, I can." So for about ten days we talked about the two characters in his book and how they'd met. We just worked that up, and I went back and he sold it to somebody for $10,000. I bought it from that person for $80,000. And I made a deal with Warner Brothers where I made ten or fifteen times that amount on the picture, and the next time I saw Hemingway, it happened to be in Paris, I said, "Ernest, *you* should have been working on that thing. You got $10,000. The fellow who bought it from you got $80,000." I told him what I made, and he wouldn't talk to me for three months. But, actually, anything Ernest wrote you can make into a movie. Good movie. *For Whom the Bell Tolls* was really a western. You could make anything you wanted to from what he did.

In working on the story for *To Have and Have Not*, [Lauren] Bacall was a brand-new girl. She'd never done anything before. I was very interested in seeing that we got a good introduction for her. I had a very good writer on it at the time, Jules Furthman—oh, let's say that he was a rebel in a lot of ways. And he wrote a scene that introduced Bacall as the girl in a strange port in the Caribbean who had her purse stolen. I said, "Jules, that's a great scene—that's so good. Nothing sexier than a girl whose purse has been stolen. She's all alone—" "Oh, to hell with you," he said and he walked out. And he came in the next day, and the girl stole the purse instead, and it became a very fine opening for Bacall and that character.* [Even before that] I used to try out things on her, and I wanted to make a test of her because she got so good—and I wrote the ["just whistle"] scene. It had no relation to the story—and it made such a good scene that Jack Warner, the head of the studio, said, "Howard,

---

* Hawks pointed out to us that he used a very similar introduction for the Angie Dickinson character in *Rio Bravo*—another example of establishing style through repetition.

where does that come in the picture?" I said, "It isn't in there." He said, "It better be in when you make it." So we had a hell of a time adapting that to the picture. And finally it worked in and became the best line in the whole thing.

THE BIG SLEEP

To Have and Have Not was so well received at previews that [Warner] said we should have another with these people right away. And I knew a story, and we started to make it, and it was just as successful as the first. And it was easy to do, because Bogart would help Bacall; he fell in love with her. [Usually] it isn't too easy to take a brand-new girl and get the kind of stuff that we got from Bacall.

Actually, it's just an honesty and directness, without quibbling about things. [With women like this, if] they think something, they come out and say it. If they like somebody, they come out and say it. It happens to be the kind of person that I like, and it's very much easier for me to do it, and also it makes a little something different instead of moonlight and roses and soft things on the water, and all that kind of thing. You get an honesty that kind of . . . It becomes fun. She isn't the girl that meets other girls and has cocktails and plays bridge and things like that. They like to ride and hunt and shoot, do things. They usually don't like women, other women. They like men around. I think they're far more attractive.

During the making of *The Big Sleep*, I found out, for the first time, that you don't have to be too logical. You really should just make good scenes. You follow one scene with another and stop worrying about hooking them together.

The script was written by Leigh Brackett and Faulkner. Leigh, I thought, was a man's name, and in walked this fresh-looking girl who wrote like a man. Faulkner didn't know anything [technically] about screenwriting. I put the two together; they did the whole script in eight days. And they said they didn't want to change things because the stuff was so good; there was no sense in making it logical. So we didn't.

Once during the picture Bogart said, "Who killed this fellow?" And

I said, "Well, it probably was . . . I don't know." So we sent a wire to the author, Raymond Chandler, and asked him and he told us the name of the fellow. And I wired him back and I said, "He was down at the beach when that happened. It couldn't be done that way." So nobody knew who killed that bird. It didn't hurt the picture.

You asked why scenes take certain turns that are maybe unusual. As we work on scenes, I always go back and say, "How would it be if it were directly opposite?" and sometimes it leads to very interesting things, because there is no particular reason that they have to run in a straight line—they can take a jog. We do that as a matter of course. I teach writers who work with me to do it. We just keep on doing it. Sometimes you carry it clear onto the set. You haven't realized that there are other ways, and sometimes you get out on the set and try it the other way. If you've got a good man, good girl, competent people, it's easy.

For example, in *The Big Sleep*, Bogart did this little innocuous scene of entering a bookstore. He looked at me and said, "What's the matter?" I said, "It seems like it's going to be kind of dull. [I wonder] if we could get a different way of going in there." He said, "Roll 'em again." We rolled it. He pushed his hat up like this, and adapted a kind of prissy air, and entered, and played it exactly as if he were one of those flying boys, and the scene became rather interesting.

PEOPLE THE CAMERA LIKES

I have a theory that the camera likes some people. Other people the camera does not like. And the people it likes can't do any wrong. Almost everything they think comes out when you photograph it. I met probably the most beautiful girl I ever saw, marvelous personality and everything—one look at her on the camera and I told her she might as well give up. She had no chance. But people like Bogart, who was not a good-looking man—everything he did, you seemed to know why he was doing it. Gary Cooper—things would happen that wouldn't [be visible] to the eye. Gable—all of the people who are great personalities. They're not actors as much as they are personalities. The camera likes them.

And if the camera doesn't like them, they become nonentities as actors. Some of them do, say things perfectly well, but they don't mean anything. But these great characters like Marie Dressler, like Wally Beery—the camera liked them. The camera got everything they did. And you find that happens all the time. When you're using a new person you have to guess that, at first. Then you train them a little bit, and put them out there, and you know in one minute whether they're any good or not. For instance, Gary Cooper, you'd watch him do a scene. You'd wonder whether you had it. And I'd go home worrying about it.* And come look the next day at the rushes—and there was more there than I wanted in the first place. I don't know why. Except that I think that he thought —and it registered. Some people you look at and you can tell what they're thinking. Other people you can't, but that doesn't always [translate to film]. It's what the camera sees, not what *you* see.

JOHN WAYNE AND WESTERNS

You know, a western is fun because you can get out of doors. You're not stuck in a stage, studio. It doesn't [matter] what the set is—they all have lights and people around them and the air isn't good.

The western takes, really, a couple of forms. One is how the West started, the formation of the great cattle herds. Actually, *Red River* started as the story of the King Ranch. And after you do certain things like Pony Express, some of the earlier things, you come to the period of the beginning of law and order; you had good sheriffs, you had a bad sheriff. *That's* a form. *Rio Bravo, El Dorado* fell into that. We had a lot of fun in writing *Rio Bravo* because we ran into so many good situations. We said, "We'll save that for another picture."

In making westerns, I've worked practically just with John Wayne. He is by far the best. I'm trying to visualize a pretty good western story now with somebody else in it and I'm having difficulty. I know Wayne is not suitable for it, but I'm going to miss his power and his force. He

* The film was *Sergeant York*.

makes me work awfully hard. But he is so good and I know what to write for him and more or less what to do.

Jack Ford started John Wayne. In *Stagecoach*. Wayne had very little acting to do. And when Ford saw *Red River*, he said, "I never knew that big fellow could act." And he put him in about three pictures in the next two years—made a big star out of him. Ford and I were very good friends and whenever I made a picture with Wayne he'd come down and stay a week on location. Play poker, have a few drinks, and the relationship between Wayne and Ford was very interesting. He still treated him as a beginner. And Wayne would do anything that Coach, or "Pappy," as he called him, asked him to do. He's not that easy with new directors. He knows what he wants, what he can do, and he does it. But in working with Ford or with me, he just says, "You fellows know what to do, just tell me what to do."

John Wayne has just come to be recognized for the good actor that he is. I've always thought he was a good actor. I always thought he could do things that other people can't do. If you try to make a western with somebody besides Wayne, you're not in the sphere of violence and action that you are when you've got Wayne. I think that unless he is working with a damn good actor, he's going to blow them right off the screen. Not intentionally, just because he—he does it.

In *Red River* he worked with Montgomery Clift. When he saw Clift the first time, he said, "Howard, think we can get anything going between that kid and myself?" I said, "I think you can." After two scenes he said, "You're right. He can hold his own anyway, but I don't think we can make a fight." I said, "Duke, if you fall down and I kick you in the jaw, that could be quite a fight. Don't you think so?" He said, "Okay." And that was all there was to it. We did it that way. It took us about three days to make Montgomery Clift look good enough to be against Wayne because he didn't know how to punch or move when we rehearsed.

But I've always thought that it is bad to put a great big guy with Wayne because he is then going to overpower him more. I'd like to make a picture with Wayne and Sinatra, Mutt and Jeff. We've never been able to do it, but both of them said they would like to. Dean Martin was good with Wayne in *Rio Bravo*. That was the first serious picture that he'd done and he showed he [is a] good actor. Also, he was playing a drunk, and that would be kind of weakness, you know [in contrast to Wayne].

Martin was so eager to do *Rio Bravo*. I said, "Go on, get into the kind of outfit you think you ought to have on." He came back looking kind of pretty, and like a gunman and everything. And I said, "That isn't like drunks I know. Most of them have tattered shirts, mostly they're in underwear. They've got the oldest hat in the world." "Okay, okay— will you be here two hours more?" And he came back, and he was the way he was in the picture. He said, "Now I know what to do." Jack Warner, watching the picture, said, "When does Dean Martin start to come into this picture?" I said, "That's the fellow in the awful-looking hat." "You mean, the fellow that looks like Charley Grapewin?"

Wayne said, "All right, what am I going to do all the time? While Martin gets these good scenes?" And I said, "He's your best friend, watch him. See whether he is coming through." He said, "Okay, that's enough for me." [Now] one interesting way of establishing a relationship between two characters is in little things where one helps the other. It was ideally used in *Rio Bravo* [where] Martin as a drunk who has shaking hands was trying to roll a cigarette. Wayne watched him and said, "Here," and took it and rolled it and lit it for him and gave it back to him. You knew right away they were friends. That can be done so easily on just some little thing in a relation between two people. Actually, most of the pictures that I do are like that. A relationship with two friends.

I didn't like *High Noon*. I said, "It's phony. The fellow's supposed to be good. He's supposed to be good with a gun. He runs around like a wet chicken trying to get people to help him. Eventually his Quaker wife saves his guts." I said, "That's ridiculous. The man wasn't a professional." And there was another pretty good western called *The Five O'Clock to Yuma*,* or something like that, where the prisoner said to the sheriff, "Wait'll my friends catch up with you." I said, "Hell, a sheriff who's any good would say, 'You better hope your friends don't catch up because the first man shot is going to be you.' " So we started hooking those things together and it made *Rio Bravo*.

* The film is *3:10 to Yuma*, directed by Delmer Daves in 1957. It starred Glenn Ford.

The young fellow in *Rio Bravo* was really a good shot. Ricky Nelson played him—so in *El Dorado*, when we started to work on that, I said, "Let's get a boy who can't shoot"—and that was Jim Caan. And in *Rio Bravo*, Wayne was the sheriff and the deputy was a drunk; in *El Dorado*, the drunk was the sheriff. You just take opposites of everything. And we [finally] had the scene where the jailer said, "You better hope nobody comes in here, because you're going to be the first one shot." And people liked it.

HATARI

Hatari in a way [was] a western. I knew the system of catching [animals]—it needed a truck; it needed a man on a fender. We had one of the finest chassis that you've ever seen, and a whole body put on top of it —had high-altitude carburetors and great brakes and had something like eight shock-absorbers at each end. And then, realizing the camera had to be faster to keep up with it, we designed and built two camera cars and they could go eighty miles an hour over the desert—never any trouble at all. Then we had a job taking care of the camera—the jounces, the bounces the camera was going to take, doing that. We tried using a $25,000 outfit from a destroyer gunsight—didn't work at all. We ended up by getting a big fat inner tube, putting a kind of gimbal on the camera and setting it on the inner tube, and it took everything—just rode beautifully. Probably cost about $10. And we got some remarkable photography.

The picture was very interesting because we never knew in the morning what we were going to do that day—we had three or four spotting airplanes, and just as dawn broke, they would go up and radio back to us. One would say, "I found a really good herd of rhino," and by that time we'd be on our way and he'd tell us where to go. And all of our cars were marked with numbers on top so they could be seen from an airplane, and we were equipped with communication between the cars. The man would tell me that car fourteen headed right for this thing, and I'd tell everybody to converge on fourteen, they'd fire a signal gun up in the air, and people would see where he was and we'd all start going there.

I remember on that particular day when we found some great rhino, I could hear the airplane telling this fellow who was in the lead, "They're just behind that clump of trees in front of you. Watch out. One of them looks kind of bad." Then he said, "I think you ought to take it easy. That fellow looks bad." Then we heard a big crash and metal going and the fellow in the airplane laughed and said, "I told you it was bad." But it was fun because we never knew what we were going to catch, and we had to be ready.

We had a great many chalk talks about what to do—how you had to shoot lower as an elephant got closer to you. Various things. And if we didn't have that animal in a cage five minutes after we started chasing him, well, we were out of luck. So it required instant coverage from all over, the car bearing the cage that was good for that animal had to be up there, and the camera car had to be up there—everybody had to be around. I could yell myself hoarse saying, "Duke, get in there and try to get a rope around his left leg and then turn around and yell at somebody—and you yell back; we'll put your words in later on." And we did that. He'd say "ka-sa-sa-sa" or something like that—we had fun.

ON "MALE BONDING" AND VICTOR FLEMING

I've particularly noticed friendship between men—and what they do [together]. I think it is a good thing. I learned it a long time ago when Vic Fleming made a picture called *Captains Courageous* with Spencer Tracy and a boy. I saw it again in a picture that was done on the desert about the French Foreign Legion. I became interested in the relationship of men. I saw how good it can be and how you're not getting into any mawkish thing, you're getting into something that is kind of fun. So I've done that.

It's hard to define what causes that kind of a thing. [When] I used to drive a racecar, in one race there was a fellow coming up on the outside and I put him to the fence. We weren't very polite about driving in those days. I won the race. After the race was over, I saw the fellow coming and I thought, Oh, Lord, here we go. I'm going to have a fight. Instead he came up and he said, "That was pretty good. But," he said, "you better not try it again because next time I'm going to run right into you." We had a drink and we became friends. He came up to the house for a while. He didn't have a place to stay. He stayed five years. I made him a director, and he was one of the finest directors in the world. Vic Fleming.* We used to be on the point of a fight many times, but we never quite got to it. We always had to laugh before it started.

Fleming and I had a lot of fun. We used to shoot together and fly together. We built an airplane for racing, he flew it in the first race, won the race, and landed it and the landing gear broke. And I said, "Next time you better let *me* fly it." And I flew it and won the race and the landing gear broke when we landed. We flew it in four races and won four races and every time broke the landing gear. Then we gave up on that airplane. He was funny. He came in one day and wanted a drink. "Well," he said, "I'm through flying." I said, "Why?" "Well," he said, "you know that new airplane? I landed it—perfectly good landing—right out in the middle of a landing strip," he said, "I pulled the lever and let the wheels down. What I meant to do was put the flaps up." "Oh," I said, "Vic, anybody does that." He said, "That isn't what I'm talking about. I'm so sore about doing that to a new airplane, I went in and had a cup of coffee and they passed me the sugar and I unwrapped the sugar, threw the sugar away, put the paper in my coffee cup." He said, "I have no business flying any more." But he did.

INDEPENDENCE—AND STICKING TO YOUR GUNS

I have never believed in staying under contract. Consequently, I could change or, if I liked a story a studio had, I could say in advance, "I'm going to change it." They'd say, "Well, go ahead," and if you get lucky, the way I did, they let you do about what you want to do.

One of the things that you're liable to run into trouble in is casting. People don't always see it the way you do. Sometimes you have to insist that you use somebody. In *Sergeant York* as Gary Cooper's mother a

---

* Fleming's most famous credits are *Gone with the Wind* and *The Wizard of Oz*.

woman [Margaret Wycherly] gave a marvelous performance. She was a very chic, smart English woman, beautifully dressed and everything. By the time she got through, you had no idea that she didn't come right from the hills of Tennessee. I liked her work. I wanted her. They said, "She's wrong for the part." She wasn't wrong. Very often you'd cast people that they didn't like. For instance, I can't put anybody in a picture, ask them to be funny, unless I think they're funny. [Once] I said to the fellow who was helping me, the assistant director, "I know a man who would be marvelous for this part. But he hasn't done anything, just extra work. Give him some lines and get him a costume so I can see what he looks like, and bring him in—that'll save so much time on his part and my part." He came in and I started to laugh when I saw him. [It was Walter Brennan.] I said, "I'd like to have you read some lines, Walter." He said, "With or without?" I said, "With or without what?" He said, "Teeth." I said, "Without." He turned around and took his teeth out and started to read, and I said, "You've got a job." He was supposed to do about two or three days' work—I kept him six weeks and he got [an] Academy Award.* Everything he did, as far as I was concerned, was funny.

Working with Brennan was fun. He's one of the great actors that I've worked with. In *Red River*, I called him and said, "I'll tell you the story." He said, "Where's the contract?" I said, "It isn't ready yet." He said, "After I sign the contract, then you can tell me the story." So he came in the next day and signed the contract. He said, "Now tell me the story." I said, "Go read it, you son of a bitch. I'm not going to tell you. You're signed now." And he read it, and there was one line in the story, it said the cook's name is Drood. He said, "Gee, that's a good story. Am I going to play that guy?" I said, "Yeah." "How'm I going to play it?" I said, "You're going to lose your teeth in a poker game to an Indian, and every time you eat, you're going to have to borrow your teeth back." He said, "Oh, no, we're not going to do that." I said, "Yes, we are"—and we did it. He got another Academy Award nomination.

[When] he came to work to do *Rio Bravo*, he'd been doing a very kindly old man in a television series, and the first scene we did, he started in doing the same character, and I stopped the cameras and stopped

* The film was *Come and Get It*, which Hawks co-directed with William Wyler in 1936.

everything and said, "I don't want any of that junk you've been doing on television. I want a cantankerous—" "I forgot," he said. "Okay, start 'em again"—and he went right off into a completely different character, and really enjoyed doing it.

ON BEING OPEN

We started a picture called *Bringing Up Baby* with Cary Grant and Katie Hepburn. I believe that it was Katie's first time as a comedienne. We had a man on the set playing a part who used to be a great comic with the Ziegfeld shows, Walter Catlett. And Katie was stumbling a little bit, and I went over to Catlett and said, "Walter, would you show Miss Hepburn what to do about this scene?" He said, "Oh, no. Never." I said, "What if she asked you to?" "Well, then I'd be glad to." I went to Katie and said, "Katie, there's a man that can show you a couple of things you should know—but you'll have to ask him." She walked right over and asked him and was absolutely delighted. She said, "Howard, you've got to keep this fellow around." So I had to write scenes to keep him around for three or four weeks, and he had a really good part in the picture, and Katie just adored him. Of course, she's so great. She hasn't any idea that she can't learn from somebody—and this was a man who was a master at comedy, and he told her, in a few words, some things I know she found invaluable.

When I'm making a picture, I make it known to the crew that if they've got a suggestion, for goodness' sake, make it—and out of it comes some of the best stuff. Especially if you're stuck you get some marvelous things— and you keep on getting them, provided you don't discourage them from doing it.

THE STORYTELLING VIRTUE

When they started to make some of these new sick, dirty pictures and everything, I didn't know exactly what to do. I went to John Wayne and said, "You want to make a couple of westerns till I can make up my mind what to do? Because westerns aren't going to change." He said, "Sure." Then the trend started back. For instance, the pictures that are really popular today—*Airport, Love Story, The Godfather*—they're old-fashioned pictures. You don't need all the junk that has been made. Matter of fact, look at another picture that is very successful—*What's Up, Doc?* It is like an old-time picture. The last Bond story, *Diamonds Are Forever*—God, that goes way back to nowhere. Sure it's inflated and blown up a little bit, but that only comes with the fact that you can take more liberties today in doing things. We used to have censor troubles. When I made *I Was a Male War Bride*, the censors looked at it and said, "Howard, you can't get away with that stuff." And I said, "Well, think about it a little bit." And they called me the next morning and said they decided that they liked it and enjoyed it so much that I could get away with everything in it. Now, today that would be absolutely no trouble. I wouldn't have had to do all the work to tell the story of *I Was a Male War Bride*. But I still claim that if you made it today, it would be just as good as it was then. Sure, audiences have changed. But, I don't know, I think a good story, if it is well told . . . There are too many people telling stories today that don't know how to tell them. There's companies that have four or five pictures on the shelves that don't make sense. The men who made them were not telling a story, they were telling something that they had in the back of their minds. But I don't worry at all about that.

AGAINST SELF-ANALYSIS

The French have been very kind to me. When I go over there, I meet with ten or fifteen, twenty directors [and critics]—have a few drinks, dinner—they ask questions—and they attribute an awful lot of things to me that I have no thought of. "Why did you do this?" "Well, I liked it. I thought it was funny." "You didn't think it out?" "No, I didn't think it out. I found out that if I liked somebody, then the people do. If I like a girl, think she is attractive, the audience likes her that way. I don't do the analysis that you fellows do. I am always very interested in listening to what you say caused this thing, but I don't want to analyze it too much, because I've seen too many people that are ruined . . . I used to play tennis with a world's-champion tennis player and he could hit the ball harder than any man I knew—until he wrote a book about his serve. From that time on, he couldn't serve—any woman could return his serve. It's very dangerous to stop and think of so many things. Just one question: Do you like it or don't you? If I don't like a scene, I stay there until I do like it—until I think it's going to be worthwhile."

Spencer Tracy and director Vidor pause during making of Northwest Passage *(1940).*

KING VIDOR

IN a break during our interview with King Vidor, he turned to the bookshelf behind his desk and took down a collection of F. Scott Fitzgerald's short stories. He was proud of the fact that the author had inscribed the volume to him, prouder still that the inscription acknowledged that one of the characters therein—the doomed director in "Crazy Sunday"—was at least partially modeled on King. In it, Fitzgerald said this director had the only "interesting temperament" among Americans plying that trade.

I'm sure King would be the first to acknowledge that there were other temperaments as interesting as his, but it is easy to see why Fitzgerald, or any other serious writer, would respond to King's special spirit. His mind is the most literary that I have encountered among movie people—excluding the scenarists, I suppose. It is not really a novelist's sensibility. Rather it is a more speculative one, like that of certain critics, even philosophers. As he says in this interview, he has never really been interested in storytelling *per se* and only occasionally have studies in character moved him more than perfunctorily. What he seems to me to have been searching for all along are general principles of some sort. Are there unseen but universal forces—historical and moral—that operate on all people, whatever their time and place, whatever their age, sex, religion or color? Are there certain psychological generalizations that can cut across these same barriers and form the basis for shared understanding? Since it is probably impossible to put matters of this kind into words, is it possible to express them imagistically? If so, isn't it possible that this relatively new medium, the movies, for which Vidor seems to believe he has a natural affinity, offers the best opportunity to record those images—images of feelings, really—and present them to a previously undreamed-of international audience? If this be true, then what is the deepest nature of the medium to which he has devoted his life? Isn't something more than a cash-and-celebrity nexus supported by technics and technique?

These questions are all, in their nature, unanswerable. Vidor knows that. Indeed, that may be the quality that most intrigues him about them. In any event, he loves to play with them. And I am certain that he feels silent pictures, of necessity more enigmatic than sound films, certainly less realistic and always richer in their poetic possibilities, provided a more suitable means of posing these questions than the talkies do. Less language-bound, they were undoubtedly a more universal medium than sound films, which must be either dubbed or subtitled (both highly un-satisfactory alternatives) if they are to play in countries where the film's language is not understood. He never quite says it flat-out in this inter-view or in his superb autobiography, *A Tree Is a Tree*, but the implica-tion is powerful in both places.

Indeed, he has the right to a certain bitterness. For though he made many fine sound pictures, the fact remains that he was the most sophis-ticated American-born master of the silent film. He was, I think, alone in his status at the end of the silent era; thereafter he was one of two dozen leading directors. In sound films, as he suggests, plot became more important; visual design alone could not hold a film together, or hold an audience's interest, as it did in *The Crowd* and, to a lesser extent, *The Big Parade*. It was no longer possible to interest people in archetypes as he had in those films. You had to particularize the leading actors, charac-terize them in detail. And that reduced the emphasis on them as symbols capable of conveying certain abstract ideas. In short, along with a hand-

ful of other silent masters, King was in the unique, historically unprece-
dented position of being master of an art that was suddenly declared null
and void.

But he kept on. And, good or bad, it is impossible to think of a subse-
quent Vidor movie which did not, in a sequence or two, remind us of
past glories. Not that that was *all* that was good about these later pictures.
But he was careful to keep alive—no matter what else was on his mind—
a tradition of which he was proud to be a part. He also continued to
search for vehicles that would satisfy the aesthetic imperatives of the
sound film, but which would still allow him to vent some of his idealistic
feelings, and though this led to a group of films, especially in the 1940s
(which Andrew Sarris has identified as his "delirious" period), that play
rather strangely compared to other movies of the period, they are
stamped with his own intellectual ambition and with his ambitions for
his art. They may be imperfect, they may not appeal as readily to our
nostalgic impulses as some of their contemporaries do, but *Duel in the
Sun, Ruby Gentry, The Fountainhead* are memorable attempts to expand
conventionalized genres, infusing them with metaphysical speculation
and highly charged metaphysical images. They are not "well made,"
but I think Sarris is quite right to suggest they are every bit as worthy of
our attention as the work from Vidor's academically blessed "museum"
period.

I also think King Vidor is worthy of our attention as a man. He di-
vides his time now between his ranch in Pasa Robles—about halfway
between Los Angeles and San Francisco—and Los Angeles, where a
comfortable two-room cottage, equipped with hotplate and bath, nestles
under the hill surmounted by his house. There he works on books and
on ideas for films he would like to make, paints, entertains young film
students and scholars, his easy rapport with whom he seems particularly
to delight in. There is not the slightest undertone of bitterness about the
fact that he has not worked in a studio for something like a decade and a
half. He would much rather talk about the two 16-mm. films he has
made with young people—one of which seems to be a rather abstract
work, while the other is a documentary-in-progress about day-to-day
life in Pasa Robles. Unlike most of his contemporaries, he is terribly interested in new films, and if he is aware of the economic decline of the
industry, he does not believe that it is accompanied by a moral and

aesthetic decline. Indeed, my impression is that he sees the possibility of a return to the informal and relatively inexpensive production methods that were still available to directors when he was starting out in the 1920s. And that pleases him.

All of this makes him inspiring to be with. Some of his thoughts are half formed, but one gets the impression he's so delighted by the shadowy patterns he perceives in them that he lets them tumble forth anyway, just to see how they look in the light of day, what other people may make of them. That rush of words and ideas is as much a part of the man as his idealism and his faith in the future—both commodities that are hard to come by these days, whether you look for them in Hollywood or anywhere else in the world. In a profession dominated by practical, determinedly nonintellectual men, he is a singular character, an individualist of a different stripe than all the other individualists represented in this volume. In his quiet-spoken way he is as strong as the strongest of them. Indeed, it is curious that the character Scott Fitzgerald based upon him is so self-destructive, for King Vidor is manifestly far less so than Fitzgerald himself was—far less so, indeed, than most people. In his old age, he is a man who demonstrates the possibility not merely of surviving in a difficult career, but of doing so with growing grace and openness.

HEADING FOR HOLLYWOOD

See, the movies began just about when I was born. They were invented and they came into being just about that time, but when I was a kid in my teens growing up, [wanting to direct] was [like wanting] to be an astronaut or a jet pilot [is now]. It fitted all my feelings. I have a certain feeling for the theater, a certain feeling for writing and a certain feeling for acting and mechanics also. And this was an interesting mechanical device that would make people move. And [I was] interested in photography, too. Later when I went to a psychoanalyst, he said, "How did you ever pick out anything that suited all your emotions so well?" I said, "Well, maybe it picked me up, I don't know. But this was it."

So I was in the remote part of Texas, southern Texas, and I started making films. Well, before that I learned how to run a projection machine in a theater and took up tickets. And during the projectionist's lunch hour I would go run the projection machines. It was a very dangerous job then because it was all explosive film and it was all run into a basket and the slightest bit of spark, the whole thing would explode and you would be trapped because there was only a little ladder going up into this booth. After that I met a fellow who had made a camera out of cigar boxes and the parts of a projection machine. And just about then a storm came along, a Gulf Coast hurricane, and we went out and photographed the hurricane. And we sold a film made with that [camera]. We sold it locally in two or three Texas towns. From then on I was a newsreel cameraman. We [even] made short comedies there. In those days you could spring up in a remote part of Texas without ever having been in a studio.

Well, I met a girl who had ambitions, a beautiful, lovely girl who wanted to be an actress in films, and the only thing to do was to get enough money together to come to Hollywood. And a lot of people said, "Oh, you don't want to go to that terrible place." My family particularly —other friends—[said] it was an awful place: "I hear wild parties and stupidity and other things." "Well," I said, "that's a great opportunity for somebody that maybe would not be too much interested in the wild parties." So off we came to Hollywood. And the first years I would go to a studio and I would go from one department to the other. I would go to the casting office, try to get a job as an actor. And if there was nothing there, then I would go to the extras' department and work as an extra. Or go to the production office and work as a prop man or an assistant director or "script clerk." That was the [first] full-time job I had. It was $12 a week. And we were given $25 a day for expense money for the company, to pay for locations and so forth. [It was a] little too early to try to get a job as a director—although at that time Universal had some fantastic amount of directors—sixty or some such thing—making short films. I [also] worked with many directors who had never been in a studio. By then I had a lot of experience. And then I got a job as a writer at Universal.

My first year in Hollywood I lived near the Griffith studio. At that time Griffith was making *Intolerance* and he had [on] Sunset Boulevard a tremendous set [for] the Babylonian episode and I've never seen anything like it since. It was very high, and although they had a canvas fence around the whole set, you could see the men and the chariots and the horses way up high in the set. And also you could see the balloon going up, which [served as] a camera platform before the days of the boom and zoom lenses. And I was determined to get inside. Now, as I remember, I crawled under the fence one day and I think, I'm quite sure, I worked as an extra, although I didn't like heights and I didn't want to get up on one of those high places. I thought I wouldn't be any good at that. I think I met a fellow the first day—an assistant director or somebody—and he said he'd see that I didn't have to go up high. So I got in some sort of a robe or something and I could watch and observe everything. I was in there two days watching Griffith work. And I think I remember the balloon going up on a cable—a controlled balloon with a camera in it. And I think it moved forward, too. I wouldn't swear to it. But this was a tremendous set and, of course, D. W. Griffith was my mentor and my ideal. Finally, during *Duel in the Sun*, he visited the set,* because we had Lionel Barrymore and Lillian Gish [in it]. And Barrymore couldn't speak his lines; the master made him so nervous that I finally had to ask Griffith would he mind going behind the set or something and he said that he'd been there long enough. And he upset Lillian Gish too. I mean, just the fact that he was there made them nervous.**

But this was an ideal, D. W. Griffith. All the fellows at that time thought [so]. He was certainly mine and I really studied his films. I studied his undercranking of the camera to speed up action and how he would keep a crescendo going toward the end of a picture—how fast he would have horses go or men run way beyond the normal speed that they could go. And then [his] films' great association with music and musical scores. I really developed out of watching and studying Griffith films a thing I call silent music, which was to see how I could put into a silent film tempo and rhythm and crescendo and so forth, as in a musical composition. And, of course, in the Griffith films he would have an orchestra playing with the films and he would use recurrent themes in *Hearts of the World, Birth of a Nation* and so forth. All were worked

* *Duel in the Sun* was released in 1947—thirty-two years later.
** Both Barrymore and Miss Gish had made their first movies for Griffith—he in 1911, she in 1912—at the Biograph studio in New York.

out musically. This inspired me to carry this idea on—to more study and more experimentation.

FIRST CHANCE TO DIRECT

I kept trying to get a job directing. I had finally gotten a job as a writer at Universal studios—$40 a week. Short films. And during the time I [had been] a company clerk, there had been a rule there—they couldn't buy any stories from any employees. I had to send in the stories by mail under a different name. I sold a couple that way. And then I got [the] job as a writer and there I met a fellow named Judge Willis Brown, who made some boys' stories. He was a juvenile-court judge. And then he gave me the job directing because I'd been a cameraman on a travel film. So now I made a lot of these two-reel juvenile-court films. They had mainly human interest and I tried putting these films together and making a feature film out of them.

I was trying to break through from being a shorts director to being a full-length director. It happens today [when] the television half-hour director [tries to get] responsibility for a full film. Finally I figured out: Write your own story and get people interested in the story and say I won't sell it unless I direct it. I wrote a story that had a little tinge of Christian Science to it. And [some] doctors had put up the money for the boy films [and] I got the same doctors to put up the same money—nine of them, $1000 each—for the Christian Science story. One of them, who was the president of the company, said, "Isn't this a little Christian Science?" I said, "No, not particularly." And they wanted me to change something and I said no. So they made the film. It was very successful right away and the next one didn't have any Christian Science in it. Then one of the doctors came and said, "I think you should put a little Christian Science into that story." And I said, "No, I don't want them to be the same."

But, anyway, the first picture was very successful and it's interesting, thinking back, about what sort of studio it was—what you had to have to have a studio. We'd rent a little bungalow, maybe the rent would be $50, as low as that. And in the backyard build a stage, and put up

telephone poles, and over that what they called the fuses on sort of rig-
ging, on wires. You could have white cloth or, for night, black cloth
to cut out the daylight altogether. Or you could have it diffused with
the light cloth. But when it rained—you know, nobody ever thought it
rained in California, but sometimes it rained for a month—all action was
suspended. You had to put tarps over [everything]. That was before
the closed-in set [was invented].

Well, then you had a studio. You had to have some sort of carpenter
shop and you probably used rooms in the bungalow for the actors or the
offices, but there were many studios like that in those days. From there
we went to the covered stages, and my father gave up his lumber business in Texas and moved out and he built a studio for me on Santa
Monica Boulevard, next to the Goldwyn studios there. It's now a super-
market. There we had closed stages and unit lights and movable lamps on
the stage. I built that studio. It looked like a village of some sort. Most
of the buildings could have been used as homes or stores, as fronts. And
from there I went to Metro, which was then in Hollywood before it
became Metro-Goldwyn-Mayer and finally moved to Culver City. Later
the Metro-Goldwyn-Mayer Company moved these big stages from
Hollywood itself. They cut them up, [these] tremendous stages, and
moved them to Culver City. And there they had glass stages—let some
daylight in [through] the diffusers under the glass sides or roofs and it
became a different type of lighting and you could work when it rained.

GISH IN *LA BOHÈME*

When we were moving from silent-film acting to sound dialogue and
sound-film acting, there was a lot of thought about how the transition
[was] going to happen and [how] some actors wouldn't be able to sus-
tain their careers. Later I got so used to depending upon dialogue and
the spoken word that I began to wonder how did people like Garbo and
Gloria Swanson and Colleen Moore and Lillian Gish justify such tremendous salaries? What did they do? Then I realized that there was a
whole technique of silent-picture acting that to me began to seem more
difficult. . . . In other words, if you make a test of someone, if they
have words to read, a speech to read, it carries them along much faster

and much easier than if they had to get up and do nothing but panto-mime—you know, express all their thoughts and express their individu-ality and their character and the story they are playing through panto-mime. Very difficult to do. I was so impressed when I first directed Lillian Gish in *La Bohème* [because] of her dedication. She had to think about it. She had to get herself into it. Took her a couple of days. The death scene she wanted to know [about] three or four days ahead so she could get all the saliva out of her mouth, and her cheeks began to look sunken, her eyes began to be sunken and it began to show in the physical makeup. When we shot the scene, it was so realistic I thought she had died—because she also had controlled her breathing to such a point that I was looking at her breast and I didn't see it moving. I thought she had gone just a little bit too far and died in trying to give a great per-formance. And I was really fearful to say stop and cut the scene. I [imagined] headlines: she is so good in the part that she really died. And then I saw the deep breath come, you know, and her face moved, and muscles, and I was very relieved. But this was typical—particularly of Gish.

There was a certain magic about it and a certain technique and I be-lieve that we were beginning to realize all of this [when sound came in]. That's why the music on the set would help bring a mood and would help to keep people in a mood, you know. It is easier with dialogue: "What's my speech?" "What are my lines?" And you can just go on. You can make a quick transition. When we started doing sound pictures, there was no place for the music, no place for the mood. And you had to do other things to get them in the mood.

THE BIG PARADE

When Metro-Goldwyn-Mayer was formed and began to have big am-bitions for greater pictures, then there was competition among directors on the lot. I started with the definite idea that I wanted to make a film that didn't simply come to town, play three days or a week and then was forgotten, which [so often] was the case. After you work on a film a long time, this is pretty discouraging. I never thought they would be run years later for students or for retrospective festivals and so forth.

So I went to [Irving] Thalberg and I said, "I'd like to make a film that runs longer, six months or three months or something." And he said, "Do you have any ideas?" And I said, "I have three ideas: war, wheat and steel." He said, "Well, let's start looking for war stories." So I started reading synopses of war books. It is a very unpopular subject now, but then it was a good moving-picture subject. And so—read, read, read and couldn't find anything he liked. Then he went to New York and *What Price Glory?* was playing and he got hold of Laurence Stallings, one of the authors of *What Price Glory?*, and told him what we were trying to do—and I talked to him on the telephone and gave him a little idea that I had and he wrote five typewritten pages from which the script was written. He had lost a leg in World War I and he'd written a book or two and one play—and I sort of talked with him a lot and spent a lot of time with him. And out came *The Big Parade*.

Up until that time, all the war pictures had been glamorous—fellows with shiny boots and epaulettes and medals and beautiful costumes. And there never had been one about a G.I. Just the ordinary guy. And at that time I was playing with the idea [that] the man caused nothing in this film—he only reacted. He only went through the war and observed it. And he was—I think this is more what I said over the telephone—neither a patriot nor a pacifist. He wasn't a hero—he was just a guy that went along. And he [Stallings] went for this in a big way and came up with these five pages, which I still have. And so this was the way the film was made: the guy just watching the war, experiencing it and going through being under fire and falling in love with a French girl and so forth.

Imagery was the dominant factor, along with rhythm and pace and tempo, in my mind and probably in the mind of many other film directors. I had a diagram on that picture which was a big circle like a Q with a tail—which meant that the man started at home and he went to Europe and he went through all of this experience and he came back home and then he went back to Europe. That's the tail on the Q. I used to draw the whole film out with some sort of diagram which would [help me] hold it all together. Now, there is one battle scene [to the beat of] a bass drum; I mean, every man walking on a beat [set by] a metronome. We had no loudspeakers and we had no synchronized music to go by, [so] we used this big bass drum so everyone could hear the beat of the metronome.

Speaking of that [scene], we used about a dozen eucalyptus trees that were in a park in Los Angeles [and] just by changing angles it looked like a big French wood. And speaking again of imagery and design, I sent a second unit down to Texas. See, we used to do a lot of drawing beforehand on some important shots—[to] design them. I wanted a straight line of—what was it, four hundred trucks, four thousand men? And they went down there and the Army talked them out of the straight line. [They said we should] have a zigzag line [because] that's the way it was in France. And after all this film came back, I went down and said, "We're going to find a straight line" and went out and got the straight line. We also used some of the zigzag later. But I did get the straight line, which meant more than broken crooked lines because it just went into infinity. You know, it just suggested the endless amount of the machines and men that we poured in—were poured in by the Allies. So my life was, and my thoughts were, filled with imagery. That's the way you went to bed at night, thinking about images. And that's what dialogue and sound pulled you away from somewhat.

THE CROWD

The Big Parade was running and a big success and was two years at one theater. I had my wish of not coming to town a week and then leaving. It cost $205,000 when I finished and then a night battle was added, so the total cost was $245,000. I think it took in, in the Astor Theatre in New York, $1,500,000. So I fulfilled my wish. Then, during the run of *The Big Parade*, a big successful run which had a lot to do with putting Metro-Goldwyn-Mayer on the map, I encountered Thalberg one day on the lot and he said, "What are you going to do next?" I said, "There must be other things that a man can walk through and observe and react to." And he said, "What, for example?" And I said, "Life." And he said, "Very good. Why didn't you mention that before?" I said, "I never thought of it before." [But] I did have a clear view of how I had [John] Gilbert go through *The Big Parade*. So he said, "Have you got a title?" And I said, " 'One of the Mob.' " He said, "That's not good." And later it became "One of the Crowd" and later *The Crowd*. So I approached that film, *The Crowd*, by just seeing what would happen to a man. He

Renée Adorée embraces John Gilbert as The Big Parade (*1925*) *moves out.*

To young Jackie Cooper, Wallace Beery will always be The Champ (*1931*).

The tragic James Murray moving against The Crowd (*1928*)

was born, and then [came] the responsibility when his father died, and then looking for a job, and approaching a city, meeting a girl, falling in love, kissing the girl and sleeping together, marriage (in reverse order in that day). And children, and growing up and so forth. So it was just the succession of the dynamics of life of that period.

You mentioned the Expressionism that was going on at the time. We were thinking about it, we were greatly influenced by the German films. *The Last Laugh*, *Variety*, *Metropolis*, those were the three. They were arriving from UFA here and they were influencing us. They were beginning to use perambulators and boom shots. In *The Crowd* I did no booms, but we did the equivalent of booms. I wanted to pick out one floor of a tall building and one office, one window and then one desk, and one man. But in those days before zoom lenses and before booms, how do you go up and go in a window on the twenty-second floor? In the studio we built a building lying down. On the stage, I mean—a small scale model of it, probably fifteen feet high. And then over that, a bridge-work affair with a perambulator so that the camera could go forward, up the building, and then when it tilted down to the proper floor, I think we had some sort of cables or something to let it down close to the window. Behind the window we had a still photograph already made of the interior shot—a photograph of two hundred desks through the window. With men at the desks. You couldn't tell whether they were moving in that. And we dissolved through that to a shot on a stage, a big empty stage with two hundred desks and two hundred men sitting at the desks. Now we used to have big, heavy mercury-vapor lamps called Cooper-Hewitts and they hung from tracks so that they could be moved over the set. [From that track we] suspended a camera platform and put the cameraman on that. And as it went forward, cables let the camera down and we went right up to one man. All of which you could do with a boom today in a few hours.

I was very much aware of forced perspective. We have a lot of it through the film. We also had sets built to the camera angle. The hospital corridors are built this way, and the hospital beds are in forced perspective, and even the doors in the hospital corridors got smaller and we used smaller men in the back. I can't see it in the film, but I remember there was a discussion about getting midgets to work near the small doors in the back; we did use smaller men in the back. I was very aware—

it was a time of the German Expressionist paintings, and the Picasso paintings were all with table tops tilted toward the painter, the viewer.

JAMES MURRAY: A FACE IN *THE CROWD*

In looking around for someone to play this lead, my feeling was that if I put [a star] in it, I would destroy the anonymity of the character. I wanted [audiences] to believe that this fellow was really a clerk in a big office. So I formulated [that sort of]face, and one day I was standing talking to someone and a bunch of extras were going off the lot and one fellow said to me, "Excuse me" and, instead of going around us, made us separate a little bit. And as he walked in front of me, here was the face that I'd been visualizing. Before I could free myself from the conversation, he'd gone a ways and I chased him. He was just getting on a bus, or hitchhiking or something, and I was just able to say, "What's your name?" He told me and I said, "Come see me tomorrow and this is my name." [But] tomorrow he never came and the next day he didn't come and so forth. So I finally looked over the bunch of extras and remembered the name he'd said—James Murray. And we called him and paid him as an extra to [be] interview[ed] and finally made a test and he was the follow we were looking for. And more power to Thalberg for taking the chance—but he did make a good test. The fellow had been a doorman at the Capitol Theatre in New York, fine-looking guy, wonderful actor, could have gone on to have been a tremendous star. I put him in a lead in another film with Marion Davies, film called *Show People*, and he didn't show up. So I took him out of that picture and he went on to do some other parts. And finally one day I was leaving the stage and found him in a gutter right on the studio lot. I was surprised that he had found the gutter. I didn't know they had one, but he found it. And so, not too many years later, I was getting ready to do the film *Our Daily Bread* and I wanted him again. It was the same idea and the same two characters—I called them John and Mary. I was walking on Vine Street in Hollywood and I saw this fellow coming along—by now he was a bum and bloated, he was drinking, and he came up to me and said could I let him have a dollar to get a drink. Instead I took him to

Musso's Restaurant on Hollywood Boulevard and we sat at the bar and I
told him I had a part for him providing he would drop the liquor and go
in training and get the fat off his neck. And he looked at me and he says,
"Screw you." So I said, "Okay, Jimmy. Screw you. If that's the way you
feel about it."

Then for years everybody asked me, "What ever happened to James
Murray? Whatever happened to the fellow who played the lead in *The
Crowd?*" Well, I heard rumors he had committed suicide in New York
and finally got a letter telling how he died. From a man who was there
with him. [Murray had] a group of fellows with him, three, four or
five, they [told some onlookers they] were waiting for the cameraman
and the crew and the director and they were working for M-G-M, that
he was an M-G-M star, which he had been. And they said they'd left
their money in their clothes back at the studio and would [the crowd
that gathered] let them have $20 so that they could buy some drinks or
something and as soon as the crew arrived he'd pay them back. No crew
arrived or anything, you know. [But] they got the money, bought the
liquor, proceeded to pass it around, get drunk and then he was trying
to amuse the people. He was clowning. And he pretended to slip and
fall in the river and everybody laughed, and then after a while they
went over and looked and he was floating face down in the river. They
pulled him out. He was drowned. So, a real tragic story, the whole thing.
I have an idea of making a film of his life. I think it would make a very
good film—the whole career, the whole Hollywood approach and what
Hollywood did to him. Couldn't take it—couldn't take success. He was
too much of an average, common man, you know.

HEARST, DAVIES AND *SHOW PEOPLE*

William Randolph Hearst was a tremendous influence at Metro-
Goldwyn-Mayer. He had an association with them, and they were de-
pendent upon the Hearst press. Now, when *The Big Parade* was such a
big success, naturally he wanted to get me to do a film with Marion
Davies. And I didn't want to do one of the films as she had been doing
them—they were all costume pictures, which I had no interest in whatso-

ever. [But] in trying to get me to do a film he worked on Mayer, and Mayer worked on me, and so we [went] to San Simeon, the Hearst ranch, and there I noticed that Marion Davies was a darn good comedienne. Used to entertain people and do imitations of people, and she had a great sense of comedy. So Laurence Stallings [and I] started discussing the possibilities of Marion as a good comedienne. I don't know whether she had ever done comedy before, but certainly not imitations and clowning the way I had her in the pictures I made.* They had some play, I think it was called *Polly Preferred*. No good, but they bought it and they owned it, and Stallings and I took it and rewrote it following the life of Gloria Swanson, who had been a Mack Sennett bathing beauty and then became a big star and became the Marquise de la Falaise de la Coudraye and came back to Paramount studios with red-carpet treatment and DeMille helping her out of the coach and so forth. So we did this with Marion Davies. That's *Show People*, using a lot of her clowning and a lot of her imitations, and I thought she was marvelous.

I kid myself [in it]. I kid one of the films I made, one of the love scenes in a picture called *Bardelys the Magnificent*, and I used Mack Sennett's studio, which was not being used before it was torn down. We shot all the comedy scenes there. We got the Mack Sennett comedians in those episodes and then we moved to Metro-Goldwyn-Mayer as [Davies] moved up the scale. I reproduced a *Big Parade* scene . . . and I put Davies in the part Renée Adorée played. And I played the director in the film. So I looked at myself and I said, "Gee, I was a good-looking guy. I should have been an actor." And I wasn't a bad actor in the film.

HALLELUJAH AND THE TRANSITION TO SOUND

I was born and raised in southern Texas and my father had sawmills in Louisiana and East Texas, and I had been wanting to do a film about blacks. I'd been in Arkansas, I'd been to the churches, been all around— and raised with them. I had all these memories, and I'd been trying to do it in the silent film. Well, I always was turned down, turned down

---

* Besides *Show People*, they were *The Patsy* and *Not So Dumb*.

repeatedly by the studio. [Then] I was in Paris and *Variety* magazine had a big headline, it said, "Hollywood Goes 100 Percent Sound." I moved up my ship reservations by two or three weeks, got back in a hurry, went to the head office in New York to Nicholas Schenck* and said, "Now I must make this film." I was still turned down and I said, "I will put my salary in with yours." And that appealed to him and he said, "I'll let you make a picture about whores, if that's what you are going to do." So I came back, prepared the script, but they had no portable sound equipment and this film had to be done in Tennessee and Arkansas, in cottonfields and so forth. And so no exterior, no portable [sound] equipment. So we just said, "Off we'll go and shoot it silent and we'll put the sound in later." It was a real problem. Cameras went at different speeds and how do you hold a camera at the exact steady speed of sound?—the batteries would get weak and the camera would go slower and so forth. Many, many problems. Today you sing a song, you make a recording, you make a playback. We didn't have any playbacks, we just had people sing without any equipment. It was just singing out to the sky.

Later on, [when] we tried to put this all together, [I found] they had no equipment in the studio to stop to listen. You had to go into the theater and run [it on] the projection machine. It was just maddening to try to work out the synchronous possibilities. I had no idea, when four people in different closeups were singing one song, how to cut from one to the other. So I had these big sheets of paper and I'd just put down the words that one person would sing and at [what] point [I'd want to] stop and jump over to the other person and [to] sing the other words. But we fought through this thing and worked it out and I believe it made the film more interesting. It freed us to use all the silent-picture techniques. It freed us to use camera movement, a chase through a swamp, with moving cameras in boats and things. For two or three years, I suppose, most of the films looked like stage plays photographed —in fact, M-G-M did photograph a few stage plays with very little changes, right on the studio stage. So this was a big problem and a big step back. The cameras in studios were [shut up in] big icebox deals which didn't permit [interesting] setups.

* Then president of Loew's Inc., the theater chain that was M-G-M's parent company.

THE CHAMP AND THE DESIRE FOR A STORY

You know many times—to go back to *The Crowd* a little bit—I thought, Wouldn't it be great to have a foolproof story! I said, Why don't I just do a triangle—two men and one woman? We made eight endings for *The Crowd* and never could satisfy [ourselves] and we finally sent the picture out with two. So when it comes down to *The Champ*, which was written by Frances Marion, who had written *Stella Dallas*,* here was a solid story, solid human-interest story.** It would relieve me as a director—now I didn't have to worry about the story, worry about how I will wrap this up and keep it all together. I could concentrate on little details—touches and things. I went to Tiajuana, they had a racetrack down there, and shot around the streets of Tiajuana—and also reproduced some of it on the M-G-M lot. I remember I also did some stuff off the cuff. I don't know whether you remember Jackie Cooper walking up on a roof of a house and singing a song and sticking cigarettes in his pocket—well, this was Marion Davies' dressing room on the M-G-M lot, but it was ad lib, off the cuff, because I was in the mood—"I don't have to worry, this story is so tight that I don't have to concentrate on telling the story. It works anyway."

WALLACE BEERY AND *THE CHAMP*

He had a long career and a very good career. When you put Wallace Beery in a film, you had something to work with. You had interest immediately, in every shot. And Jackie Cooper at that time was the same type of small boy. So you had a live couple of actors in there, interesting

---

* The sound version of which Vidor would direct for Samuel Goldwyn.
** It is about a former boxing champion, down on his luck, but trying to bring up his son. He takes a comeback fight in order to raise money, wins it, but dies of a heart attack in his dressing room afterward.

actors. And I remember a little incident with Wally Beery. When I talked to him about playing it, he said, "If I have to do any fighting, I can't do it." I said, "All right, we'll get doubles, I'd like to have you do the film."* One day at lunch when we were getting ready to do the prizefight scene, I noticed him with a couple of pretty girls, extra girls, having lunch, and I was having lunch with the assistant director and I said, "Go over and get the girls' names—I have an idea." We took them off the set where they were working, put them in the front row of the prizefight audience and then when I called for the doubles to do the fighting, Wally said, "What do you mean, doubles? *I* want to do it. I don't like doubles doing it for me." So he got up in the ring and did some tough fighting because these two pretty girls he'd had lunch with were sitting there. He was a wonderful character.

OUR DAILY BREAD

When I came to make *Our Daily Bread*, which was a story of the Depression and of a commune, a co-op [getting started], I took it to Thalberg and he said, "It's a marvelous story and it is a big idea, but not for Metro-Goldwyn-Mayer," because, you know, they were very much in the glamour field—big stars and all that. He just couldn't see [a picture about] a bunch of out-of-work people. So I had to leave the studio and I tried all the other studios and I got turned down. Finally, through Charles Chaplin I got a release through United Artists and then I borrowed all the money by mortgaging everything I had—home, automobiles, everything—and we got together $125,000 to make the film. The idea I think I read in *Reader's Digest*, about co-ops maybe, but it was very much in the air at that time. It was in the headlines. And remember I said something about steel, wheat and war? This was the wheat story. And you can see—*I* can see**—the early impressions of Griffith films—to have the climax a crescendo, faster and faster, more action and more active, and then cutting it off quickly with a few chords, a

---

* Beery won an Academy Award for his performance in this picture.
** In the climactic scene, in which the co-op farm is saved by the hasty construction of an irrigation ditch.

coda. That was the way this was designed. Particularly the ditch-dig-
ging. And I let the sound go to save money. And again we used the
metronome and the bass drum and choreographed picks down on one
and three and shovels on two and four. By undercranking the camera,
they would [seem to] go faster than they could go in real life—double
the speed that would be realistic. That built up the interest. You shoot
out of continuity, out of chronological order, as you know, but if you
lay it out with a metronome, you can go to any scene you want in this
whole sequence and you have an idea about how fast it should go.

SOUND — AND THE CHANGING AUDIENCE

In a silent film you had to pay strict attention to the screen, you had to
interpret, you had to figure out what was going on—what they were
meaning and what they were saying. Then came the explicit dialogue,
explicit words, and with it came the popcorn and the candy and the noise
of the wrappers, because you could turn away and talk to the person with
you and drink drinks and not miss anything, because they could still hear
without looking at the screen. Silent film, you had to look at the screen
every moment, you couldn't turn away or you'd miss something. Also,
silent pictures could be interpreted in different ways by different levels
of intellect, and so forth. You've probably heard the old story about
John Gilbert—they said his voice was too high and therefore he couldn't
be a talking-film star. That was not true at all. His voice was not high;
he had a good voice. But, you see, his image was the passionate lover,
the great lover, like Valentino. And you can't put that into words. In
the beginning they tried putting it into words—such as "I love you, I
adore you, I must have you"—and they become funny; they're very
funny. But if they're left out, then the audience puts in their own words
or no words and he was all right. The studio didn't know anything else
but to say his voice was too high.

ON THE STUDIO SYSTEM

Actually, I never found it oppressive; I found it very helpful. Irving Thalberg once expressed it by saying—I was making some film, it might have been *The Crowd*—"You know, we can afford an experimental film." And they could—they could well afford it. They made about fifty a year, so what's one or two films that are not going to make a lot of money? See?

And another thing about it, they had wonderful departments—art department and special-effects department—they were great. And they had the money. When they said go, you didn't have to do any promotion. I'm not a good promoter at all, and that's really what happened to my career. I didn't like to spend so much time promoting, packaging things, [so] I sort of lost interest. But then at M-G-M [you could make something like *The Crowd* just on the basis of an idea]. Well, a few years later it was "Let's see the script; let's see the play; let's see what stars you've got"—and you had to package a thing more. And I found that not so suited to my taste. So big studios, to me, were a big help. And you had enough competition right in the studio itself.

ROBERT DONAT

The Citadel I made in England for Metro-Goldwyn-Mayer. I had seen Robert Donat on the screen as a romantic type of hero, and when I met him he was far from that. He had a concave chest and slender little arms, but as he started to get interested in the film, he blossomed out and filled out—he had ways of making himself look robust. And he was the only actor I ever knew who wanted to go out looking for locations with the director. He wanted to know all about the scenes; he wanted to look at them too—and study the people. We went to Wales together. And he laid out his entire emotional rise and fall, how he would play each scene. It was interesting that he would have a mirror right on his lap and keep working on his makeup—the makeup around his eyebrows and hair and all that—right up until the cameras were going, and then he'd drop it and immediately give a superb performance. I never was more pleased with anybody's performance than I was with his. I said to him one time, "I can't help but think what would happen if you didn't keep that mirror up there until the last moment." He said, "I'd probably be worse." And I said, "Well, I don't want to change anything. You're too good." He was a superb fellow, very much like Tyrone Power, who was also a wonderful guy to work with—a real gentleman and a pleasure to work with. Robert Young, Gary Cooper were too. But in that film were Rex Harrison and Ralph Richardson and Rosalind Russell and a whole lot of wonderful actors. At that time, in England, you could go to the theater and if you saw somebody playing a lead in the theater, you could get them to come out in the morning or afternoon and work in the films. That was a great thing for casting. I thought *The Citadel* told a good story—an A. J. Cronin story*—and I was very much interested, and I felt very good about it. I thought it would win an Academy Award, and it almost did. It just missed by a few votes.

FIRST COLOR—
NORTHWEST PASSAGE

We had worked for a long time in black and white (it shouldn't be called "black and white" because there are many shades of gray, and different tones), [and] along, suddenly, comes color. I was getting ready to do *Northwest Passage*, and I realized, having felt that a director should be knowledgeable and in charge of every part of a film, that I didn't want to be subject to asking people about what does red mean, what does green mean and so forth. I had heard things about cool colors and hot colors, [but] I thought the only way to do it was really to try to learn about painting, and I started in. It was just the same transition we had to make when dialogue [came in]. You know, we spoke in the silent-picture days. We spoke with gestures and words like comic strips

---

* The story is of an idealistic doctor who temporarily loses his way—taking on a fashionable Harley Street practice—then reasserts his idealism by accusing a colleague of malpractice and winning the battle in court.

—zing and powie and pow. Fellows told stories that way: a dame comes in and "Wham" and "Take 'em"—and so forth. So here we were [again] and I wanted to know about it. [Because] Mr. Mayer [would say], "When I pay for color, then I want color," so they would have glaring reds and so on. [For example] in *Northwest Passage* the green costumes were supposed to blend into the hills, the shrubbery and the growth, but when we made tests they were so blatantly green—Killarney green—that they stood out; you could see them miles away. I tried to investigate this and finally we found out [from Technicolor] this was the green Darryl Zanuck liked. So we had to get busy and get our own green back. To make these costumes blend, we sprayed them down to change the color. We began to use colors to help tell the story, help make sequences move.

Northwest Passage was a peculiar thing—it's a book in two parts.* I made all the first part, which was the prologue: we were still supposed to do the second part of the book, and the producer, Hunt Stromberg, never could make up his mind about the second part. It would have been fun, because [in the first part] the man (Spencer Tracy) is built up to be a hero and the last part is his downfall. But they just couldn't see it. For a while they held the actors, I think for a couple of weeks, and said, "We'll have this fixed"—and I started shooting, believing they would send me the pages up there, and they never arrived. I went to New York for some reason, and they had another director shoot the ending. So we came home. And then they released the prologue.

THREE WEEKS WITH *THE WIZARD*

In the case of *The Wizard of Oz*, Victor Fleming was wanted very badly by Clark Gable and David Selznick to take over *Gone with the Wind*. Cukor had been on the film and had some disagreement, so they stopped, and they wanted me. I spent the weekend studying the script. Came Monday, and I didn't want to take the job on short notice, and

---

* Based on Kenneth Roberts' best-seller about a guerrilla fighter in the French and Indian Wars.

so then they said, "Well, would you take over *Wizard of Oz* if Fleming comes over?" And I said I would. Victor Fleming was a good friend, and he took me around to all the sets that had been built and went through the thing. He left that night, and I took over—it was, as I remember, about two and a half weeks, three weeks possibly. Which included the "Somewhere over the Rainbow." It's run all the time, and whenever I hear it, I get a tremendous kick out of knowing that I directed that scene. I always wanted to do a musical film. I wanted to keep the movement going, just as we had in silent pictures. And I was able to do that in that film, [in] my contribution to it. I did some of the cyclone scenes, and "We're Off to See the Wizard"—working with Bert Lahr, Ray Bolger, Jack Haley and Judy Garland. But I did not want any credit, and as long as Victor was alive, I kept quiet about it.

DUEL WITH DAVID

David Selznick was one of the greatest fellows for casting a film. He would just get marvelous actors, marvelous stars in the tiniest parts—no matter what he had to pay them—and he was great at persuading them to do a little part. And also the money thing never worried him at all. That was one of his great faults. But he did give you tremendous support. I won't say that in the early days I didn't scrounge around and raise money and all this sort of thing, but I think, after you've established yourself, that someone else ought to do it, and somebody who's good at it. In fact, I didn't appreciate the role of producer until years later—the business part of it.

David Selznick was [also] a very difficult fellow, although he was a good friend and really the only man I know who had the right to call himself a producer—or one of the few. [Anyway] he called me over to tell me about [*Duel in the Sun*]—it was a little book by Niven Busch, a little paperback. It was about the length of *High Noon*, and he said, "I want you to do this as an intimate story of these people, and I will let you alone. I will have nothing to do with it, it's your film." I saw it as a possibility for an intense new angle on a western situation—a small, really small frame. He said no big stuff. But as we got into it, he wanted me to run *Gone with the Wind* and he wanted to have the biggest ranch and the most cattle and the biggest cast and the script was being rewritten and he suddenly had the idea this should be another *Gone with the Wind* of the West, you know. And it was a question of blow up, blow up, expand, expand, expand. In fact, the beginning, the opening shots, I didn't shoot—you know, big Mexican border dance hall—but he had become the writer then and it just got blown up all out of size and got a long way from [that] intense little study.

He was a sort of perfectionist. We all are mostly, but he would want things done over and we would have to do them over—even though he hadn't changed [them] very much. He would write endless memos that you didn't have time to read, and sometimes you'd get scenes at three o'clock in the afternoon which you'd spent all day shooting. He'd been changing them during the night, and before he could get them typed, you'd have shot most of them.

I used to get memos out on top of mountains—cars running back and forth, you know—and I'd put them in my pocket, and he'd always say, "Did you read this, did you read that?" And I'd say, "David, I don't have time to read it—I'll read it tonight." He'd say, "It'll be too late." One night I got a memo to come up—we were in Tucson, in a hotel there—and when I got in, he said, "Come up to the room, I want to see if you'll make a compromise with me about the way of shooting some scene." And I was tired, and he had a good sense of humor, and I said, "David, I'll compromise on anything if you'll let me have my way." That's what I felt about it—and we got along. We were good friends, but he would blow off on the set, and I walked off *Duel* the next-to-last day of shooting. I went back and made a television film for him after that. [Selznick] was a great one to get other directors—if you had horses, he'd get a specialist with horses; shooting a gun, a specialist with shooting a gun. Josef von Sternberg I had as an assistant director on the picture. People wanted to know what he was doing. And they want to know since. Well, he was just doing whatever I left him to do.

THE TROUBLE WITH INDEPENDENCE

As the big studios broke up and became fragmented all over the place, it meant we had to package and put together independent pictures—get a story, get a script, get a star. And this became something that I didn't particularly like, wasn't trained for. With a big studio supporting you and supporting you financially, you could go ahead and plan. But I did this for a while. I got together three or four scripts—financed the whole business. Did a very good script of the early life of Cervantes. But to get the stars, you had to give them a date, and in order to get the date, you had to have the money. It was a vicious cycle—sitting on the phone and wooing people, money people and stars and so forth, endlessly. I wasn't cut out for it. And although I'm interested again in making a film, nevertheless I'd like to get somebody else to package it.

WAR AND PEACE

I had read about a hundred pages of *War and Peace*. I think I talked to David Selznick [about it] years before, but I hadn't done anything about it. One day I received a call from Dino De Laurentis, who produced it, and at that time Mike Todd was making announcements, and Selznick, that they were going to do it, but De Laurentis said he'd send me a script, and he sent me a six-hundred-page script, and it was so awful, put together in a hurry just so he'd have a script out. And I read it and said, "Don't show this to anyone else. If you want to make it, I'd love to do it." So I started reading, studying the book—about six weeks, that took for me—and we arrived in [Italy] and we were sort of scaring the other people away—the Mike Todds and so forth. The reason De Laurentis went into it was because Mike Todd came to him and tried to get him to put some money in his project. De Laurentis said, "If he hasn't the money, why don't *we* do it?" It's a long book and a long picture—enough for two or three films. But I did manage to get the [revised] first-draft script out in about a month. [So] I had a script that was able to persuade Audrey Hepburn to play the part. Then we continued on with the script. In fact, until the last day of shooting [we were] still writing. That's painful to have to do, but you sign up an actor—stars, you know— and you have to go. Whether you're ready or not.

I was in accord with, you might say, what Tolstoy was trying to do— which was, as it were, a search for truth on the part of Pierre. I had this theme that interested me always, but even though it is, for me, the greatest novel, nevertheless it is not something that [came] out of [my] own insides. But then you approach the thing as a craftsman, and I am aware of all the difficulties we had in putting this together, and the amount of money we had to spend, and so I got a kick out of that—being able to finish the picture and put it together. I liked working with Audrey Hepburn tremendously—and Fonda, too.

A TASTE FOR SPECTACLE

It's the early training and the ability to make big masses of people mean something definite. I think that's what's really behind it. I'm guessing, too, but I was able to work out big groups as individuals, as it were. And I always kept the direction straight and simple—not depending on the design of uniforms to identify who was what. It was always one army moving right to left, and the other one left to right. In *The Big Parade* all the fellows going to France from the U.S.A. were left to right until they got in the battle; the Germans were always moving right to left. And then when they came home, the Americans were moving right to left again. But it's more than that. I was talking about the long line of trucks —four hundred trucks in a line, four thousand men—graphically it meant something definite. Let's see, in *Duel in the Sun* there's a gathering of the clan—a lot of horsemen coming together. Instead of just making it a confusing jumble, I was able to design it. I was always thinking of choreography, too—no matter how many people I had, I was putting stakes in the ground and [saying]: "You go from this point to that point." Each thing is choreographed, as it were.

One problem I ran into in Italy was, if we had anyone shoot second-unit, it always looked to me like confusion. Therefore I shot the battle scenes myself, the important ones (although I let a second-unit director take over the actors for some scenes) because I wanted the battles to be clear; I wanted them to mean something. All the *War and Peace* battles were worked out with a stop-watch; this group of men go from here to there on a certain count—you know, the zero bomb plus twelve seconds, and so forth. I enjoyed that. I liked doing that. Always a lot of blueprints, a lot of diagrams of what each company, what each fellow, must do. Someone once asked me if I'd rather direct five thousand men than two actors—I said, "Always." I preferred it because they don't give you arguments, they don't talk back to you. Someone again, on *War and Peace,* asked if I ever felt like Napoleon, and I said, "Hell, Napoleon could only direct one side of a battle; I can direct both sides."

I AM A CAMERA

I had the feeling, always, to have all the pictures made from the viewpoint of the leading character, and I discovered, always, that they never got a day off, because no scene happened that wasn't observed from their viewpoint. This was not so of *War and Peace* because in *War and Peace* there were three or four stories going on. But *The Big Parade* and *The Crowd* and all these films, the leading character sees it all happen—first-person technique. And in *The Fountainhead,* the solipsistic idea, the integrity, the divinity almost, of the artist is another theme which I've always been interested in; that the whole universe springs from the individual—what he's conscious of, that's reality; what he is not conscious of doesn't exist. It was strange that they selected me to direct *The Fountainhead,* because this is a thing that I was always playing with and thinking about, although I didn't agree entirely with Ayn Rand's approach to it. I didn't agree with the fact that they let the main character, the architect, go [after] he blew up a whole housing structure. I didn't think that was acceptable.

I think the clarification of this [is] my life and my career. I think I wasn't fully aware of the solipsistic idea, until along about *The Fountainhead.* Earlier, when I would tell a story to a star, he'd say, "But I don't prompt any of these situations— I don't motivate them." He'd say,

"I want to motivate them—I am the hero." I didn't understand it, because I felt that life motivated [them]. I'm still interested in this—that life creates a situation and you have to live [it], you can't fight it. That's what neuroticism is: fighting the life that we have to live, you know. In other words, in simple words, we make our own world; we make our own universe. Whenever you get a problem, you can say, "Well, this is my own consciousness." And if you have opposing forces, you try to integrate them. I think [all this is] reflected in the films. But in a growing way. And I would like to make *The Crowd* over again today—a man facing life, but in the end realizing that he's faced himself.

I can remember back to my first film, I remember someone saying— I think it was a writer for William DeMille—something about plot, and I said I wasn't interested in plot as such—the maneuverings of people. I don't think I've ever had a villain in my films. I can't remember one real villain, you know. It's the straw man we set up to knock down—and we don't need that. We don't need to symbolize or to construct one just to knock him over—kill him, you know. Life is enough of a battle in itself.

Something about the lens is very akin to the human consciousness which looks out at the universe. "I am a camera"—we are all cameras. We are recording eyes, you know, we look out and record and we use our consciousness to do this. The motion-picture camera is the [tool closest] to the human sense of observation and sense of the universe. When the men land on the moon, I land on the moon—because I am conscious of it, and I take it into myself, and I am landing on the moon. This is what happens with a motion-picture camera. It approximates the consciousness that everyone has. I am sure all the young kids today, they're realizing it more and more every day. You point the lens, you take it in the film, take [the film] in the cutting room, you assemble it, organize it into some meaning. And the motion-picture camera is the really solipsistic instrument for awareness and for realization. That's why the career of motion-picture directing is appealing to many youngsters in grammar schools, high schools, colleges today—it's a career that [allows them to express what] they are consciously realizing is happening to the world. You can't just say, "that war over there"—way off in Asia. You can't say that any more. You can't fool people any more. It's *my* war. That's why people felt responsible individually, you know. We are taking these things into ourselves.

LOOKING AHEAD

I am not horrified at sex on the screen. I think it's probably pointing toward some sort of terrific honesty. I believe that the motion picture speeds up the process of realizing reality. As I said before, it's only an illusion, but so is life. We look out upon the world, and it's a drama, it's a story, it's a script, you know. But then, it's what you do with it. It's what you do with it in your own computer or your own cutting room. And we think the motion picture is responsible for [showing us] this. You know, now you just can't have the same old plot, the same old story over and over. People won't go. You have to open up new cans of reality all the time. They have to delve a little deeper. Otherwise people say, "I'll stay home and look at television." So [movies are] the instrument for enlightenment.

I am very much interested in the new films, because I don't feel any differently than I did when I was beginning. I think if I made a film, it would be the best film I ever made—and this is because I haven't frozen myself at some past period that was happier or freer or something. I didn't stop back there. I've tried to keep an open mind about what's going on and see it as progressive. I think it's a beautiful world; I'm interested in everything that's happened. I can only be terribly optimistic about it, and terribly appreciative about it. And I think that age is the gap between freezing oneself back at some period and saying, "I'm going to stop there" and then they look around them and they see other things going on—such as *Last Tango in Paris* or *Deep Throat* or something—and they say, "I'm frozen back there! I'm going to be shocked with this." And the gap in there is what makes people old. I went to see *Last Tango* and enjoyed it. People are going and paying a lot of money and standing in line, and that's a fact of life, and I can't call it bad. I'm not going to call it bad. I don't believe in life being bad. I haven't seen *Deep Throat* yet, but I probably will. But I'm not going to call it bad; I'm going to call it progress and call it good, and I'm going to call it revealing and enlightening. It's got to be. I don't believe in a bad world.

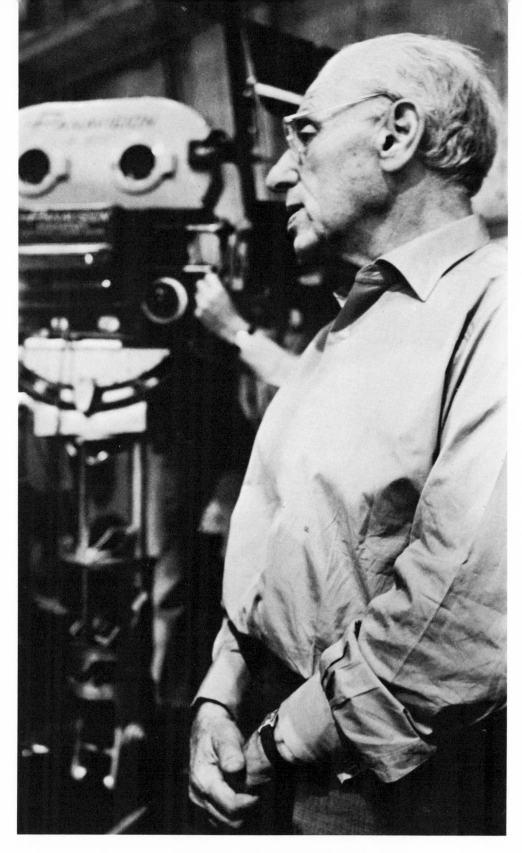

Director George Cukor

GEORGE CUKOR

OF the directors represented in this book, George Cukor lives with more self-conscious taste than any of his colleagues, and I don't think I have ever been in a home more enviable than his. Hidden behind a high blank wall on a not overwhelming plot not far up in the Hollywood hills above the Strip, it rambles comfortably around handsome Romanesque gardens alive with color but planned in such a way that you're unaware of the planning. In that sense, the gardens are rather like his best films— and it's amusing that the art director precisely duplicated the exterior of Cukor's home as the principal setting for one of his films, *Something's Got to Give*, the movie left unfinished when Marilyn Monroe was fired from it shortly before committing suicide.

The interior is a succession of large, dim, comfortably furnished rooms. In the living room, where we photographed our interview with him, a Rouault glowed on the wall behind him. In the library, where he served a light lunch after we had finished the interview, he keeps a collection of books autographed by his large circle of literary and theatrical friends—among them Somerset Maugham, Aldous Huxley, Noël Coward. His taste in literature runs toward the English moderns, and he was at the time mulling over the possibility of making a film based on the life of Virginia Woolf.

Unfailingly gracious in manner, Cukor nevertheless displays a toughness of mind and spirit that I found enormously attractive. As this interview shows, he finds it difficult to say precisely what it is that sets him apart as a director, precisely how he achieves what he has achieved—an unparalleled succession of entertainments which show him as a master of dry comedy, strong melodrama, warm romance. Of all the directors we talked with, it seems to me Cukor has entertained the widest range of the Great Audience. By and large, his pictures exclude no one—man or woman, child or old person, sophisticated or unsophisticated in taste. His movies, for the most part, can be appreciated (no, *liked*) at one level or another by just about everyone.

There is an irony in this, for, of all the directors we talked to, he has a reputation in the industry as the most limited, frequently being dismissed as a "woman's director." That's a fair example of the kind of stupidity about its own work—and its most gifted workers—that has so long afflicted Hollywood. Do they really imagine that *David Copperfield*, that robust and brilliant adaptation of Dickens' novel—featuring W. C. Fields' most endearing performance—appeals only to women? Or that men are exempt from the charms of *Pat and Mike* and *Adam's Rib*, the wonderful Tracy-Hepburn comedies? Or that the Philip Barry plays which Cukor so expertly adapted to the screen—*The Philadelphia Story* and *Holiday*—do not speak to the masculine sensibility? Perhaps this misconception is due to the fact that so many women—Greta Garbo, Katharine Hepburn, Judy Holliday, Joan Crawford, Judy Garland, among others—have given some of their best performances for Cukor. But Fields, Cary Grant, James Mason, Spencer Tracy, Ronald Colman *et al*. have never been better than in films directed by Cukor.

Cukor is the only director represented here who had extensive experience on stage handling literary material and dramatic actors before coming to the movies. He is, therefore, extremely acceptant of theatrical conventions, perfectly content to photograph stage plays—if they're good ones—and quite unconcerned with the aesthetics of so-called "pure" cinema. Doubtless he would agree with Hitchcock that "galloping horses" are not necessarily more purely cinematic than a drawing-room comedy, since it is both theoretically and practically possible to impart subtle cinematic movement to the latter, through cutting or montage. This, of course, reverses the conventional wisdom about what accounts for the "movieness" of movies, but Cukor has blithely proceeded to do so in his most characteristic work, without fussing much in public over the hows and whys of what he does.

And more than most directors Cukor seems to feel the movies are primarily an actor's, not a director's, medium; that his function is to serve actors as a sort of on-set critic, discouraging their excesses, encouraging their better instincts. Such modesty about the director's task also downgrades him in the eyes of some colleagues and critics.

But in Cukor's case his view of the director's role is the sign of a strong and serene ego. He easily shares praise for his work with colleagues and appears to have no hesitation about working with strong-minded creative collaborators and no hesitation, either, in confessing a certain vagueness about what he contributes to the process of making movies. He knows it is important, all right, but it is hard to put into words. Perhaps his major contribution is the creation of a salubrious climate for creative work—an air of confidence, trust, focused energies, an atmosphere in which everyone feels free to chance his or her instincts, knowing that the director will encourage what seems interesting and valid in the explorations, but squelch notions that are unsound.

Cukor's method—or nonmethod—is surely responsible for the easiness of his comedies, the spontaneity of his romances, the insinuating agreeableness of his best work. Of course, there is never anything sloppy about his films, never a sense—so often present in the work of younger directors when they are setting out "merely" to entertain (as if that somehow demanded less art than a heartfelt statement of personal feelings)—that the director is just fooling around. He speaks in this interview, as he has elsewhere, about probing beneath theatrical conventions, to the core of authentic human experience.

Cukor is often, and quite correctly, praised for his "taste"—though there is a faintness in that praise which is puzzling, as if taste were common in the popular arts. The famous good taste of his is something more than a keen eye for dress and décor, something more than a matter of his unobtrusive technical virtuosity, something more than his keen sense of where the best values in an actor's performance lie. It consists most significantly of a judicious but never ponderous sense of balance. This gives his films a firmness of pace, a shrewdness about character which prevents, for example, comedy from overpowering sentiment, or a star actor from overpowering his cohorts, or the demands of plot from diminishing characterization.

SOUND AND CUKOR ARRIVE TOGETHER

There was the extraordinary thing that a rather established profession, or what they called industry, was suddenly split apart. And there was a good deal of discomfort about how they would handle dialogue. Lionel Barrymore was very witty. He said, "Speech has been a success for thousands and thousands of years. And now they are testing it." So I came out when everything seemed very strange. Everybody had been thrown for a loop—the actors weren't trained, the places were not equipped and the sound technicians, as I remember, had been radio operators on boats. So it was rather clumsy. And it was not flexible. I was a dialogue director when I came out and there was no camera movement at that time because the cameras were not silent. And they had these booths that were soundproofed. And then these cameras would go inside, so that the pictures lost a great deal of flexibility that they had before. As I remember, we shot at night because the sound stages were not insulated [from exterior noise].

So it was very primitive at the time. There was a great deal of hocus-pocus and mystery [and] it was [a] very advantageous [time] for me to come out.

I was very curious, although I'd been a rather successful stage director. I'd done a stock company in the summer and then I worked for Gilbert Miller and I worked for Ethel Barrymore and Laurette Taylor, but the theater was in one of its periodic dips, and when you came out here you felt this enormous vitality. They were going great guns and one is always relieved to find that. So it was rather pleasant, but in the theater I knew my way around. I'd been a stage manager and I ran my own stock company, but here it was completely alien. . . . But I got used to it, and I liked Hollywood the moment I got here. I felt lucky here, and then I had thick skin and a lot of determination and stayed on.

I found there was a demand for people's services, which is always encouraging, and I liked the people here. They were thrown, but they were interested in what was going on.

THEATER PEOPLE VS. MOVIE PEOPLE

I still encounter [what] I think is stupid snobbery. As though everybody in the theater was enormously aristocratic and they were all to the manor born. They did work with distinguished material, so therefore that rubs off on them. But I think that the movie people were just the same breed really. Except [that] as I remember it, and also (it is really before my day) Ronald Colman, who was a young man [when] he came out here, said, this was the most glorious place [in] the [earlier] rather free, happy days. It was before the Arbuckle scandal. And he was just thrilled by it all.

THE MOGULS

I thought they were very shrewd; they were extremely good businessmen; were very knowledgeable. And they had their own curious kind of taste. I think they really knew or thought they knew for the most part what the public wanted. And they had very definite ideas and very solid, intelligent ideas. And they were anxious to get whatever you could offer. That is what I liked; if you had an idea at all, they would encourage you to give it to them and they were very, very anxious to get the best in people. Also they realized that the coin of the realm was talent and they respected it. Now, they weren't all dreamers, they were tough too. But I think every businessman is tough. And I found working with them very pleasant and one felt faith with them. They were men who could make decisions. They were in a position to say, "Yes, I'll make this picture" and "Yes, I will spend money." And they had people around them—they had the most distinguished writers. But they had aspirations and one mustn't despise aspirations. It shows that they have hopes of doing the proper thing.

LEARNING THE ROPES

I knew nothing about the camera. [I had] to learn from these people about cutting and camera techniques—and a great deal of that is an eternal fascination. I was a dialogue director [at] first and then I codirected. I was a dialogue director with a very gifted man, Lewis Milestone, on *All Quiet on the Western Front*. I was observing all this time, without any of the responsibility. I liked that enormously and it was a marvelous training for me.

ADAPTATION AND ADAPTABILITY

There is a trick of adapting a play to the screen.* I don't see why they are so hoity-toity about it. Griffith originally started from rather old turkey plays. If you photograph a stage play, you have to adapt it and give it a movement—and sometimes a very subtle movement—and yet keep the cohesion of the play. And because I came from the theater and I knew a great deal about the theater of that time, I suppose they assigned me to [adaptations], and also I was rather wisecracking—I suppose I still am—and they felt I had no soul. I [was] this brittle person. And then I was catalogued. It is easy to catalogue people. And I was

---

* Cukor's first credits—as codirector and director—were on films adapted from plays. Throughout his career he has returned to theatrical material for films.

catalogued as being [able to] do comedies and sophistication, you know, as though I had come from a great aristocratic background. But then after a while I did some costume things—*Little Women* and *Camille* and *David Copperfield*. Well, I was put into *that* category. One is always being put in some category or another. Now, we all have our limitations, there are things for which you think you have a sympathy or think you understand, but it is easier [for others] to put you in these boxes. I don't know quite what category I'm in now.

You have to say, "Look here, just give me a crack at this." They would listen to you. They were not inflexible. You had to have some common sense about it, [but] they would be inclined to listen, they would also go along with things and they were pleased to see a kind of flexibility [on your part]. They realized that this was good showmanship—to bring out different facets, especially in the actors, but also the directors—and they were for the most part good showmen. And they were sensible enough that if a thing was not sympathetic to us, they would not force you to do it. I was under contract to Metro-Goldwyn-Mayer for years and, right or wrong, when I found a property didn't interest me, I would ask to go elsewhere. They rented me out—for a profit, I should think.

A DIRECTOR PREPARES

Most of my education comes through the research that I do—and that leads you up fascinating byways, you know. You suddenly find yourself knowing this and knowing that and it opens up a whole world. Then, when you know really as much as you can assimilate, you've got to shut it off and then start doing it. And the audience senses it. They say, "Well, yes, this must be real, this must be the way it is." And I'm not aware of it, you see. But some of it seeps through subconsciously. So the power of thought in pictures is very important.

For example, in preparing *The Actress** we went to Ruth Gordon's

---

* Based on *Years Ago*, Ruth Gordon's autobiographical play about her adolescent infatuation with the theater.

house, which she hadn't seen for a long time, for the first time—she'd left there in about 1914. We went there with our camera to do research. And it was marvelous. It really didn't make sense. It was much smaller than she'd thought and the kitchen was a room that had eight doors. Now, no architect or art director would have imagined that, but it had the texture of reality. There was one door to this and one door to that, and we reproduced it. I think the audience feels if a thing is real. And we did all sorts of research on that trip, as we do on every trip, to places that really didn't appear in the thing. Ruth Gordon's father had worked for the Mellin's Company—Mellin's Food—and we went to where they were dismantling it. We went to see the neighbors. You do a complete research so that you really know what you're doing, and even though you don't use it, as I said before, some of it seeps through. That way you don't limit yourself. And then it's a well-rounded picture. You are authoritative.

In *Born Yesterday* when I first saw the Jefferson Memorial, I was very moved by it. I was very moved by what he said. And I said, "Let's photograph that." And we did, and I'm sure the audience was moved as I was. And then I was moved at the people looking at the original of the Declaration of Independence and the tourists and the tourist guide in the dome of the Capitol, all of which adds a sense of reality. In that case, *Born Yesterday* was [set] in Washington and that was [a play] in one set, so you had to move as much as you could. And we got as much of the outdoors [as we could]. We played scenes in the National Gallery, we played them on the steps of the Library of Congress, and that's how you adapt, or try to adapt, stage plays and still not make them static.

When it is appropriate that one goes outside, one does. And it was very imaginative of a company to realize that if you do New York, you can't fake that. There was a tendency to try to do it on the back lot or to do it in process, which is always phony-baloney. Now, of course, I think the passion is, for no reason at all, [to go on location]. There is a tiny room and they insist on inconveniently going [to it]. Subconsciously it may have some effect on you, but I think that's a self-indulgence and a kind of nonsense that is fashionable at the moment.

DIRECTING ACTORS

First of all, you cast them. You get the actors who can play comedy. Or who can play in costume. They, too, have a style. You can't [have them] do it in the old-time, stagey way—you have to make it conversational, and palatable to the screen because the screen is realistic. They may have [had] a certain amount of [stage] training, but you can stop them from orating because that alienates the picture public.

I know when Sam Goldwyn (whom I respect a great deal) did *Wuthering Heights*, he had a problem with a very, very distinguished actor, Laurence Olivier, in the part [of] Heathcliff—one of those somber Victorian heroes with cloaks on and a great many problems. And he flung himself here and there on horses and all that. Olivier had done this sort of thing on the stage and Goldwyn would see these things and thought they were overacted. And William Wyler, who is a very good director, would try to persuade Olivier [not to, but] Olivier simply didn't know that you had to [underact]. And then Goldwyn told me that one day he just called the company to the set and he said, "Now look here, the rushes I'm getting are not good," and he said, "I'm going to call the picture off. It's just not believable—all this rhodomontade, all this acting." And Olivier said, "Well, I think you're speaking of me, Mr. Goldwyn, and may I come up to you and talk to you about it?" And Goldwyn and he had a conversation and then he adjusted his acting, still having the vigor, the flair, but also the reality that is needed for screen acting.

I don't think that directing is all that easy. Everybody thinks it is a snap. And I have been at it quite a long time and I'm not sure of the results. Handling actors—now, I don't mean handling, but working with actors—people have the odd idea that the director is a kind of lion-tamer. Actresses say, "No, no, no, I will not do zat" and then you say, "You *will* do zat" and all that absurd thing. These people are all intelligent people and you've got to create a mutual trust. And they've got to believe that you know what you're talking about and deliver the goods, and if they do anything intelligent you'll likely notice, and if they do anything foolish, there is the good critical eye that will discourage them.

The director's function, among other things, is to get them out of themselves. And very often people think they have limitations and the director sees that they are not limitations. But it's a very fine point, about how to handle actors. Some actors, you've got to give them their head. And some actors, you've got to know what they are likely to do when they are off the beam. And you guard them from that and also you have to watch them and see what they can contribute out of their own gift. And then you respect that. There are some who are inexperienced and you have to coach them. Really. And then you've got to know—you've got to know psychologically—how to behave with an actor. Now, certain actors give their best in three or four takes, or five takes. And others are better the more repetition they have. And you've got to know when they are at the best, when that's all you can get out of them. And you don't dog them.

Finally, the director should feel, he should show, a conviction [about the work], but not in a phony way, because they'll smell you out. Also [he should have] the self-possession, when he doesn't know what he's talking about, to say so, to own up. Very often, you know, actors say, "Well, you told me that yesterday, and now you're telling me this." And then you have to say, "Well, I was wrong yesterday and I'm right now." But, by and large, you give the tone of the whole thing. You give the vitality. And if a director sits down, everybody else will sit down. And that is among his other duties, to keep it going.

Oh, I'm pretty tough. I'm plenty tough. I'm determined. I'm being at my best behavior here, I'm being absolutely charming for educational television, but people are wrong; they have a picture of a movie director and are always surprised that we're not [all] exactly the same, you see. I think there's a new type of young director who talks a good deal about integrity and his own vision and sincerity. Well, I think, depraved as we were, we were sincere and we had our own vision and it's just the difference in fashion [to talk more openly about it]. But I think the animal is the same.

I think there are certain directors who accomplish things visually, with the camera, and I accomplish things sometimes through the actor— through the acting gift—which, like all gifts, is a great eternal mystery which is denied us. I don't know why a painter can make a certain line and I can't make a certain line, and why an actor can call on something in himself that I cannot. If I were asked to read a script from the beginning out loud, I'd do it very badly. But I go great guns if I have to make the hot suggestions, you see. Also, there's another funny thing—there is a new civil-rights law that [says] it's very bad form to give an actor readings. I say why in the hell shouldn't I give you readings? If you misread it, then I'll read it correctly. The director has the enormous advantage of hearing it. You see it and you hear it. So you have that detachment. But there are all kinds of limits now which a director is supposed to observe which I have to learn.

One doesn't know [the actors'] methods. They may be great friends of yours and you trust their work, but you judge it after the fact. You don't peep in on them and say, "Oh, well, this is what he's doing." I think you appreciate it very much and you look at it rather knowledgeably and rather critically, and sometimes with jealousy. You don't know exactly how they accomplish things. You see the end result and you judge from that.

JOHN BARRYMORE

In the first place, I had a great admiration for John Barrymore. From the second balcony I saw him do these wonderful things that Arthur Hopkins produced in New York—*The Jest* and *Hamlet* and all these wonderful things. I was, in a sense, brought up with John Barrymore. So that when I worked with him,* at first I was a little nervous, but I was a friend of Ethel Barrymore's and I went to see Jack and he said, "Now, look here, you watch me." He said, "You know, people say that I'm this and I'm that and I'm a ham"—all the unkind things that people had said about him. He said, "Watch that, kid." And then we began to work on this thing and I found that, as with all first-rate actors, he was very open and you could meet him on a common ground. He was not inflexible. And very gentle, curiously enough. [Later] in *Dinner at Eight*** he played a second-rate cheapish actor, which God knows he wasn't. And

---

* In *A Bill of Divorcement* in 1932—the film was Katharine Hepburn's movie debut.

** An adaptation of the Edna Ferber–George S. Kaufman play about the intertwining lives of a diverse group invited for "dinner at eight."

he did it with enormous wit and very subtly. I said, "Oh, that is wonderful, Jack." And he said, "Well, it ought to be. This is a combination
of Maurice Costello," who was his father-in-law, a rather undistinguished
gentleman, a silent-picture actor, Lowell Sherman, his brother-in-law,
who was a rather slick Broadway actor, expert actor, "and me. So," he
said, "it should be rather easy for me to do." But he did the nuances of
it and he was creative and in a very interesting way. The very first
shot, he is on the telephone and he's what they called at that time—I
shouldn't say it—a Lambs' Club actor, pretending to be very grand to a
society woman. He said, "Let me put this phrase in. 'Yes, yes, yes, dear
lady.' " He was being very grand and hambola. His speech was very well
observed, very accurate. When he wanted a drink and he talked to the
bellhop, all this grandeur, all this fake suavity left him. And he played,
as I say, an ignorant actor and he found out that another actor got the
job that he desperately needed. And he'd say, "I can be English. I can be
as English as ahnybohdy." Then he'd say, "Ibsen, Ibsen. *I* can do Ibsen,"
and he had just heard vaguely of Ibsen, and he would strike this absolutely inappropriate pose and he said, "Mother dear, give me the
moon." Whereas the Ibsen line was, "Mother, give me the sun"—to
show that he'd gone over, he'd become mad. And Jack was also very
encouraging. He would listen sympathetically and try anything the
director might suggest. I remember the very touching end. *I'm* the hero
of this story. I said, "I think he [the character in *Dinner at Eight*] can't
even die satisfactorily." I said, "Something awkward and awful should
happen to him, [even though] he was imagining this great death scene
where he was going to kill himself." And I said, "I think it would be
awfully interesting if he did this very ugly, middle-aged-awkward
sprawl," and he did this so wonderfully. And [then] he pulled himself
together and died showing his profile. Jack was a man with no vanity,
and enormous knowledge and humor as all the Barrymores had. They
were all fascinating creatures. They were really magical people.

KATHARINE HEPBURN

Katharine Hepburn is human in every way, and she was gifted at that
time and had the originality that she has and the force, but she'd been

acting only for some [little] time and she had clumsiness and she certainly had never been acting in front of a camera. And Barrymore was enormously kind to her. I'll never forget the first day she worked. We had seen a test of her in which she was like nothing we'd ever seen before, and the first day she was required to look at her father who had returned from the hospital, and she looked at him with this infinite compassion, and then her eyes filled with tears, and Jack Barrymore winked at me. He said, "She's okay." And then he was charming with her. He encouraged her. He instructed her and made things very easy and pleasant for her. He did appreciate [that] this was a very gifted girl, and indeed she [had] a wonderful part and she made an enormous impression.

There was an interesting moment in the picture where they have first seen her, and she spoke rather forcefully, and the audience wasn't quite sure whether they liked her or not. And then there was, mercifully, an interval where she said goodbye to her mother, who was troubled. And you saw this girl go to the door and she smiled. And you saw that she had this lovely smile. And the audience had time to take stock of her when she walked across this big room and took the cushion, as I remember it, and lay on the hearthstone, and then they could see that she moved beautifully and she had a lovely figure, and there was a nice interval to take stock of her. And it was at that moment that Katharine Hepburn became a star. Not *because* of that moment, but suddenly the audience saw this is somebody to be reckoned with. That didn't mean that she didn't have a lot to learn. And she's been learning all the time and she is a very adventurous actress and extremely intelligent and is still working without any vanity, although she is a great, great star.

She is on to herself and she bears no grudges. She is an extraordinary human being. And she prepares intelligently. Now, there was something that I had nothing to do with, but she was going to do a musical comedy. And she'd never done that before. And she was living here. She is my tenant—lives down the street. And she would go every afternoon with her dog to a remote place and let her voice out and speak the lines. She believes in intelligent preparation, technically learning the lines and probably thinking a great deal. [I'm] not telling you how an actor prepares, they prepare themselves subconsciously and consciously, but she did all she could—she didn't want to sound like a little canary bird in the big theater. And she must have thought about it. She is not opinionated, although as she gets older she has more and more definite ideas. But we've done six or seven or eight pictures together and we happen to be great friends and I happen to have a great feeling of affection for her. [I'm] amused by her. And I think we're pals.

SPENCER TRACY

With Spencer, we would rehearse and occasionally he would let you in on what he thought, and he was also creative, but neither he nor Katharine Hepburn do all this business of going into things and exaggerating and examining themselves, which I think lets a lot of the magic out. Spencer would, I'm sure, be preoccupied with the part. I'm sure he would be mulling it over. But he didn't articulate it because he felt that "if I talk about it an awful lot, then when I do it it won't have the freshness." They rehearse, they rehearse the mechanics of it, but it never really comes alive until it is played, and you [as the director] discover it as well as they do. And that is the immediacy and the sense of improvisation that good picture acting has.

I'm not talking about [verbal] improvisation. [Spencer] spoke every "if," "and" and "but" in the text. Judy Holliday, who gave the sense of just saying things that came into her head, was very meticulous about it. She would even observe the question marks. To allow people to just chatter and go off the deep end—I can always detect it. I can always say, "Well, they're stalling." And I should think that they would not be as witty as a good writer who has thought about [their lines] for a long time. I think you want to give the illusion that it is improvised, that's what an accomplished actor does. But you hew to the line, to the text—it's very, very important.

There was a moving, wonderful scene in *The Actress** and technically [Spencer] did it very well. He was eating his lunch, as I remember it, and he made the bread, the butter, the way he chewed, part of the scene. He made it so eloquent. He was funny and he had the authority to switch

---

* Cukor is speaking of a scene in which Tracy, as the crusty father of a romantically inclined girl, talks about—as he never has before—the meanness of his own childhood and youth.

from comedy to rather serious [material] and did it wonderfully. He loved and respected Jean Simmons, who gave a wonderful performance, and there was a scene when she wanted to be an actress and she stood on the steps in their house and she was starting things off rather badly. And Spencer looked at her and he did something very funny: for no reason at all, he looked at the mother as though she had talked this girl into doing something. But then he looked at her with this eloquent face of his and his face changed color. And I said, "That was lovely." He said, "Well, I remember when I told my father that I wanted to be an actor and he looked at me, this skinny kid with big ears, and he said, 'Oh that poor little son of a bitch; he's going to go through an awful lot.' " He drew out of his own experiences.

[In *Edward, My Son*] he played a cold-blooded monster and Spencer was very funny. He said, "It's rather disconcerting to me to find out how easily I play a heel." He said, "I'm a better actor than I think I was. When I was doing Father Flanagan, that was acting. This is not acting." But he had a very sharp sense of humor and [he was] on to himself— no delusions, because if we are deluded we're sunk. And people who have a sense of where they are and what they're doing are forearmed. That doesn't mean that disaster doesn't strike, but at least you're not fatuous and stupid about it.

LITTLE WOMEN

When they asked me to do *Little Women*, I don't think I'd ever read it. In fact, Katharine Hepburn said I never really did read [it], which is a vile thing to say, [that] I never really did read the Louisa May Alcott novel. I thought it was sort of like Elsie Dinsmore—a little-girls' book. But there's always a reason why something has lived. So when I read this thing, I was absolutely startled, because it had all the American virtues— duty, love of family, love of parents, respect for parents, hard work, all the staples that I think are admirable. The pitfall of that picture was that it could have been like a valentine; it could be very sentimental. But, first of all, there was a very talented art director who reproduced the house in Concord that Louisa May Alcott lived in. Now, that was done here—snow and all. And the New England woods. And done so expertly that you didn't have to run to New England to do it. And [Katharine Hepburn] cast something over that in that part of her career. I think she loved her family and she believed in all those virtues, and it was a wonderful part which she played extraordinarily well. I think it was a picture of Americana and I enjoyed doing it very much.

It was sort of naïve; it was awkward in certain ways. I mean, the little heroine—the little sister—seemed to have died twice, and the hero is introduced in the last quarter of the picture. But I find that when you do talented books, you do some of the weakness as well as the strength. You don't slick it all up, you see. You've got to understand what the material is about and then get the essence of it. And that means sometimes doing it rather awkwardly; not making it smooth.

DAVID COPPERFIELD

People have approached me saying the second part of the picture wasn't as good as the first. "Well," I said, "the first part of [the novel] *David Copperfield* is more appealing than the second, and if Dickens didn't solve it, I don't think we should try to, because we must [respect] his extraordinary genius and then just have faith that we'll do it well enough that it will carry you on." I think it's always a mistake to make too clever adaptations. Because [then the audience] really [doesn't] know what the vitality of the work that you're doing is. But you've got to know what the virtues of the thing are. The cragginess, the awkwardnesses—not that the work is wonderful because of those things, but they're part of it. And the naïveté of it and the crudity of it gives it a kind of strength that one should not [tamper with]. The work itself loses because that's not the original thing that you've undertaken to do.

I hope to do another Dickens. I think Dickens is a man of genius and of richness, of things that have not been done, and there it is for you. And if you can do it with the toughness, with the edge that Dickens had, I think they're wonderful works. I think Dickens in the twenties was out of favor, but now the scholars are saying that it's glorious—and I didn't realize that he had such an effect, that Dostoevsky and Tolstoy were enormously affected by him.

FIELDS AS MICAWBER

He only worked for about two weeks and he was an absolutely charming man. He was born to play the part; he *was* Mr. Micawber. He'd always played himself or things he created [until then]. And I found him very sympathetic, very nice and very inventive, but never outside the character of Micawber. He would do little inventions that I thought were awfully funny that Micawber might have done. Fields played the sort of a scalawag who was having a tough time with life. And also he wasn't too honest and he was trying to get away with things. And I'll never forget, right before he did a scene where he was working at his desk—a high desk, bookkeeper's desk—he said—he was supposed to be writing in ink—"Could I have a cup of tea here?" And he put the cup of tea there. And then, "Could I have a certain kind of wastepaper basket?" So then he was using the teacup as the inkwell and confusing it. And then when he got off the stool—he was bugged by all kinds of inanimate things—he'd get his foot into the wastepaper basket. And that was true to Dickens. Fields was not a great friend of mine, but he was marvelous, hard-working and would try anything. And this was not his own territory. But he realized that he was working with something that was a classic and he behaved that way.

GARBO AND *CAMILLE*

Well, that was another case where the actress was born to play that special part. Oh, I don't flatter myself that I am the expert. She did very well before she ever saw me. But it was a happy collaboration. I've seen bits of it on television, but I saw that picture for the first time [in many years] when they had the retrospective of my pictures, as they do for all old gentlemen, and I was staggered when I saw it on a large screen—at [her] lightness of touch . . . the wantonness, the perversity [of] the way she played Camille. That usually is a sort of sobbing part; a victim part. But she played it [as if] she was the author of her own misery. And had enormous eroticism and boldness. She was supposed to be dying— eventually she does die of TB—but she just did a very delicate—she

Judy Holliday in the process of proving she wasn't Born Yesterday *to Broderick Crawford (left) and Frank Otto (1950)*

Judy Garland playing with her beloved drunken husband in A Star Is Born *(1954)*

The frail Camille (Greta Garbo) in the arms of her lover Armand (Robert Taylor), 1937

Katharine Hepburn, unhorsed but unbowed, with John Howard in Philadelphia Story *(1940)*

cleared her throat and [in] some way you knew that this woman was going to die. And then also she was unsentimental about herself. She was tough, she said to the young man who idealized her, she said, "Look here, I'm just a girl like all the rest. I'm a tart here like all the rest. And don't fall in love with me." And she was trying to protect the young man from himself. But she was hard on herself and realistic and not self-pitying, which is a most attractive quality. I think now there's an awful lot of self-pity going around, and self-righteousness. Everybody is put upon—which is a great bore. I think you admire people who have a certain amount of guts and character.

In the first place, Garbo is very intelligent, very disciplined. She'd never done a picture outside of Metro and her relationship with the crew was remarkable. A director makes a climate in which she can work. Also, I think you watch very carefully what she's doing. You make suggestions, but you let the impulse come out of her, as you do with all creative actors and actresses. Oh, I had something to do with it—exactly what I really can't say.

SEXUALITY, EROTICISM, ATTRACTIVENESS

Eroticism is the whole climate of attractiveness, of voluptuousness, of sensuousness, that you achieve in various ways, and [some] people have that in their personality. I don't think a beautiful girl like Ava Gardner has to huff and puff and do an awful lot; she carries that with her. And it touches their imagination. I think Garbo had that to a degree, and the audience feels it. I think very often bold sexuality is off-putting, and all these great movie queens—none of them seemed to undress. I mean, all of the goddesses of the screen—they were plenty goddess-like. Some of the limitations that were put in the [old] code were absurd, but it guaranteed that the people had built-in attractiveness. And I deplore the lack of beauty and attractiveness today. Now, [there was another] extreme—I mean, you'd see people in terrible snowstorms and the hair, the marcel, was always there and they were sexy at every moment. But by and large

I think it is pleasing to see attractive people, and that does not mean, because a girl is attractive or beautiful, or a young man handsome, that they're talentless. That is a cliché that I don't understand—when you think of all the beautiful people [who] were pretty damn good actors. Nobody could be handsomer than John Barrymore and all these great, historic, lovely faces.

You know, that part in *Camille*—Armand—is always a stick of a part and it is [always played as if he were] rather a sap, because it was always played by men of forty-five pretending to be young boys, so that they looked like asses. But Robert Taylor, who was very young at the time and very picturesque—you understood his plight very sympathetically because his folly was the folly and the impetuousness of a young man. And Robert Taylor gave a very, very good performance. It was a smart-aleck thing to say, "Well, he was so beautiful—Robert Taylor." Well, indeed, there was nothing wrong with that, because he acted very well. He liked, he wanted to play sort of rougher parts, which he did perfectly well. But when people have this gift of picturesqueness and beauty, I think it should be exploited.

CARY GRANT

We did a picture called *Sylvia Scarlett* and [until then] he was a successful young leading man who was nice-looking but had no particular identity. In fact, if you see him with Mae West,* he's rather awkward. But in the meanwhile he had been working and had experience and acted on the stage, and suddenly when he got the right part, in *Sylvia Scarlett*, he flowered; he suddenly felt the ground under his feet. It was a well-written part, well directed, and he knew what this character was, and he gave a marvelous performance. Then later on he developed this style of comedy and this dash, this dapper thing; he worked with fine directors, with Leo McCarey, who was a master of comedy, and Hitch, and he would learn things from all these people, and he developed his style. But you know, he was very young and very inexperienced when he

* In *She Done Him Wrong* (1932) and *I'm No Angel* (1933).

started, and he mellowed and he grew, given the opportunity. You see, he didn't depend on his looks. He wasn't a narcissist; he acted as though he were just an ordinary young man. And that made it all the more appealing, that a handsome young man was funny; that was especially unexpected and good because we think, "Well, if he's a Beau Brummell, he can't be either funny or intelligent," but he proved otherwise.

[*Sylvia Scarlett*] was a terrible failure when it was done, with Katharine Hepburn, and now it's one of those rediscovered treasures. Every time they show my pictures they say, "Oh, we want to show *Sylvia Scarlett*" and I'm rather surprised that they do. Katharine Hepburn and I are very amused by it. But it has its virtues.

A CRAFTSMAN'S RANGE—AND A FEW WORDS ON COLLABORATION

I think if you are a workmanlike, competent director and you're called upon to do melodrama, if you understand it, yes, you can do it. And things with tension. I think that we all have limitations, but I don't like it when people put artificial limitations on you. Why shouldn't I be able to do a serious dramatic thing? I mean, I've been at it a long time and you kind of know what you're doing. Now, there are certain melodramas that if I were asked to do, I'd say, "No, no. I can make a stab at it, because of competence, but I think there are a hell of a lot of people who would do it better than I would. And I think you ought to get them."

I would have said offhand, "Well, I'm [not] awfully good at doing westerns," but I did a western and was absolutely fascinated by it.* But it was a special kind of western. I think you have to find out for yourself and don't become infatuated with yourself, don't say, "Well, I can do anything." There are some things that you can't do. I think what you can't do are things that you have no real sympathy for, you know.

I did a picture called *Pat and Mike*** and there were gangsters in that,

---

* *Heller in Pink Tights.*

** In which Spencer Tracy plays a gambler attempting to convert Katharine Hepburn from an aristocratic amateur sportswoman into a premature Billie Jean King. Needless to say, he succeeds and they fall in love.

but they were comic gangsters. And you mustn't get the idea that I was from this old aristocratic family (which I was, of course)—that I was saying, "Oh, this is how the lower people work." No, no. [It arose out of] my collaboration with the Kanins.* They wrote about this cut of life. And I think that you can see [it] with understanding and compassion, but also with humor. I don't think their problems were tragic, although in some of the pictures there were real problems. The breakup of a marriage, the loss of a child within a comedy can be very, very moving, and I think, in fact, in all successful comedies there is always a touch of heart. I think Judy Holliday was so wonderful in that she unexpectedly made you weep. And in fact if you are a great comedienne, there is always the emotion underneath it, unless you're doing a farce. And all these first-class actors have that in their personalities. Spencer Tracy and Katharine Hepburn—there was always the human thing in it, the human comment on marriage, on whatever they were dealing with. And to do that in terms of comedy is a very interesting thing and it's not easy. You have to have witty writing.

It was a very happy collaboration, but I consider that the Kanins were the authors. If I had written the things, I promise you I'd been here taking a lot of the bows. But I did respect their talent and their originality, and I think you're always a better director with good material. If you do good scenes, the actors are better. You rely on, you lean on it. I'm the better director if I have a wonderful cameraman and wonderful actors—then I shine. It's just great. It doesn't take anything away from me. It shows that I'm smart and I'm clever enough to get people who really do their job well. I'm not the Renaissance man and I don't think it's a failing in me. I don't think there's anything wrong with me that I'm not the greatest writer or musician or anything.

---

* Ruth Gordon and Garson Kanin frequently worked with Cukor in the late 1940s and early 1950s. They collaborated on the scripts for *A Double Life* (1947), *Adam's Rib* (1949), *The Marrying Kind* (1952) and *Pat and Mike* (1952). Cukor also directed the film adaptation of Kanin's play *Born Yesterday* and Miss Gordon's adaptation of her autobiographical play, *Years Ago*, under the title *The Actress* (1953).

JUDY HOLLIDAY

Judy Holliday was an extremely intelligent, intellectual person—very well educated, very highbrow, very musical, and she was unique. Some actresses are very talented and some actresses are talented and are artists. Judy Holliday was an artist as well. And it's a pity that she died so young because she would have done wonderful things. She showed you truth through comedy. There was a scene in *Born Yesterday* where just in a kind of a few steps you saw that she had been a chorus girl; that she had no talent, but she was a professional chorus girl. That is what an actor can do. And then, of course, she was a master of comedy and subtlety, and of understatement. She was a brilliant actress. And then with the other pictures I did with her, I found her marvelous and modest and, in retrospect, infinitely touching.

THE MYSTERY OF TALENT

[On *Pat and Mike*] Katharine Hepburn took lessons from [Bill] Tilden. Of course, he was a wonderful tennis player, but he described what the sensation of playing might be. And then also I stood at the side and I watched him play. And the tennis ball seemed to come to him. He never did any movement and it seemed to come to him. And Babe Didrikson was there, and she was an absolute charmer, and then I got to know these people. I don't think I could have done, you know, *The Pride of the Yankees*, but maybe if the story were good, maybe the subject would interest me. So therefore it's not only theatrical talent [which interests me. I am] drawn to the mystery of what causes human beings, some human beings, to be able to do something and do it superlatively well after they've had training and others with the best intentions in the world can't do it. As I say, I cannot draw a straight line, and then I watch people who do something wonderfully, and when I work with people I watch the art directors do all kinds of things that I couldn't possibly do, and I very shrewdly grab them to me.

THE AUDIENCE

Well, I don't think you spend your money to be tormented in the theater. Now, I think if you're going to see great eternal tragedies, the Greek tragedies, or Dostoevsky, or the things like that, well, you might submit to that. But to be tormented by people trying to make a buck and whose intellectual opinions and whose skill is not to be particularly respected—the pomposity of it puts me off. And also the unattractiveness. You're not doing Gorky's *The Lower Depths;* you're doing a fake version of it, you know—a fake, sentimental, soft version of it that is supposed to pass for great truths. And I just find it repulsive [when] people behave in an unattractive way. I don't want to see it. I don't want to see a lot of bums and things unless they have humor or you become a better man before you leave the theater.

I hope the pictures that I make are not special. If they are for a limited audience, it's no good. I think the movies are going through perilous times. They [once] meant a great deal to the people in their lives. Now I think that maybe some of these people have been alienated, and that is what the wise old moguls knew, that this was a family entertainment. That's obscene to say these days—but an entertainment that isn't just for the kids, for this or that group. It should interest everybody. And the successful ones do. And I had a letter from a lady whom I just met, who lives in the backwoods of a small town. She came from Akron, Ohio. And when she found out I was a movie director, that I was a friend of her son's, she wrote me a letter that I think makes this point. It has all sorts of flattering things about me which I will spare you—but she said take, for instance, *The Philadelphia Story* starring Katharine Hepburn. "Akron, Ohio, where I grew up, of course was in the rubber industry, six factories. These people there were in the depths of the dark Depression of the thirties. And when these movies of yours arrived at Loew's and at the Palace, and the new and beautiful theaters, there were long lines waiting to get in. Thankfully, the admission was small, as no one was making large amounts of money, but everyone loved to see a good movie. You see, Mr. Cukor, you probably never thought about how great your work was and about how the poor working people were depending on great talent. Back in Ohio, as well as other states—I know this, for I lived through this period." I hope that my actors would read things better than I do, but it was close to the emotional life of this country. And it was an important part of people's lives. And maybe these people have been alienated, for what reason I don't know, and I hope that we can get them back, to involve them.

THE REALITY BEYOND CONVENTION

I think if you get the human truths, the human experience, if you can evoke that, no matter how artificial [the context] might seem to you, [then the work is] valid, and also one must have a sense of history. One must realize that a lot of these [older] pictures [we] now think absurd because life has changed. And therefore we think, "Oh, well, this is just theatricality." But things did exist in that way. I remember when I saw plays that had things that I thought just theatrical nonsense. For example, *Tosca*, where there was a secret police and there was this and that. Well, [in] the Second World War we discovered there were secret police and there was melodrama. You have to dig out what is real and valid. Let's say, *Camille*. There were things in that that were conventions—that a bad woman would ruin a young man's life—but if you do it so that everybody understands that, then you [can] dig out the reality and the truth of it. And I am a great believer that the truth will move people. I know that when I see other pictures, when I see pictures about Italy or France, about life that I know nothing about, I sense if they're real. *The Bicycle Thief*—I didn't know that little children worked, but it was done so well that I said, "Oh yes, this is it. It touches me." And that is the great thing that movies had. They weren't just being clever or being sensational or playing on just a small part of the human emotion. I'm not saying that sex and eroticism is not part of human emotion, but it is not the beginning and end of everything. There are other things.

It's awfully nice if [a picture] looks beautiful—gives the impression of verisimilitude, but if you've got some good stuff, that is [where] the vitality is. That is the heart's blood of the whole thing. You can do, let's say, a picture about movies—like *A Star Is Born*—well, that's a very special experience. Her problems are special to movie actresses. But if you get beyond that to the [general human] truth of it, then you move the audience. And Judy Garland did with this extraordinary performance.

A CONCLUSION

I suppose fundamentally I am the same, but you vary; you learn. I had a funny experience. I had to get a driver's license [recently] and I sat in the classroom and I felt exactly the way I did when I was a kid. I had the temptation to copy and cheat as I did then, and to look over at the other person, and all the fears and all the misgivings, and I thought, "Well, really, you haven't done anything since you were eight years old." [So] fundamentally you are the same person. [But] then you either deteriorate or you educate yourself. And also occasionally give yourself a long hard look and try to be a little fairer, a little better.

I think some of us are lucky. We don't get atrophied; our mind doesn't become atrophied. We still have this enormous curiosity and interest in what goes on; and there is a zest for life, if you're well. And I'm full of curiosity. I read the morning papers and laugh at them, and get excited by them, and I'm aware of what goes on; otherwise you are half dead. And I don't feel one bit older than I ever felt. That is the one thing I think would be lamentable. I know that certain things—I'm not as agile; I find myself clumsy in various [ways]. But I try to overcome it. And if you look life square in the face and say, "Well, I lack here and I lack there," and you take a sharp account of yourself and you try not to be envious or resentful and sorry for yourself, I think you stand a chance. I said [to another interviewer], I said, "Christ Almighty, you know you've got to keep going."

Director William Wellman

WILLIAM A. WELLMAN

THE week before *The Men Who Made the Movies* was scheduled to premiere we invited the directors it featured to come to New York for a party to honor them and to help publicize the series. Howard Hawks, Raoul Walsh and Bill Wellman were able to make it, and one morning I did a half-hour interview show with them for broadcast on WNET, the Public Broadcasting channel in New York, while the series was running. When we had finished, the producer of that broadcast popped out of the control room and asked Bill if he would mind taping a pitch for the station's quarterly pledge week, when viewers are asked to send in contributions to help finance its operations. Bill agreed, and I retired to the control room to watch him. I found myself standing next to Howard Hawks, and midway in Bill's pitch he jerked a thumb at the monitor and said to me, "Remember when I told you there are some faces a camera loves?" I remembered, and Howard jabbed his thumb at Bill's image and nodded again.

And it's true. Besides being a handsome man with a good voice—he's proud of his ability as a singer—he has that magnetism which communicates itself through a lens and onto film or through a cable into our living rooms. Douglas Fairbanks, Sr., was quite right to try to make him into an actor when Wellman turned up, a devilish young war hero, looking for work in Hollywood right after World War I. So was the producer who called him after he saw him on *The Men Who Made the Movies* and offered him a part in some film he was shooting this year. In the beginning I think Bill was afraid of what his buddies from the Lafayette Escadrille would say when they caught him working in a profession he-men don't regard as entirely worthy of a real man's attention (which is, of course, why from the beginning so many male stars have gone to such lengths off-screen to prove their skills as athletes and outdoorsmen). I also think that Bill, who has more than a touch of the ham in him—deny it though he will—feared that he might get to like the work too well, that it might bring out a side in him that he doesn't admire. It is also possible that he feared the idleness, the long periods "at liberty" which are a part of every actor's life, for as a young man he was a considerable roisterer and wencher and he needed the sublimation which constant hard work offers.

There is an element of role-playing in Bill's manner. He likes to think of himself as a really tough guy, and his yarns are all of creampuff actors who tried to pull egocentric tricks on his sets and how he refused to let them pull that stuff, of producers who tried to tell him how to make a picture and where he told them to stick their ideas. I haven't the slightest doubt that when the occasion warranted it, he could enforce a strict order on his sets, that he could singe a producer's ears whenever it was required. On the other hand, the roll-call of actors whom he simply adored is a long one, and you can find not a few producers scattered through his memoirs that he thought weren't bad sorts. And as for wife, children and grandchildren, the men he flew with in the war, the crews that worked with him picture after picture, he is downright sentimental about them in a way that the other directors—none of whom was ever called "Wild George" or "Wild Alfred"—never were when our cameras were around.

Which is not to say that "Wild Bill" is a fraud. He bristles with temper and temperament. But the crust on this crusty old gentleman is not very thick, and underneath it there is a large dollop of marshmallow in the left chest cavity. Moreover, both the colorful anecdotes about his own outbursts of temper and his sentimentality are, I would guess, diversions designed to distract us from the tempered-steel spine of his character. He loves talking about the camaraderie of the Lafayette Escadrille, and about the heroic things he saw others do, and about the beauty he found in the skies above France, but the stories he tells about himself tend to be about screwing up. I don't know exactly how he won his medals in that elite squadron. Similarly, though he uses a long and dangerous illness that threatened his life about a decade ago as a sort of framing device for his recently published autobiography, *A Short Time for Insanity*, and though he is quite open about the pain he was in, he minimizes the difficulty of his long fight to free himself from addiction to the painkillers that were prescribed for him. In Bill Wellman's code, a man makes light of bravery if he talks about it at all.

It has been good knowing him, not merely because he is a fine companion, an open, funny, warm, eccentric human being, but because he makes you realize that, though Hemingway and the novelists who followed him and the movie-makers who followed them turned the "code hero" into a literary archetype, that stylization was based on a kind of American man who really existed in the early years of this century. It's no wonder that Bill—and Howard Hawks—tended to make movies about the type. To them there was nothing literary about it. It reminded them of their friends and of good times gone by, and was therefore congenial to employ in their work.

Bill's marriage to Dorothy Coonan has turned out to be one of the great true-life romances of Hollywood. I think Bill loves Dotty so deeply because after four unsuccessful marriages she saved him from becoming that self-parody that so many men of his breed became as their youth faded and as changing times rendered their unique gifts less appreciated in our society.

GROWING UP

I was born in a fourposter bed in Lyndon Place in Brookline, Massachusetts, and my poor mother had a very tough time with me because I have such a big head. In high school I was a good athlete: I was shortstop in the ball club, and I was quarterback on the football team, and I was rover and captain of the hockey team and we won the New England championship. Rover is the lightest, the fastest skater and the dirtiest player. And a very dear friend and I used to borrow cars at night. You know, there was the Stutz Bearcat and the Mercer. We always brought them back, but we were caught bringing one of them back and I was put on probation for six months and had to report to the probation officer of the city of Newton, who happened to be my own mother. That was enough to make me realize that things were not so hot in Boston. So I then tried selling candy. The candy had the frightful name of Fish's Green Seal Chocolates—but anyway I worked for this company and they told me to go up and down the lines of gals that were packing and eat as much as I wanted to, which I did. For three days I would eat candy, and I haven't been crazy about candy ever since. And I went out on the road, never sold a pound. Worked for a cotton belting company, belting that was supposed to take the place of leather belting in machinery. I never sold a yard of that. My brother was big in the wool business, so he got me in that line and sent me down to Philadelphia, which was a frightful mistake. They put me on the road, and I never sold whatever the hell the term is, a pound or whatever you sell wool by. Then I went to work in a lumberyard, the Bucket Lumber Company, in the middle of winter in Waltham, Mass. And I was a lumper and I was very good at it. The lumper is the guy that takes the lumber and carries it over to a man named a piler, who is piling it. I didn't have to use my brain. Used to crawl in—two of us in a freight car—and unload South Carolina pine flooring. You started on your belly [near the roof] and you ended standing up. All of these things I did beautifully and I was a big success in the lumberyard.

But then there was a man named Earl Overton, whom you can look up. He was one of our early fliers and he was flying out of Waban, which was very near Newton Highlands. And I used to fiddle around his airport. He had one flying machine. He'd fly over every once in a while. And I got to know him and he gave me two flights and that's all I needed. Then I had to be a flier. My dad didn't have enough money for me to become a flier in the regular way, so I went into a war to become a flier. I joined the Lafayette Flying Corps. That wasn't easy, but one of my uncles, Francis Wellman, was a big lawyer who wrote *The Art of Cross-Examination*. He got me in, so that I got to Paris and joined the Foreign Legion and became a second-class soldier. And then from there on you became a flier.

THE GREAT WAR

It's a very tough thing to explain, and it really isn't talking about pictures, but when you're in the Lafayette Flying Corps, you join the Foreign Legion and then, if you're lucky, you're sent to Avborg—down in the south of France, the most frightful place I've ever been in my life. You learn the preliminary part of flying, and you never fly with an instructor—the instructor tells you what to do and you go and do it. If you pass that, you get your wings, you're a second-class soldier, but the minute you get your wings, they make you a corporal. And then you're a hell of a man. Then you go to Po, which is down on the borderline of Spain, to an old English hunting resort, one of the most beautiful places I have ever seen in my life, and they bring you in and the first thing they do, they take all your clothes off. You never see them again, because you're lousy. And then they completely scrub you so that you are absolutely clean. And you know, the strange part about it was, I was uncomfortable then. I was much more comfortable when I was dirty and lousy. But then they give you a uniform and you learn acrobatics. They show you what to do and you go up and do it. Now, there were six Russians that were just ahead of us, and they had a nurse with them, I think, and a man that could speak the language and understand everything. And we hated them. In acrobatics you're supposed to go to a certain altitude and then go into a vrie, a spinning nose-dive. Watch your altimeter and at a certain time you neutralize your controls and you bring yourself out of it. But one thing they insisted on is don't look out of the cockpit, not until you get used to this. You're supposed to do six of these dives. We watched the Russians and the six of them went up. The little fifteen-meter Nieuports were so cute you could almost say they were beautiful—wonderful stunting planes, you know. And we watched them go into their vries and we could see one, two, three heads stick out—and those three guys never came out of it. It was the most wonderful sight I've ever seen in my life. They dug a hole in the ground. We applauded—frightful thing, you know. But when I got up there, you can rest assured I kept my noggin in there until I got used to it. Then you can do what you want to. And it's really amazing.

They give you about two or three weeks of just going out and flying and doing whatever you want to. Then they send you to Plassie Belleville, which is just outside of Paris, and you sit there and wait until somebody gets bumped off in the sixty-six fighting groups, the fighting escadrilles, along the whole front. And if you're next in line, that's where you go. I was sent down in the south to the Black Cat group, very famous group. They didn't even know what an American was like when I came down. They were nice, but it was strange. And then one of the Frenchmen got killed and Tom Hitchcock happened to be the next in line. He was the great polo player. And Tom joined me down there and the two of us had a lot of fun and it was very exciting.

We did one historical thing. We had a man that takes care of two of you: they called him a réformé—lost an arm or a leg or half a face, but he was still doing what he could do. And this man had half his leg gone. He had a wooden leg and he used to be a great athlete and with that peg leg he took care of Tom and me, woke us up, got us to the field on time, did whatever was necessary. And this foot coming down the floor was almost the sound of fate, you know; you never knew what it was. One time very early in the morning he came down, and he'd nudge you with his wooden leg. If you didn't wake up, he'd tap you. He didn't tap you, he'd hit you. And you'd wake up damned fast, you see. And he told us the captain wanted us—something very important. Of course, Tom spoke French. So, we put our clothes on. We went back and all the pilots were there. There were fifteen pilots in the escadrille. And the captain—wonderful guy, he'd been an infantryman, he was a lousy flier but a great captain. And there were piles of pamphlets there and he started to talk about them and for the first time he really got excited and everybody got excited. It was fantastic. Didn't know what the hell they were talking about. Finally I said to Tom, "What the hell is it? Is the war over?" He said, "No, it's just begun. That's President Wilson's message to Congress. We're going to drop it in the front-line trenches. America's in the war." Well, then we went nuts, you know.

But then it changed, because as we went out, the captain was talking to Tom because Tom understood French and I was following behind. And I saw that they were taking out Tom's plane and mine. And I knew that we were going to be the heroes of this thing. After the captain had left him, I said, "What is it?" He said, "He thinks that we'd be insulted if he gave any of the other pilots the opportunity of dropping President Wilson's message in the front-line trenches." I said, "Look, to hell with him. I'm sorry. I love this patriotism, but he's got a hole in his head." You know, you get everything thrown at you but their helmets. Fifteen guys could do it quickly. He said, "Look, c'mon, we've got to do it." I said, "Okay."

We flipped for the half of our sector [each of us would take] and I won the flip, so I took the easy one, which was very lovely and quiet and no trouble. You couldn't get away with anything because the military outposts and the balloon observers were watching you. Well, the oldest soldiers they had [were in that sector] and I guess the oldest Germans, 'cause they were even fraternizing. And so I decided to give them a little alcoholic acrobatics. I went up in a loop and was going to throw the leaflets down. But when you get to a certain point, you have to cut that motor off or you won't have any wings left. Just before I was ready to cut it, something broke and the motor stopped. I didn't know whether I was going to land in Germany or in France. And I didn't have much time to make up my mind 'cause I was very close to the ground. Fortunately, I was going into France and I went in and lit just on a dime. You can't make much of a landing in no-man's-land, you know. And I hit it, went over, upside down in the third-line trenches and my belt was stuck. I couldn't get unloose and I knew they were going to put their equivalent of the one-pounders on me. They did. They started to edge in on the plane. And all of a sudden I saw this bearded guy with a knife in his hand, like a butcher knife. And he performed a minor appendectomy on me and released me and I fell in his arms and then we went and got safe and I think about a minute later they blew the plane to pieces.

I spent a couple of days with a guy that looked like—what's this wonderful football player that used to be on USC's great football team? Frank Gifford. He looked exactly like him, no beard, no nothing. And we celebrated, and people came in and he finally had somebody read him the message and it was wonderful. I was kissed by everybody in the whole god-damned brigade. I went out and shot a seventy-five into Germany. I forgot to call in and say I was all right. My poor mother heard that I was brought down and missing, and then finally I did call and the captain came over and got me. And we went out and showed him where it all happened and he congratulated me on landing with a bad motor. But I didn't tell him I was upside down when it happened.

Now, if you brought down a German, you'd get to Paris for ten days. You'd go to the Folies Bergère. It was just full of military and women of ill-repute, if you want to call them that. And it was a great place for fun, but it was sad because it was quick fun, you know, and you'd get sort of into that phase of not knowing whether you're going to be there tomorrow or the next day.

Now, you weren't frightened or scared, particularly. Sometimes you get in a spot in the air, you know, where . . . then you get a little worried, believe me. The best way I can explain it all, you learn an awful lot. You see your friends get killed. Dave Putnam, who I went to school with; Rankin Drew, Sidney Drew's son, who was in love with Anita Stewart, who was an old-time star who'd thrown him down. We loved him, but he was very quiet all during training, and when he got to the front he got into a dogfight, he dove into a German. He didn't shoot at all, he just dove into him. He killed the German; killed himself. Unusual and rather rugged way of committing suicide.

COMING HOME

When I was a kid Doug Fairbanks was playing at the Colonial Theatre in Boston in a thing called *Hawthorne of the U.S.A.* and he used to come down on Sundays to the Boston Arena and watch the hockey games and, for some reason or other, he asked to have me skate over and meet him and the people who were with him. So I did. I came over and he asked me to come backstage. I was only eighteen years old and I didn't even know what backstage meant. But I went backstage and met him and we became very dear friends. And then one time months later, when I was in the Lafayette Flying Corps and flying actively in the Chat Noir, the Black Cat group, I got lucky one day and the newspapers built it up as they always do and you'd have thought I had won the war, which naturally I didn't. And Doug sent me a cablegram which said, "When it's all over, you'll always have a job."

[A little later] I joined the American Air Corps. They got me to switch from the French to the American because they wanted two instructors over here. They made me a first lieutenant and they sent me down to Rockwell Field in San Diego, and I used to fly up [to Los Angeles] on the weekend and land on Doug's polo field. And that was my first insight to Hollywood. I met everybody, Mary Pickford, Harold Lloyd, Charlie Chaplin, you name them—all of them. I had a limp, and if the girl was pretty, very pretty, it was an exaggerated limp, you know, it helped a little bit. But anyway, when I did get out of the Air Corps, I went to Doug and he made me an actor.

Now, I don't want to speak disrespectfully of actors, but I became an actor in *The Knickerbocker Buckaroo* and they put on a frightful yellow makeup then. They put it on for me and I played this part with Doug. I didn't like it, but it was a way of making money that I'd never heard of before. And I unfortunately was married then—unfortunately for both of ourselves, I was married to Helene Chadwick, who was a very blossoming young star. And then I went from that into Raoul Walsh's picture *Evangeline* and I got four-weeks' guarantee and the first thing I did was to wade out into a very easy, very soft surf and take the leading lady in my arms and carry her in. I was [wearing a] white wig. I looked like a fairy and on the way in she smelled so nice, she was lovely, and I held her a little too tight and she liked it, so I went, as you might say, on the make. And she was kind of cuddling up and everything else. And suddenly I kissed her and I walked into a hole. And this beautiful little thing became a tigress, because she didn't know how to swim. And when she did come up, the only thing I could do was to cold-cock her and carry her in and deposit her at Raoul Walsh's feet. It happened to be his wife. So they fired me, you see.

Then I saw myself on the screen in *The Knickerbocker Buckaroo*. I sneaked into the Egyptian Theatre, I *think* it was the Egyptian Theatre, and saw the picture. And I was so frightful, really, to me, that I just stayed for half the picture and then I went out and vomited for no reason at all. I'd never done that—for no reason. And I decided then that I didn't want to be an actor. So I went to Doug and said, "Look, Doug, I don't want to speak disrespectfully of actors, but I just don't want to be an actor." He said, "Well, what do you want to be?" And I pointed to Albert Parker, who was the director, and I said, "I want to be him." I wanted to be a director because I had heard what he made. It was purely financial. So he got me a job as a messenger boy in the old Goldwyn studios.

[Doug was] wonderful, but I was sorry for him because I suddenly realized his life was not his own And any of the stars today or anywhere else, their life is not their own completely. And I think that's why a lot of them get into a lot of trouble. They go overboard and everything else because they do have to sign autographs, they do have to cater to the people that are supporting them. That's why I wanted to be a director, and when I became a director, I stayed behind the camera.

I had a row with Duke Wayne. I made three pictures with him, *Island in the Sky*, *Blood Alley* and *The High and the Mighty*, and in *The High and the Mighty* he suddenly wanted to become a director—he has that inclination. And I yelled, "Cut." And in front of a whole crew, which is a big mistake, I chose him. I said, "Look, you come back here behind the camera and do my job, and you're going to be just as ridiculous doing it as I would be going out there with that screwy voice of yours and that fairy walk and being Duke Wayne." And it quieted him down. And I meant it. And he behaved himself because he's a—sometimes—nice guy. And I doubt very much if I could be included in the sometimes-nice-guy category.

BEGINNING TO DIRECT

(*Bill Wellman's career as a messenger boy was brief. He was given a chance to direct, claims he did poorly, and was out of work for over a year until he got a chance as an assistant to a man named Bernie Durning, who specialized in action films.*)

We were inseparable. He made me—got me my chance to direct. Eventually. He had one problem—used to get drunk every once in a while and lay in bed for five days. On one of those days I took over and it gave me my chance.

You cannot believe—[Durning] had the first two teeth that were put on a delicate gold thing—you know this was years ago—and it looked like a beautiful dental bra, really, and he used to show it to everybody. We were making a picture with Dustin Farnum way out in Eureka and he lost it when he was scrubbing it—fell down the god-damned drain. And he called work off, and we got the company together—he used to have an organ and a violin and a cello that would play and get you to cry. The whole company came up and we took the plumbing off from the second floor down to the first, couldn't find it. From the first floor right down to the god-damned cellar and then if we didn't find it there we'd have to go out and start excavating in the street, which I can assure you we'd have done, and I stuck my head down and I took it out of the god-damned drain—the only bra bridge I've ever seen in my life. You can imagine what was down there, and I got it. That took the whole day. God damn, that was when pictures were fun.

(*Wellman's chance to move from assistant director back to director came on another Dustin Farnum picture*, The Twins of Suffering Creek.)

I don't remember it. I give you my word of honor. Can you imagine what it was, with a title *The Twins of Suffering Creek?* If I could remember that far back—good God, that's 1920. I remember that another one I made was *The Man Who Won.* I can't tell you a single thing about that, either. I'm sorry. I can't tell you anything about all the Buck Jones pictures I made except the one that was written by Frederic and Fanny Hatton called *Big Dan*, which was a beautiful story. But I made one with Buck Jones called *Cupid's Fireman.* You make all kinds of things, you know. And that, I think, is what gives you the background to eventually make some very lucky picture.

[After those] I got fired at the Fox studio because I went in and asked the old man for a raise. I was getting $250 a week and he raised me right out of the studio. He fired me for asking him for a raise. So then I had a tough time getting a job and I made a picture for the late Mr. Cohn, Harry Cohn, who was the big man at Columbia, and I'm one of the few guys that was crazy about him. He was a rough, tough guy, but he was a hell of a producer, I thought. And I made a picture for him in three and a half days and nights.* We stole long shots from pictures that he'd made, we put our scene, you know, in between them and made it look big, and it was a wonderful story. Ethel Wales and Tom Ricketts, two

* *When Husbands Flirt*, 1925.

character people, were the stars. Forrest Stanley was the leading man, and the leading lady, I can't remember her name except that she was Cohn's girl, and the sum and substance of the story was that the old man had taken a laxative and [the whole story is] his experiences from his home to his office. This is literally what the story was about. It was released in six reels and was a feature and wasn't a bad picture.

B. P. Schulberg was an independent producer then. He saw it. He and Cohn started a fight about me. They were fighting about a $50-a-week raise. And finally Schulberg gave me a $50-a-week raise as against what Cohn was going to give me, which was $35-a-week raise. So I took the $50. And then he had this sexpot, beautiful little gal, Clara Bow, and I went with Schulberg. Paramount then was in trouble, with a fight between Zukor and Lasky, and Schulberg came in there to take over the studio and he brought in Clara Bow, who was a sensation, and me, who was a problem and a question mark, you see. And the first picture that they gave me was a thing with Betty Bronson. I can't remember the name of it, thank God, but it had Betty Bronson and Ricardo Cortez.* Now Betty Bronson, you remember, played kid things beautifully. And they sent word down to me that they wanted me to put some sex in her. I sent word back, "You don't want a director, you want a magician." Peter Pan—that's what she was. She was a delightful little actress, but that's what she was, and, to make a long story short, when she tried to be sexy she looked like a little girl that wanted to go to the bathroom. Well, they saw the picture, it was pretty wretched, and they were going to let me go, but Schulberg fought for me and got *You Never Know Women*, with Florence Vidor, Clive Brook and Lowell Sherman, which was a very successful picture. Got the artistic award for the year.

Then they suddenly got hold of *Wings*, and since I was an artist and had been a flier, they gave me the picture to do.

WINGS

Now I had a producer and a writer to contend with, you see. And I got rid of both of them. The writer got rid of himself and I made the pro-

---

* It was called *The Cat's Pajamas*. Between it and *When Husbands Flirt*, Wellman made *The Boob* at M-G-M; it featured Joan Crawford under her original screen name, Lucille Le Sueur.

ducer realize that he'd better get in the cutting room because that was much more important than just sitting down and watching Wellman work. I was on one of my domestic holidays and this was my big opportunity and I was going to make that god-damn company suffer if it was the last thing I ever did. We're down in San Antonio, Texas, and they wanted me to do the dogfight and I wouldn't do it because there weren't any clouds there. To do the dogfight against a blue sky would be like photographing a lot of flies. I waited thirty-three days. They sent some of their envoys from the studio. One of them came down and I said, "I'll give you two choices. Either you go home or you go to a hospital." So he went home. Finally I got the clouds with this wonderful bunch of fliers I had, and we had a dogfight that still stands and I think it is just as good as the one I did with all the stuff that I had—the process backgrounds and everything else—in *Men with Wings*.

So I stayed with it and I stayed on it and they sent all the biggies, the money men—Otto Kahn, William Stralem, Sir William Wiseman. They came down when we were doing the big battle of Saint-Mihiel. We had an area there in Texas that looked exactly like it, and I'd rehearsed it and rehearsed it. For those days, it was big. I had sixty-five airplanes in the air. I had over a thousand men. We'd rehearsed the thing. Had the trenches, you know—and when you are in the Army, they dig the trenches to the right length. They don't let up on anything. And all I needed was sun. Right at the apex of the thing I had a camera platform with four levels—the third level was mine. I had a board that I pressed buttons on so that I could keep the barrage ahead of the troops, and I had rehearsed bits of business. And the thing had taken days—doing beautifully. But I couldn't get any sun. And suddenly I looked up . . . Now, I'd been watching sun breaking through clouds when I was a flier, and I just saw this thing breaking and I knew the sun was coming out. I called everything. The planes all came up and they were in their proper positions, the soldiers all got ready. The man who was the head of the thing came up and said, "What are you doing? You crazy, for Chrissakes? What are you going to do?" And I said, "I'm going to shoot a scene." He said, "But there isn't any sun." I said, "You get right back where you were. We're going to have sun." Took five minutes to do this scene, exactly five minutes. And all of a sudden [the sun] broke. It was beautiful.

I gave the word. You could have heard my voice in San Antonio. We started the thing and it was absolutely magnificent. And I gave orders for no one to come up where I was, because I didn't want to be disconcerted. Someone came up and spoke to me in the middle of the thing and I pushed the wrong button and I saw a couple of bodies fly up in the air and they weren't dummies. I kept on pressing buttons, but I said, "You son of a bitch, get off this thing, whoever you are, or I'll kill you." And he got off and I pushed the last one and it was over and the sun went right down. It was absolutely sensational. You won't believe it. The sun went down, it was all over. Bedlam. And all I did was to climb down and try to go to where I committed the error. Ambulances were going out—fortunately, the men weren't badly hurt. But they were hurt.

And there was one crazy bastard—I don't even know his name—one of the pilots. He came down and he went crazy. He flew so low he made lines of troops all fall down. The one thing I'd forgotten, which I shouldn't have, he had flown at the front. And he went absolutely nuts. And he smashed up. I went over. There he was with his arm in a bandage and he looked at me and he said, "Bill, I'm sorry." I said, "I understand. I should have warned you. I understand perfectly."

Now, they told me, "You know who kicked off the thing?" I said, "I don't know who the hell it was." And they said it was Otto Kahn. I said —I can't tell you what I said—"Bleep Otto Kahn." And that night, when I was taking a shower all alone, [it came over me]. I was only twenty-nine years old, and the whole burden of the thing was gone, I'd licked them. I knew I had a beautiful thing and I knew I was the only guy that could put it together. Because no one knew anything about it. They couldn't fire me. And all of a sudden I got lonesome loaded. Have you ever done that? All by myself. And then I said, "Oh, Jesus, this isn't doing me any good," so I went in to take hot and cold showers to try to sober myself up, and there was a knock on the door and I yelled, "Come in," and I went out with a towel around me, half loaded, and it was the three money men. I thought, "Oh, Jesus. But at least if they fire me, they're going to have five minutes that they'll never forget as long as they live." I said, "I'm sorry, you want a drink?" I said, "I'm a little loaded, but I can't help it." Otto Kahn, whom I became great friends with later, said, "I don't blame you, but all we want to say is we've got to go home, we're on our way back to New York, and you can have whatever you want for as long as you want it, you're a very, very wonderful man."

And with that they went out and I fell down on the floor and cried like a baby.

GARY COOPER MAKES AN IMPRESSION

I had to have a performer [in *Wings*] who played the veteran, who said goodbye to Buddy Rogers and Richard Arlen, who were a couple of kids, and went out and forgot his lucky piece—left it on the bed—[and then was killed in a crash]. As he said goodbye, he stopped at an entrance of the tent they were in. And he turned around and smiled and saluted them. Not a real salute, you know, but it had to be something that an audience would remember. Now, that is a tough thing to get. I must have seen at least thirty-five actors for the scene, and then suddenly I saw Cooper and he'd been in one picture. He'd played in a western with Colman—a very small part. So we signed him and I took him down to San Antonio and I kept him there all the time because I liked him. He was getting nothing. And I carried the tent around with me, wherever I went, in case I'd have to get to [the scene], and I never did get to it. I didn't want to because I was very fond of him and being in the picture as long as he was built him up; it made him important. And I kept him there until finally all the actors were gone and I had to do the scene, just the two boys and Coop. They were the last ones. And I called him up and he came up in my suite and we rehearsed it that night and then the next day [Wellman snaps his fingers] "Print" like that. It was all over. And he thanked me.

I went up and I took a shower. And as I came out, there was a knock on the door and I yelled, "Come in." And in came Coop, and he said, "Mr. Wellman, couldn't I do that scene over again?" I said, "Look, Coop, you're the only one who could get away with this in the whole troupe. I'd tell everybody else to go to hell. But you must remember this, let me give you a little lecture. I know my job. I'm your mirror. You're the actor. You don't know what you're doing. I do. I see it. I know it was good. It was great, or I wouldn't have printed it. But just because I'm interested, I'm curious, because of you." He was getting a little scared. "Tell me why you didn't like it." He said, "Well, in the middle of the scene, I picked my nose." I said, "Listen, you son of a bitch, you keep right on picking your nose and you'll pick your nose right into a fortune. And always back up. Never be the aggressor. Always back away from everything until you can't back any farther." And he did. And he became one of the greatest stars we've ever had.

WRAPPING UP *WINGS*

When I got back to Hollywood they had nothing to do with me. I went in, cut, figured out the picture, but they had forgotten to take up my option and for six weeks I worked for nothing. And I went to Myron Selznick, who was my agent, and said, "What do I do?" He said, "Just keep your mouth shut. Don't say a word. Finish it all up."

They previewed the picture in New York. They didn't invite me. They had thought they had a bust, they literally thought they had a lousy picture. It was sensational. Then Schulberg called me in to tell me how great it was, that he was sorry about this misunderstanding, the frightful things he'd said. I said, "Look, Mr. Schulberg, let's cut this crap out right now. You've forgotten to take my option up, I am not under contract with you." He said, "Oh, there must be some mistake." I said, "There isn't any mistake," and he called Mike Levy, who was a studio manager. They had those intercoms—they had to cut the thing off if they didn't want to hear his voice. And he said, "Mike, Wellman tells us that we didn't take up his option." "Well, you remember, Ben, you told me to—" and Schulberg cut it off. And I said, "Look, Mr. Schulberg, I have a guy named Selznick out here. If you want to talk to him, I know he'd love to talk to you and tell you what a great man I am." So I walked out. And then I heard the word come over to the secretary out there, "Send Selznick in." And Myron said, "Tell Schulberg I'm taking Mr. Wellman somewhere else. We've got other people that are interested in him." And when we went out I said, "Mike, you're crazy." He said, "Bill, will you just behave yourself? When I get through telling New York what he's done and what they've done, don't you worry." So about a week later he went in and signed me up a contract for seven years and I hate to tell you, and I won't tell you, what I got the seventh year of that contract. I never knew there was that much money—I jumped from $350 a week to $1500 a week. That was the first jump, the first year. And it went up in that way until the end of the seven years. Boy, I tell you, I put it in annuities and we squawked like hell because the government was taking ten percent away from us—no kidding. Can you imagine what it is now?

I think the thing I'm most proud of is *Wings*. Those were the days, if you had a big road show, it was really a road show. You'd take a theater over and the orchestra would come up, you know, and play. And you'd see a news weekly and a two-reeler of some sort and then the big picture would come on. And then you'd go out in the middle of it and smoke and have a drink or something and come back and finish it. And I got a screwy idea that if the picture could just enlarge itself as the dawn patrol took off, it would be something unforgettable. And, by God, Roy Pomeroy* did it. He really did it. I don't remember if it's on it now or not, but that's the way it originally was. And we had the sound effects—guys were behind the screen, you know, they saw the thing cockeyed. TRRRRRR—the scream of a guy that went down and all those kind of sound effects and the orchestra playing. And if it wasn't an orchestra, it was a magnificent organist. Once in a drunken moment with Hal Skelly** years ago, I said, "Look, someday these god-damned pictures are going to talk. They've got to. They have a phonograph, no reason why they couldn't." Tried once to synchronize my voice with a guy on the phonograph just for fun to see if I could do it.

When we first started [sound], the booms were camouflaged. They hung from chandeliers or something, you had to get your action underneath there. That burned me up—you can't make a picture that way. You've got to have some flow. So I came in and I said, "I got news for you sound men this morning. I'm moving that god-damned mike." And I got my grips, got me a big high ladder and went up and took [the mike] and put it on the end of a broomstick. And I moved it and it worked. And that was the first. Overnight it changed our studio. They got booms and they got all kinds of things.

* Head of the trick department at Paramount at the time.
** The actor best known for his stage performance in *Burlesque*.

ON TO WARNER BROTHERS

(Wellman did not stay the full seven years on his Paramount contract. By 1931, four years after Wings *was released, he was at Warner Brothers, where he made one of the most famous films—containing one of the most famous scenes—of the time. That was* The Public Enemy.*)*

There's a man named Darryl Francis Zanuck who was a great producer at one time, and I worked for him and I never called him Darryl. I can tell you all kinds of experiences I've had with him. I admired him very much, and I liked him, and I thought that when he was active he probably was one of the greatest reportorial producers. You understand what I mean? He could take a headline in a paper and make a picture faster than anybody in the business. I made a lot of pictures for him. And I'm going to tell you this because I said to myself, "Should you be out of character and be nice?" and I said, "No." So I'm not going to be nice. I'm going to be lousy about a couple of things because this burns me up. He has made I don't know how many pictures. Great pictures. I'm talking about Darryl Francis Zanuck. But why the hell he should pick out one bit of business out of all those pictures that he's made and say that he was responsible for Cagney pushing the grapefruit in Mae Clarke's face is something that I can't understand. He's like Babe Ruth striking out. So I want to tell you about this thing. And I want to read it for you. In the scene both Mae Clarke and Cagney were seated having breakfast. And in this [the script] they're walking around and at one point Kitty, that's Mae Clarke, says, "Maybe you've got someone you like better." And Tom stares ferociously for a second, then reaches over the table, picks up a half a grapefruit and throws it at Kitty's face and strides out. That is the way it's written. Now, whose idea it was to *throw* [not mash] a half a grapefruit at Mae Clarke I don't know. But I would bet it's Bright and Glasmon,* the two writers, or Harvey Thew, who wrote the script. I can assure you it wasn't Zanuck and I don't think it was me. But it might have been. However, it's in the script [that way].

---

* John Bright and Kubec Glasmon were given "original story" credit on screen. Thew, who apparently did a "polish job" on their script, was billed under them and given an "adaptation" credit.

I was married then to a very beautiful girl who was an aviatrix. That shows you how crazy I am. Two fliers marrying one another. It's like committing murder. She was beautiful, and whenever we had an argument she had a wonderful way of handling it. This wonderful, beautiful face became like a sculpture. There was no movement in it at all, it just was beautiful and dominant. Just quiet. And it stayed that way for two or three days and that's a frightening thing to have to overcome, you know. You go absolutely crazy. And many a time when we had breakfast and we used to have grapefruit, I wanted to take that grapefruit and mash it in her face just to make her change just for a minute. Just to do that, I'd be completely happy. But fortunately this sequence came and I said, "Oh, baby, I can get rid of it here. I won't do something that will cost me money," so I did it, and Mae Clarke became the recipient of the half of the grapefruit. That's the story of that part of *The Public Enemy*.

The other part that I'd like to tell is this. I was met by these two writers, they were druggists in Chicago.* They were there on the lot and I was going to lunch and they came up to me and introduced themselves to me. And they seemed like nice guys and they said, "Look, we got a story and we want you to read it. Called *Beer and Blood*." That was the title: *Beer and Blood*. And they told me about the neighborhood that their drugstore was in. I said, "Come on and have lunch with me." So they did. I said, "Fine, I'll read it and let you know." I went right back to the office 'cause I was cutting on a picture, and I read it and I went crazy about it, so I immediately went to Zanuck and I said, "Look, I got the best title, *Beer and Blood*." I told him the story. "I've got the script, it's wonderful." "Bill, I can't do another one, I just did *Little Caesar* and *Doorway to Hell*, I can't. Tell me why I should do it." I said, "Because I'll make it the toughest one of them all." He said, "Okay, you got it."

When we got all ready to shoot, Eddie Woods was the lead. Cagney was playing the second part. Eddie Woods was engaged to marry Louella Parsons' daughter. Now, Louella Parsons I despise, but she was a big figure, you've heard of her, at that time, and I guess this meant something. I don't know. Anyway, we did two or three days' work and

---

* John Bright and Kubec Glasmon were not actually druggists, but they had clerked in a Chicago drugstore.

Zanuck was in New York and I didn't look at the rushes till the weekend. But when I finally looked at the rushes, I said, "Good God, we've got the wrong guy in the wrong part." It was so evident, so I went into his [Zanuck's] office, got him on the long-distance phone and told him. And he said switch, and we did. I put Cagney in the lead, and that made one of the biggest stars we've ever had. These are the things that happen in pictures that are unbelievable. Eddie Woods [took] the other part and he was great. But Cagney was the one who was wonderful. And when he realized that here was his chance, it was a great performance.

Another thing about it—Mike Curtiz, the director, and [Jack] Warner and Zanuck and I went to the preview of *Public Enemy*. First preview. And it was a smash. But the last scene* Warner said, "You've got to cut it out, it made me sick. It'll make everybody sick." And Zanuck fought for it, and I fought for it. But Zanuck was the one—Zanuck was a tough little guy, don't kid yourself. And my fellow director was smoking a cigar. And Warner turned and said, "Mike, don't you agree with me?" Mike said yes. Zanuck hauled off, knocked the cigar right down his throat. I'm not kidding. That's what made pictures [in those] days. They don't do that any more. And, by God, it scared Warner and we had no argument about it, it stayed in the picture. He hauled off and let him have it. I said, "I can love this guy, I don't care what he does from now on," and that's a true story of *Public Enemy*.

A STUDIO ROMANCE

Most women don't want to work with me, you know, because I wouldn't let them wear makeup. They said, "What'll we do?" I said, "Make up the way you would if you were going to go out and have lunch with someone." "But then my lines will show." I said, "You're damn right they'll show. It's a little bit of character." There's no character in these models. Honestly and truly, I look at models and it makes me sick. You

* Where Cagney—dead and bound in grotesque bandages—is delivered to his family's home and propped against the front door. When his brother (Donald Woods) opens the door, the corpse Cagney falls into the parlor—a shock ending to his shocking criminal career.

know, they probably got the passion of a pelican—these faces that are made up and there's nothing about them that suggests good strong legs and freckles like my lovely wife. Beautiful gal with freckles. If it hadn't been for Dotty, my wife, I know I wouldn't be here. Whether I'd be in jail or in a home or dead I don't know—it would be one of the three. Because we've been married for forty years and she was only nineteen years old when I married her. And that [Walter] Winchell, great pal, he took a picture of each one of my wives and over their heads he put the amount of money that I had paid—for our divorce settlements. And they earned every dime they got, I'm being very honest with you. And over poor Dotty's head, nineteen years old, they put a question mark. And the question mark is still there and that was forty years ago. But she absolutely, literally housebroke me, and she had some rugged times, she was wonderful. She was a magnificent dancer, a leading dancer of the Busby Berkeley chorus. She was the one that Berkeley would say, "Take a bunch over there and show them what I mean," and she'd do it. And she was the only one that didn't have a contract. Now, I never went on a Berkeley set. I used to have some drinks with Berkeley off scene— Berkeley was a wonderful director. I never went on a Berkeley set, but one day this little freckle-faced thing skated by me on roller skates. It was Dotty and I took a look at her and I finally went on the Berkeley set.

There were all kinds of gals that were mixed up with everything, and Berkeley said, "Gee, what are you doing here, Bill?" And I said, "I want to meet that little freckle-faced girl over there." And he said, "Dotty Coonan?" I said, "I don't know her name." He introduced me to Dotty and I said, "I'd like to take you to dinner, how do I ask you?" She said, "You just did ask me." "Well," I said, "will you go?" She said, "No, you're married." I said, "Now, wait a minute, I'm going through that horrible year period that you have to wait for before you can get the final decree." She said, "Well, when you get it, you come and talk to me." She wasn't kidding.

Later on, I was making a Dick Barthelmess picture. I had a set, I was all ready to go—we were going to start in about two weeks. And I opened the big door there, because it was right opposite where Dotty and all the girls were. And I just waited for her to come out, and she did come out and I chased her. She was on roller skates again. They were doing a roller-skate number, and she went in the executive building and I chased her down there and she ducked into the ladies' room. And I sat down in the corridor and waited for her. She finally came out and I said, "Look, why are you being so nasty about it, give me a chance, will you? For God sakes, you hardly know me, invite your mother or all the Coonans, I don't care, but let me take the whole bunch of you to dinner. Just give me a chance to make your life miserable." And she finally said, "You can meet me at seven o'clock." And I met her at seven o'clock and it was the first dinner we had of, I don't know, thousands of dinners. It was as if we'd been dining together for a long time. Wonderful romance. And she didn't want to act. She hates it. I finally got her to play that little girl in *Wild Boys of the Road* because she looked like a boy, and she was wonderful in it. In England they absolutely went crazy about her when they saw her. And then I got her to do one more thing in *The Story of G.I. Joe*. But that's all, she said no more.

When I asked her to play the part [in *Wild Boys*] I told her, I said, "Look, I've looked at all the girls that they've got and I couldn't find the girl I wanted." I wanted a girl that had beauty and still had boyishness about her and an athletic something about her and still had a softness about her. A tough thing to get and I said, "You've got it, Mommy. You're not as pretty as these girls, but you're prettier to me. The freckles, you've got long black hair and you're built where it should be and got good strong legs, you, to me, are absolute perfection and you'd make a wonderful-looking boy, from a girl's standpoint." Well, I talked her into it and she did it beautifully.

Now, they all accused me of doing something [in *Wild Boys*] that the Russians had done.* And I never even saw their pictures, nor have I ever seen them. Or heard anything about it. I don't know what the hell they were talking about. I didn't write the story, Zanuck gave it to me. He said, "I'm not sure of this, Bill, do you think you can make a picture of it?" I said, "I can make a great picture." And it was very successful. That's all I can [ever] say to myself. For instance, it was well written. You can't make a picture unless you've got beautiful writing, I don't care who you are. Then you got to get a hell of a cameraman and a guy who likes you and you like him and he knows how you want things. He's your right arm. And I think we counted in a hundred pictures we could

---

* Nikolai Ekk's *Road to Life*, the first sound film made in the Soviet Union.

just remember twelve cameramen. I had Archie Stout as long as he lived, almost. And I had Bill Clothier until I quit. And every single one of them were my right arm. They are—because they photograph what you're thinking. And I've had all the best, they're really wonderful.

ON AUTHORITY AND SIMPLICITY

I had a reputation of always knowing what to do, always knowing what I wanted to do. Which, of course, is a lot of baloney, because I didn't. But George Chandler was a very dear friend of mine and he played in thirty-six of my pictures—he played everything from the stone-faced messenger boy in *A Star Is Born* to that crazy husband with Ginger Rogers in—what was the name of the thing?—*Roxie Hart*. And we had an understanding whenever I got stuck I'd give him a high sign and he'd do something that would give me an excuse to lose the temper that was well known. And then I'd call a coffee break and go into my office and work like hell and straighten it all out. And this happened time after time.

He'd do anything. He'd miss his lines or he'd tell a lousy story in the middle of the thing or he'd do something that would give me a good chance so I could put him where he should be and all within laws and everything else and it was wonderful. And if he wasn't on a picture, I resorted to a cameraman and *he'd* do something that would burn me up and it was a great help. And then I fooled actors, too. I always did camera rehearsals. That was number one with me. Rehearse it until I got it right, get it built up and then take a camera rehearsal and say, "Fine, now is that all right?" [If the actor didn't like what he'd done, I'd say], "Great, we'll do it again." Then we'd do it again and he'd straighten himself out, but I'd print the camera rehearsal. Now, George Stevens is exactly the reverse. He'd take a thing over and over and over again and go and look at them all. I printed two takes, one to see and the other one in case something happened, you know, in the lab. I couldn't see a thing over four or five times—I'd get absolutely screwy, I wouldn't know which was the better take or anything else. I'd seen enough and done enough to know what I was doing.

Some of these directors take four- or five-walled sets. They take one side out; when you get through shooting that, you put that side back in and go around and do the reverse on it. How the hell are you going to cut them? You've got guys going in from left to right on one thing and you come back and they're going in right to left. It's going to be awful tough. They're going to meet and bump into each other. It's going to be very funny. But some of the directors do that, really. I don't know whether they do it today. If they gave me a four-sided set, I couldn't choose.

I bet you can't guess how much footage I had on *Public Enemy* that wasn't in the picture. Zanuck told me this. I didn't believe it. Three hundred and sixty-some-odd feet that was not in the picture. Now, that's shooting the picture pretty close to what you want. I didn't do that all the time, believe me, but I knew what I wanted—you take the long shot, your principal shots, you visualize what you want, where you want to come in, whether you want to come in to a medium shot or whether you want to get a shot of something different or a close shot. Close shots in my pictures you'll find are very sadly missing. Because to me a closeup is an exclamation point. And if you don't use it for that, then you've lost it, but if you use it properly, it's a great thing from a directorial stand-point because then it means something. You use closeups to bolster a sequence, to get a point over. Cut in to a closeup and it means something. Some kid came to one of my kids and I heard them talking some months ago. A girl was telling about one of the pictures she'd been in in TV and she told how good it was because of the number of closeups she had. And I couldn't believe it. I interrupted. I said, "You mean that your performance is valued by the number of closeups that you get?" "Yes, that's what it is on TV." I said, "Well, thank God I wasn't in TV." And yet they have to have, I suppose, an overload of closeups because it's such a little screen.

Jack Ford called me up—this was years ago. [In the 1920s at Fox] he was directing Tom Mix pictures and I was directing Buck Jones and when he got through with his company they'd come over and I'd make the Jones picture, and when I got through they'd go back and make a Mix picture. Well, this is a long time after that, some years ago, twenty years ago. He called me up once very late at night. He said, "Listen, you idiot, I just saw your last picture and you saw my last picture, didn't you?" I said, "Yeah, what was it?" Well, we told each other what the pictures were and I said, "What's wrong?" And he said, "We're beginning to get too tricky. Moving the camera too much. You're doing it more than I am. So let's stop it. Let's do what we used to do. Make the picture the simplest, easiest, nicest, most quietest, most natural way you can make it and stop all this stuff. Do you agree with me?" I said, "One hundred percent." And I've never been on a dolly since. Truth. He had the same feeling.

Another thing—you said you'd seen a lot of my pictures. Did you notice there's an awful lot of rain in them? It was always raining every picture. I don't know why. But when you see Jack's pictures, it's all wind. You know, when you see people come out, wind is blowing the hair. He's wind crazy and I was rain crazy. It's an odd thing, yet I don't remember doing it. But they brought that to my attention in London* and then they named the pictures in which there'd been rain sequences and, God, they were right. Yet I don't remember [consciously doing them] except that I do love the rain. I love the rain especially if you're in love with someone. A rainy night in love is great. That'll encourage anyone, be free of all your troubles. There's a certain romance, to me, about rain, and there's tragedy, and coldness and everything.

A STAR IS BORN AT M-G-M

(*In 1936 Wellman moved briefly, and unhappily, to Metro-Goldwyn-Mayer, remaining there just long enough to get into trouble.*)

When I was working at Metro-Goldwyn-Mayer, the director, I can't remember his name, on one of the Tarzan pictures got sick. And Eddie Mannix** called me up. He's a very good friend of mine. Eddie said, "Look, I hate to ask you, Bill, but will you take over for me because we're right in the middle of it and there is nobody else who can get in and

---

* Where Wellman recently attended a retrospective of his work sponsored by the British Film Institute.

** A production executive who functioned mainly as Louis B. Mayer's chief assistant and troubleshooter.

do it." I said, "Oh, shut up, I'll do it." And I did. I went in there and it was the Tarzan with the little midgets, you know. Well, I can't remember the name of— Oh, God, what was the—not the gorilla, not the monkey—what's between them? The chimpanzee. Oh, what was his name?* I don't know, and Johnny Weissmuller was Tarzan and Maureen O'Sullivan was the girl and the other girl was the girl that married Colman and I can't remember her name**—she is wonderful. Tall, stately.

I never had so much fun in my whole life. It was absolutely fantastic. The little chimpanzee, you know, was taught to spit at people if Johnny didn't like them. They let all the people come in to see the Tarzan set because, you know, what the hell—they didn't mind. So anybody that was there, and Johnny would take the little guy along and he'd give him a nudge and he'd spit and he could hit a dime. And the little-bitty people that we had in the thing I fell in love with. I fell in love with the whole thing, and when it was all over—and I did a good job on it too because I loved it—I went in to Mayer and I said, "I want to do the next Tarzan." He said, "What are you talking about? It's beneath your dignity." I said, "To hell with it. I haven't got any dignity." And I begged him to let me do another Tarzan and he wouldn't let me do it. I never had so much fun making a picture. God, swinging across the thing on vines and doing all these silly things. I did all of them. Fell in the god-damn pond that they had and everything. Had more fun than I've ever had in my whole life and they would never let me do another one.

The story of *A Star Is Born* I wrote because I had gotten in wrong with Louis B. Mayer. Mayer's secretary called me up and said that he wanted me and Woody Van Dyke***—you've heard of Woody, one of the finest directors we've ever had. Very good pal of mine. Said Mr. Mayer wants you and Woody Van Dyke up in his office and no one could find Woody Van Dyke. Didn't know where he is. I said, "Yeah, I can find him." Woody was asleep on the couch in my office, getting over a hangover. So I woke him up and said "Woody, one of the Napoleons wants to see us," and he said, "Which Napoleon?" and I told him

* Cheeta.
** Benita Hume.
*** W. S. Van Dyke directed, among other films, *Trader Horn, The Thin Man, San Francisco, Journey for Margaret*. He was, by reputation, the fastest director in Hollywood, earning the nickname "One-Take."

and he said "Oh—" a four-letter word. We went up to Mayer's office. I wondered what the hell the big guy wanted us for. And it's the kind of an office that when you get up and the secretary opens the door, you don't hear it open. And then you suddenly come into this mammoth office—you know, it's a good place to have mothers' meetings or you could even put wings on it and fly it. It's a hell of a place to chase dames in and it was soundproof and then there's this huge desk and he was going over figures.

Finally he stopped finger figuring and he said, "I want to tell you something. We're going to give you two directors that are God-given talents great exploitation. You're going to have exploitation such that no director's ever had because I'm going to try to shame these other directors to be able to make pictures as fast and as competently and for the amount of money that you two do. And maybe we can shame them into it." And then he said, "So I'm your general and you're my two sergeants." Well now, that's not a thing to say to a guy who's been in the Foreign Legion, the French Air Corps and the American Air Corps and, thank God, got out of the thing with the brains still in my head where they should be. So I got up and walked over and I said I'd been a second-class soldier in the Foreign Legion, I'd been a corporal and a sergeant in the French Air Corps and I asked for and got a complete divorce from anything like that. And on top of which you hired me for my so-called talent, but if you hired me for my personality, you're behind the eight ball, and if you think you're hiring me for a fink, you're nuts. So old Van Dyke woke up and he started to clap and we walked out of that office and then we were in the doghouse.

Now, to show you what these guys will do, I was getting a tremendous salary, but Mayer wouldn't let me make another picture. He kept paying me every week. This went on week after week. So finally I made a deal with Eddie Mannix. I said, "Look, Eddie, give me a break, I'm going crazy. Let me write. If it's good, you buy it from me. If it isn't, I keep it." So he did. I wrote a couple of things and I got a young writer that was in the so-called college of writing there at the studio, named Bob Carson.* Didn't know how to write a script, but he could at least do the tough work, you know. And I wrote a couple of things that we

---

* Robert Carson would later go with Wellman to Paramount, where he wrote *Beau Geste* and *The Light That Failed* for him. Still later he would become a writer of popular novels and nonfiction works.

did sell and that they did make—one of them was *The Last Gangster*. I didn't do it, but they did it. And I wrote *A Star Is Born*. They didn't like it at all. So then Myron, on the outside, had been doing his business and he got me out of there because his brother, David Selznick, married Mayer's daughter Irene, who was a charming woman, really and truly, and a very brilliant woman. I was crazy about her. They let me go to David.

David Selznick I got along with. I got him his first job at Paramount and a year and a half later he was running the studio. I dared Schulberg and Bachman, those were the two men that were running it then, to hire a man with the name Selznick, 'cause they broke his dad. And I was very fond of his dad. I probably was the only good Irish pinochle player they'd ever known. I played pinochle with his dad until I became a great pinochle player. And I was crazy about him and I loved his mother. And Myron Selznick was my agent. I think I was his second client. He was the greatest agent of them all, and he hated producers. And David—I didn't make any pictures for David, I made them *with* him. And Dore Schary, until he let politics screw him all up, was a magnificent producer. He and I got along very well. We did *Battleground* together.

But when I gave David *A Star Is Born*, he said, "No, Bill, I don't like it. I'm sorry. But we're going to do the Ben Hecht thing* anyway. Irene and I are going to Honolulu for six weeks and when we come back we'll start working, and [meanwhile] you go play golf." I went to Irene and I told her the story, and she went crazy about it. I said, "I'll leave it," and so then I went and played golf. Six weeks later they came back and I got a call from David: "Come on over here. I've been thinking this all over, we want to do *A Star Is Born*." And that was the way it was done. Now, in his memoirs** he said he wrote it. He did like hell! He had a couple of guys come in here and they rewrote it and I rewrote it right back to the way it was, so it finished up just as it was. And that's the truth. [It was just based] on things that happened. John Bowers*** was living with a beautiful gal and he had a bad voice, a John Gilbert bad voice, and when he went into talk they said he was through. Bowers just took his shoes off and his bathrobe and swam out into the ocean—

---

* *Nothing Sacred.* See below.

** *Memo from David O. Selznick*, not a memoir but a collection of the producer's business papers.

*** John Bowers was a leading man in silent films.

committed suicide.* The scene of March being reprimanded by the judge**—word for word, that happened to me. And all these things were things from memory. To be very honest, I thought it was a hell of a story.

Well anyway, Jock Whitney was the man who was giving the money and David was making the picture. So it previewed and it was a success. When it was all over, the cards they got were complimentary, they applauded and applauded. But despite that, David said, "Look, it's all wrong. The first half is comedy and the second half is tragedy and nothing has ever been done like that that has been a success." I said, "I don't care how it's written, if you can do that with an audience it must be a good picture." So they said, "Well, we'll give you one more chance," And I said, "Where is this chance to be?" David, knowing all the places, said, "Long Beach." Now, that is not the Long Beach of today. That's the Long Beach that was full of sailors on a Saturday afternoon with their dames, half loaded, coming in to look at a picture like that. I said, "That's the cruelest way, but you know something? I think, despite that, I'm perfectly willing to go and preview it if you two bastards will come there and see it." And they showed it—the drunken sailors and their dames and everything else—and it was a complete success. It was wonderful.

Now, all of these things are the things that give a guy like me what is called a director's stomach, and unfortunately I still have it. If I were making a picture, I couldn't eat a meal. I was eating soft stuff, soft cereal, slept two or three or four hours a night, worked every night as hard as I was working when I was working shooting the picture. Just trying to think of some way of doing things differently.

BEAU GESTE

(After doing two pictures with Selznick, Wellman decided to try his hand as a producer-director, but says the former role started interfering with the latter and so abandoned the idea of performing both functions.

* Precisely what Norman Maine, played by Fredric March, did in Wellman's film.
** For drunkenness.

The first of these dual-capacity productions, Men with Wings, Beau Geste *and* The Light That Failed, *were made at Paramount.* Beau Geste *starred Gary Cooper in the title role, with Ray Milland and Robert Preston as his brothers, who join him in the Foreign Legion, where he is hiding to draw suspicion for a jewel robbery he knows was committed by a beloved aunt. Brian Donlevy played a sadistic sergeant tormenting the English gentlemen.)*

That was a rugged picture. You had to be tough. We're out on location in the middle of the desert near Yuma. Only men. We wouldn't allow a woman in the camp. At the beginning, I ran a bus to the house of ill-fame in Yuma, and the first couple of weeks it was packed. They were riding on top of it. But after they had been there for two or three weeks there was only one guy who would go there, an old stunt man. He was the only one, and he ended up burning it down.

Everybody slept in tents—four to a tent—except me. I had my own tent and office. I had to. But everybody hated Donlevy—because he lorded it over everybody. Everybody moved out of his tent. They wouldn't even sleep with the guy. Despised him. I've never seen a guy that could completely get everybody to dislike him as he did. Yet he was good in the picture, so I kept him right in. I wouldn't change him. And I made him behave himself to a certain extent.

Well, Milland hated his guts, and Milland is one of the toughest guys I've ever known in my life, believe it or not. He is an Englishman, you know, but he is a rugged guy. If I got into any trouble, I'd be glad to have Milland with me. And I've had some pros with me. Well, Milland discovered Donlevy was afflicted with this thing some people have, where when they see blood, they faint. Now, there was a scene in which he fenced with him, with a bayonet. And we had his [Donlevy's] whole chest covered with this thick thing so if Milland stuck the bayonet into him, he wouldn't be hurt. But Milland found out that part of Donlevy's arm and both sides were not padded. Now, Milland is an expert fencer. So we started the scene—he didn't let me know about this and I didn't find anything out until it was all over. They went into this scene and they got to the end of it, and Milland went through there and Donlevy saw the blood and he fainted. He fainted dead away. We sent him to the hospital and I think they took two stitches, it wasn't very serious, but he saw the blood and he fainted. That's all Milland wanted. Milland got drunker than anyone in the world ever got drunk celebrating that night. He had accomplished one of the biggest things he's ever accomplished in his life.

When Donlevy came back, Coop and Bob Preston, who is another wonderful guy, and Milland all were on one side of the fortress—I was doing scenes there when up came Donlevy in the car. Now, we'd all been looking for dames, but there weren't any around. But he found one somewhere. In the hospital or something. It was this beautiful-looking young nurse and he brought her up and they opened the door. And then he walked over to the other side and he gave her the glasses and he explained all the scenes, the big fight scenes and everything else. And all the guys were watching it, you see. No one ever said one word to him, nothing. It was just crushing—there was absolute silence. We just went on with the scene as if he weren't there. He got into his car, went down to his tent and she drove away. And then that night at the dinner—I got to say this because there was something big about him—he stood up and said, "Could I have the floor for a minute?" Everybody became silent. And he apologized. He said, "I apologize for everything. I'm very sorry and I really mean it and I hope that maybe you guys will accept me if I can be a regular guy for a change." And they all applauded. And he became all right. The three guys moved back into his tent and it was just wonderful.

THE LIGHT THAT FAILED

I'd refuse to see it again. Do you know the story—that Colman and I did not like each other? It is an odd combination—Colman and Wellman. Kipling—you know I'd never read it?* I got kicked out of high school, and I just read things that I was going to make pictures out of. I don't read any stories. They bore the hell out of me because I've done all of them. I can tell you exactly what the plot is going to be the minute I start reading, so why read it? Anyway, the memories [of this picture] are very unpleasant.

A girl came bursting into my office when I was working on the script

---

* *The Light That Failed* is the story of a popular Victorian artist whose eyesight begins to fail just as his career begins to prosper.

and she said, "Can you be Ronald Colman?" I said, "Don't be silly."
She said, "Well, I can be Bessie." And she said, "You can at least be
decent and try." And she had a little English accent, and I said, "Yeah,
I'll try." So I tried to be the best Colman I could and I read the scene
where he drives her half crazy. Ida Lupino—she played the most beautiful
scene in my office I've ever seen in my whole life. I said, "Where the
hell did you come from?" She'd been doing musicals, little lousy musicals. I took her right into Schulberg* and I said, "Here is our Bessie."
And I told him the whole thing and he said, "She's fine. She looks wonderful." Made her a star.

But Mr. Colman had another girl that he wanted, so he objected. He
came to me and said, "I don't like her." I said, "You don't even know
her. And I don't know this dame you want. I'll tell you what we'll do.
This I'd like to do. We both will go into Mr. Schulberg. If he agrees
with you, then you're doing fine. You've got your girl and you can get
yourself another director. I'm not fond of you. I don't want to make a
picture with you anyway and I know you don't want to make the picture
with me, so we might both of us come out on the right end." He said fine.
So we went in and I told Mr. Schulberg, "Mr. Colman can tell you his
story. I'm not going to tell it for him." He said, "I have a girl that I like
much better than the girl Mr. Wellman likes." And Mr. Schulberg said,
"Well, I'm very sorry, but Mr. Wellman is a very competent director
and he brought me this girl and I like her. And if you don't like her, I'll
sue you." Just like that, you see. Once in a while they would stick with
you, you see. So that's all. I got up and left and he left and that was it. He
didn't want to get sued.

Now, Colman is like Stanwyck. Stanwyck doesn't know only her
own part, she knows the whole script. Got one of these retentive
memories that is absolutely fantastic. So they were doing the big scene
where he [Colman] drives her [Lupino] crazy. And in the middle of
it he forgot his lines. It was where she was going absolutely hysterical—
you remember the scene. And I said to myself, "Wait a minute. Maybe—
maybe he was as impressed as I was. And I got to be decent about it." So
I said, "Okay. Too bad. If we do it again, can you get into it, Ida?" And

---

* This is the same Schulberg (father of the novelist, Budd) for whom Wellman
had worked earlier at Paramount.

she said, "Yes, if we do it quickly." So we started all over again, and I'm telling you the truth, got to the same point, he forgot the line. Well, that was a mistake. I said, "Okay, cut. All right, fellows. Take ten minutes." And I said to Mr. Colman, "Mr. Colman, will you come take a walk with me, please. To the next set." So I walked him over to the next set and I said, "Listen, you son of a bitch, I know what you're doing and don't you do it again. Because you've got a lovely face. It has to be in front of the camera. My face doesn't. Mainly I'm behind the camera. But I'm going to make a character man out of you if you don't behave yourself. And I'm going to give you one more chance." And I walked away from him. The ten minutes was up and we did the scene and she did it beautifully again and he did it beautifully. But it was Mr. Wellman and Mr. Colman from then on.

Now, I didn't let it influence my directorial chores, you know, because he was magnificent, a fine actor. Sometime later in the thing he had a long speech. I rehearsed it and then we did it. And while it was going on, I just put my head down and I listened to the most beautiful voice I've ever heard in my whole life. It is absolute magic. I don't know any other greater. And then it was all over and I yelled cut and, and they applauded it, the electricians and everybody else. And Mr. Colman said, "Well, what did you think of it, Mr. Wellman?" And I said, "I didn't see it." He said, "You didn't see it?" And I said, "No, no, I didn't see it. I knew what you were doing. And I just put my head down and I listened to the most beautiful voice I've ever heard in my whole life." And I walked off the set and left him with his mouth hanging open. And it was true, you see. But later on he was doing a radio series called *The Halls of Ivy* and do you know the heavy's name? Wellman. Really and truly, the heavy's name was Wellman. But then Frank Capra, a very dear friend of mine, had made a wonderful picture with him.* He brought us together. We finally got together and he married a girl that I was crazy about.**

* *Lost Horizon.*
** Benita Hume, with whom Wellman had made his Tarzan picture.

THE OX-BOW INCIDENT

No one would let me do *The Ox-Bow Incident*.* You know how I bought it? There was a producer at Paramount, when I was under contract there too, making the B-type of pictures. There's no need to mention his name. One of the few producers I kind of liked. And he got into some argument with a biggie, I don't know who it was, Zukor or Lasky or whoever the big ones were then, and they fired him. I admired him very much for it because I'd always got into arguments with those guys, too. And then some weeks later he called me up and said, "Look, Bill, I've got a story I've just bought written by a man named Walter Van Tilburg Clark"—who unfortunately died about a year and a half ago— "called *The Ox-Bow Incident* and would you read it and if you like it, would you like to do it for me?" I said send it over. So he sent it over to me and I loved it. I went absolutely crazy about it. And I called him up and said, "You got yourself a pigeon, have you got money?" He said, "Yeah." I said, "Who are you going to use in this picture?" He said, "I'm going to use Mae West." I said, "Now, wait a minute, maybe you haven't sent me the right story, what the hell are you going to do with Mae West?" He said, "I'm going to build a barbecue pit, a sunken barbecue pit, and when these poor tired cowboys come in, she'll sing them a song, you know, and give them something to eat." And I said, "Look, get yourself another director, I'm sorry. I just don't agree with you." He said, "I'm sorry."

About six months later Dotty and I went up to the old Arrowhead Hot Springs when it was great and he was there. And he was having trouble. I said, "You sold *The Ox-Bow Incident?*" He said, "No, I can't. No one will buy it." I said, "I'll give you"—the only time I've ever spent any of my own money in my own business—"I'll give you $500 more than you paid for it." He said, "You've got yourself a deal." So I paid him $6500 for that beautiful story. I came home with my wife, made her sit down, I read her the whole god-damned book. Right through from the beginning to the end. It took me almost all night long.

---

* *The Ox-Bow Incident* is about the lynching of three innocent men—strangers passing through a small western town—for a crime which turns out never to have taken place.

Left to right: Dana Andrews, Anthony Quinn (on the rocks) and Frank Conroy (in uniform) in The Ox-Bow Incident (1943)

Clara Bow driving to the front in Wings (1927)

Left to right: Gary Cooper, Ray Milland and Robert Preston on the set of Beau Geste

I was so crazy about it. I said, "Mommy, this can be the best that I've ever done." It wasn't, but it could have been.

I went to everybody that I'd made pictures for and made money, including David, Metro, the whole bunch. They all thought I was nuts. Now, Zanuck and I had a terrible beef two years before and we hadn't even spoken to each other. I probably made more pictures for Zanuck, I guess, than any director, and I called up the studio—he was at Twentieth Century-Fox. I called up his secretary, a rather old gal, and when I was working there I used to sneak her a drink every once in a while to find out what the hell was going on on the lot. I called her up and she said, "This can't be— Is this— Are you Bill Wellman?" I said, "Yeah." She said, "Well, you crazy bastard, what do you want?" I said, "I want to talk to your boss." She said. "You're crazy." I said, "Well, try it. Try it. Just call him." So she called him, and, by God, he spoke to me, said, "What do you want?" I said, "I've got the greatest story I've ever had in my life. I want to read it to you." He said, "Come on over." So I went over. Never mentioned any of the trouble, and we had a pip. Far bigger man than I was, would be, about the thing. I told him the story, he said, "It sounds great, give me the book." I gave him the book. He said, "I'll let you know." Three or four days later he called me up and told me to "Come on over, you've got yourself a picture." Said, "I don't think it'll ever make a dime, but it's something I want my studio to have. I want to have my name on it and I know you want to have your name on it. But you got to make two pictures for me sight unseen. At your price." I said okay, I'd do anything for it. One of the two pictures was *Buffalo Bill* and the other was that air picture—Preston Foster and that lovely gal—oh, Jesus—Gene Tierney, beautiful gal.* And so I had to make those two. They just gave me the script and I made them. I made them as best I could.

BUFFALO BILL

This has nothing to do with *Buffalo Bill*—the actual making of it. This, I think, was before that time. I had finished my allotted number of pic-

---

* The film was *Thunder Birds*.

tures to do and I was playing golf. Gene Fowler called me. Oh, yeah, it *was* long ago because [in] this neighborhood there were about two or three houses around. Dirt road out there and another house here, but the same six acres. I hate to tell you how little I paid for this whole thing I got now. But anyway the front acre, it was an acre there with those orange trees, I paid $3400 for the one acre. It was owned by an old lady in Pasadena and I went to buy it from her and she said, "What is your business?" And I said, "I'm a director in the motion-picture business." She said, "You can't have it, you can't have it, I hate everybody in the picture business." So I got my secretary to go over and buy it and then I bought it from *her*. Anyway, Gene lived a block up from here and he was my pal and Bill Fields and Greg LaCava* and all that wonderful group, they used to come down and play pool in my place down below, we used to have great talks, wonderful times. And Gene called me up and said, "Look, I want you to come up, you're not working, I've got something that we can do together." Now, Fowler was to me one of the most brilliant writers, but he hated picture writing. But he did a couple of very fine jobs and Zanuck would pay him immense money just for ideas. So I went up and Gene opened a drawer and he brought out a sheaf of papers on Buffalo Bill, the real Buffalo Bill, that he'd been saving and writing on for several years. And he said, "I want to write a story and make a picture on the fakiest guy who ever lived, Buffalo Bill." And, boy, I'm telling you, when we got into that thing, it was true. So we worked on it for almost three months, and we had half a script that was absolutely beautiful. And one day he called me up and he was loaded, and he says, "Come on up here." And I walked up to that place and said, "What's wrong?" It was in the winter and he had a lovely den, and a little fireplace was going there. He said, "Bill, you know, you can't stab Babe Ruth, you couldn't kill Dempsey, you can't kill any of these wonderful heroes that our kids, my kids, your kids, my grandchildren, your grandchildren, everyone else worships and likes. And that's what we're doing. Buffalo Bill is a great figure, and we cannot do it. What do you say, what do we do?" "Let's burn the god-damned thing." So early in the morning we got drunk and we put it in, page after page. And burned up three months of the most wonderful work I've ever done with a writer in my whole life. And he was right.

* The director. He specialized in comedy.

I should be ashamed of myself, but I didn't like the picture I finally made for Zanuck. Having been through this thing with Fowler, it was fakey. I loved Tommy Mitchell in it. And I loved the two girls. I thought the relationship of the Indian girl and the other girl* was very interesting. I tried to do the best I could with it, but when that poor little crippled kid at the end stands up and says, "God bless you, Buffalo Bill," I almost— I said, "Do I have to shoot this?" I went to Zanuck, I said, "Look, will you get someone else—will *you* come out and do it?" He said, "Remember we made a deal." I had to do it, and when I did it, honestly and truly, I turned around and damn near vomited because I think that's the fakiest thing I ever heard in my— Poor little crippled kid—"God bless you, Buffalo Bill." And then Zanuck told me later on it was the second-biggest moneymaker we've ever made.

Did you like the Indian fight in it? We were in a little valley—again I was on location. I can't remember where. Somewhere way off and there was a valley we were in and I could dam the stream coming in there and I wanted to get very shallow water in it, you see, spread over a wide acreage, because I could visualize, as a cameraman could, when those charging Indians come in and the cavalry from the other side and they fought in the water. And it was absolutely brilliant. But, we had the flash floods and they washed me out three times. That cost a lot of money, you know, to dam up the stream. And the studio called me up and said this is your last time, it's too expensive. So I did it once more and this time we just did get it. And the next day they had another flash flood and washed it right out.

A THEORY ABOUT ACTORS

This is rather silly maybe, but it's a true thing. An actor looks into a mirror all the time. Says his lines to this guy [in the mirror]. Makes himself up in front of this guy. He looks and studies his face to see which is the best side to be photographed, and he does this day after day after

---

* Played, respectively, by Linda Darnell and Maureen O'Hara. The former has some speeches about the unconscious racism of the whites that were remarkable for the time (1944). The title role was played by Joel McCrea.

day. And one of two things has to happen. Either he learns to hate that son of a bitch he's looking at or he falls in love with him. He usually falls in love with him. Now, a girl can look into a mirror, you know, because that's what they should do, fix themselves up to look pretty, but when you do it day after day after day, picture after picture after picture, something's got to happen. Is that silly? They don't like it when I tell them that. I tell that to a lot of them and it's true. Now, I can't shave in a mirror—I shave in the shower. I look in the mirror when I comb my hair, but I comb my hair. But they talk to this guy. I talk to myself all the time, but I'm not seeing myself.

I can name two of them I was very fond of. And I have not been very fond of actors and they're not very fond of me, so it's sort of an even-steven thing. I was crazy about Bob Taylor. I think Bob Taylor's probably one of the finest men I've ever known in my whole life. And he was an actor. And he was probably the handsomest one of them all—at least that I know of. He had no trouble that way. And the other one is Joel McCrea. He used acting, you know, as a way to make money. Joel McCrea is a very, very wealthy man—I don't know what he's worth, he's worth millions. And he's a rancher, and he's just not an actor and, strangely enough, Bob Taylor wasn't either.

THE STORY OF G.I. JOE

I love it. I love the man who wrote it—Ernie Pyle. Let me tell you—I got to tell this right. I was home here doing something, I don't know. And the doorbell rang and I opened it and a little guy said, "My name is Lester Cowan, I'm a producer." Well, the minute he said that, you know, he's not very welcome because there's never been a producer in any of the homes I've ever lived in. I said, "Well, what do you want?" I didn't ask him in. He said, "Well, I'm going to do Ernie Pyle in *G.I. Joe*." I said, "Well you're very lucky." He said, "Well, can I come in?" I said, "Yeah, for a little while." He came in and sat down. I said, "What do you want?" He said, "Ernie and I have been talking about it, we want you to direct it." I said, "Now, wait a minute, you're talking to an old broken-down old flier who hated the infantry." Because in the war I was in, the

German infantry would do everything but throw their god-damned helmets at you and the French did the same thing, because they thought you were back living the life of Riley. We lived in little stinking rooms and there weren't many girls around. There was one girl for this whole crowd, you know, and she wore wooden shoes, and she did all the laundry and you knew if you were a one-shoe man or a two-shoe man. But, anyway, what was I talking about? Infantry. So I said, "I hate the god-damn infantry and I don't want to have anything to do with them and please thank Mr. Pyle, but not for me." So he left.

Another couple of weeks and the bell rang again and I opened it and there was this silly guy again. I said, "What's the matter with you?" This time I really got mad at him. I said, "Get the hell out of here." And I slammed the door so hard it almost cracked the ceiling. And then he came back the third time. This time it was in the middle of the summer and he had his arms full of presents for my kids. Anyway, I said, "Get out of here, I don't want my kids to have any more presents. Good God, I have enough trouble not spoiling them as it is." So he left. And then I thought to myself, "Life is a crazy, lousy trick. If I was a kid, I wouldn't have done that."

The phone rang a couple of days later and it was Ernie. He said, "Look, Bill, please come down and be my guest at Albuquerque." I talked to him and I said, "Ernie, I'll come, but I'm not going to do it. I'll come to see you because I want to see you. I'd like to talk to you. I don't like your god-damned infantry, but I want to talk to you and I want to meet you." So I went down to Albuquerque—train or a plane, I've forgotten. And there he was to meet me in his car. He said, "You don't remember me, do you?" I said, "No, Ernie, I don't." He said, "I came to see you when you were doing *A Star Is Born*. I was working for a very small string of newspapers and trying to write something that was a little different and not doing very well. And I got to wondering how an old flier who made *Wings* was doing a thing like *A Star Is Born*. I got very curious and I got them to pay my way out there and I interviewed you and you were very noncommittal and very polite. When I left I saw a sigh of relief and I didn't get very much of a story on it, did you read it?" And I said, "Well, yes, I remember, I did read it. It was sent to me." He said, "What did you think of it?" I said, "I think your writing has improved." And he didn't say anything and he drove on for a few more blocks and then he turned and he said, "Bill, that's the nicest thing anyone's ever said to me. Ordinary guys say they thought it was wonderful, and I appreciate it very much." And I loved the guy right from then.

He drove me to his home and it was one of these FHA homes—they're all the same, only his garage he'd turned into a room where he slept, and his car slept outside. And I went in and I met his wife. And just for a moment there was something sort of strange about the whole thing. I met her and shook hands with her and she turned immediately and I noticed that there was a little stagger. Just a little. I didn't say anything about it, naturally. That night he said, "Bill, I've got a room here in the garage." I said, "I don't want to sleep in your room, *I'll* sleep out in the garage." He said, "No, that's my refuge out there. This is where I want you to sleep." I didn't answer. It was a beautiful room. It was *his* room, and he slept down in this room in the garage. That night I was restless and I turned around and I picked up his book, the one we made the picture of—*Brave Men*. I started reading it, and in the middle of it I hear footsteps outside and the tinkle of a glass. The door opened and closed. And I kept reading it and I began to realize how wonderful it was—the writing was so pathetic. So tragic, so wonderful, about the doughfoot, the fighting kid. I couldn't put it down. And I heard those footsteps three times and I knew what was up. She was an alcoholic.

The next morning I got up early. The coffee was on, I just had to turn the gas on, and I went out and got the newspaper—you know, it's never on the lawn, it's always mixed up somewhere. I found it and I went in and I started reading the thing and in came, without ringing the bell, Lester Cowan. "Hiya." Walked right by me and said, "I think I'll go up and wake up Ernie." Well, I knew now that if Ernie liked this guy there must be something about him. In came Ernie in a bathrobe and he had a couple of—what do you call them?—Bloody Marys, and Cowan and I had some orange juice. And I just suddenly realized that Cowan wasn't saying anything. Keeping his big mouth shut. And then Ernie started to talk—not about the picture—telling me about all these kids in the war, not thinking about the story or the picture, just the wonderful stories. The wonderful spirit of this guy who was as unfit to be out where it was really dangerous as anyone I've ever known, he only weighed about a hundred twenty-five, thirty pounds.

Suddenly [we became aware of] this car circling and circling and circling the house, and finally it got to him and he got annoyed and said, "I'm going to go out and kick him out of here, doggone it." I just sat there and waited for Ernie to come back, and he came back in a few minutes and he was a very subdued man, and I said, "What was it?" He said, "You won't believe this, but that was a little old man and his little old wife, driven through three states and came over here and just thanked me for a lousy little paragraph I put in of their son who was killed." And he said, "I invited them in and they said no, they didn't want to come in, they just wanted to thank me for it." I cry when I tell it to you, and I cried right then, and I said, "Look, Ernie, you've got yourself a pigeon. I don't know whether I can do it as well as I should do, because I don't know the infantry—I can do anything with a flier, because I was one and I know them all—but I'll break my ass to do a good job." And I did a good job. I had real [soldiers], they all came in and I made actors out of them and then all the actors had to live with them and learn to be like them, drill with them, and then they went on to the other war [in the Pacific], as did Ernie.

Ernie was right in this house. The last time he was in this country, literally, he was here. We were working on the script, giving it the polishing, and Ernie worked with me for three weeks on it, and one day we both found ourselves looking at the ceiling and seeing nothing but ceiling. And he said, "Look, let's call it off. You go play golf and, look, Bill, I hate to say this because this is the stock question they always ask somebody. In Hollywood there are two people I want to know. . . ." I said to myself, "He hasn't spoken of any dame, it isn't like him." And I said, "Well, look, Ernie, if I know them, I'd be tickled to death. Who is it?" He said, "Bill Fields and Gene Fowler." And I said, "Oh, God." And I said, "Well, Fowler, I'll call him right up, but I can't handle Fields for you." He said, "You mean you don't like Bill?" "Bill's one of my best friends, but I've been on the wagon for six months and he won't even speak to me." Which was true. He was up there in Bel-Air dying, literally, and he was spending all his day on one of those things that they put the women on when they don't want to muss their evening gowns. He had his liquor beside him and that's where he was, looking out the window. I used to go up and yell at him from the front porch and he'd throw everything he had except his bottle at me. He even threw a chamber pot at me—full. And he called me a coward and, you know, a selfish guy—I was thinking of myself, wouldn't join the real guys, the men that knew what they were doing. I wouldn't drink, I'd gone on the wagon. I said, "But I'll call Gene." I told Gene who it was. Gene said, "I'll be there in five minutes." Down he came and he said, "You want to see Bill Fields, come with me, baby," and he went there—Ernie, Bill Fields and Gene Fowler, no dames—just talking for three days. If you could have had a tape of those three guys, could you imagine what it could have been? And when he came back, he was exhausted. I said, "Did you have a good time?" And he just looked at me and smiled. Never said a word. Never asked him any more.

We went on and finished the whole thing, and the last night he was here we had dinner with Gene and with Mommy and my kids—he loved my kids—and when I came in that afternoon they were in the front room. My kids were rough and tough, there were four of them [then]—Pat, Bill, Kitty and Tim. And I had a couple of horses and they used to play Indians and horses and do the damnedest pratfalls—[playing dead]. Ernie was shooting each one of them. He'd shoot Pattie, that's my oldest one, first and she'd do some terrific fall. Then Bill, then Tim, then Kitty. Doing the most sensational falls you have ever seen in your life. And then it was their turn to shoot him. And he made a deal with them. He said, "No, a man only falls dead once." The exact words he used. "A man only falls dead once." So they all did "baam" and he did a tired, exhausted fall. And that's what happened to him. He went on to San Francisco, to the front again, destiny unknown, and that's when he was killed by a sniper. But that one line, "A man only falls dead once"—I'll never forget it as long as I live. He was the loveliest, nicest, finest, most brilliant man I've ever known in my life.

A lot of people think that *Battleground* is better than *G.I. Joe*, but I don't. Because *G.I. Joe* had a message. It's a good picture. You know that [recently] this producer sold it to CBS for four years to be run once a year because it is a picture against war. The last speech of Ernie Pyle's— they bring the poor captain down frozen and this poor little Juan [the Italian kid that I had] tried to get him together. This to me is the best picture I ever made in my whole life. And I firmly believe that I could never make another one like it.

Now, *Battleground* was bigger and full of laughs and all that sort of stuff. And it had a hell of a finish when those poor guys [who have been in the Battle of the Bulge] march by the new replacement, it had a certain ring to it, but nothing like that last scene in *G.I. Joe*. Oh, *those* poor guys. Most of them were soldiers, and most of them were killed. Every one who was in that picture went into the last battle they had—the last one, you know, Okinawa—and most of them never came back. And I worked with all those kids. And I feel sort of guilty about it. I got them a little more money, but it was a strange feeling about the whole thing. That's a picture that I did that you can't criticize. I did that on a lousy little stage over at the Selznick studio with forced perspective. Ernie never saw it. Ernie got killed and he never saw it. He would have loved it. *Battleground* I can't talk about because to me it was the cutting the bread, you know the way I did with that French gal [Denise Darcel] and she was wonderful and you hoped she wouldn't cut herself,* but there was nothing like that in *G.I. Joe*.

TWO FLYING PICTURES

Well, Ernie Gann, I hadn't met him, but they got a hold of the story. I'd signed a contract with Batjac, which was Duke Wayne's corporate setup, for six pictures—three of them with Wayne and three of them with whoever we got. The first story they had bought was Ernie Gann's *Island in the Sky* and they sent it to me to read. Wonderful. His writing about anything to do with the air is absolutely tops to me. And so we worked on the script together. The only thing I can tell you is that it's a true story and every one of the characters was really true. There was a flier down and they all left everything, they left their wives, they left their kids—you saw the story, I can't tell it any better than it was done—and they went up in there and they found him. That's the whole story. They gave up everything to find a pal. And that was fliers.

Fliers are the greatest people in the world if you know them. They're screwy, most of them, but they're the nicest, nicest guys and they're all married to good-looking dames. I've never seen a flier with an ugly girl in my whole life. Including myself.

We did that picture and it was very successful, and in the middle of

---

* In a scene where she is slicing bread, drawing the knife toward her bust.

it, when we were writing it, Ernie said, "Look, Bill, I want to tell you a story, just for fun so we can take our minds off of what we are doing. A thing I call *The High and the Mighty*. I haven't written it yet, but I can tell it to you." And he told me the story of *The High and the Mighty*. I said, "Stay right here, baby, I'll make the quickest sale you've ever had in your life." I called up to be sure that Wayne was there with his then partner, wonderful guy, can't remember his name. The two of them were there, and I said, "This is Bill Wellman, I've got to come down, stay there for a minute. I've got the greatest story to tell you you've ever heard in your life." I went down there full of enthusiasm and I told them the story of *The High and the Mighty*. They bought it like that. I said, "That's going to be my next one, with you playing it," and they said, "No, we'll let Tracy play it." I said, "I don't care, Tracy will be great." But anyway, they said, "What does he want for it?" I said, "I don't know, $55,000"—I didn't know what the hell he wanted. "And he wants at least five or ten percent of the profits, if any." He [Wayne] said okay. So he gave the money and Ernie got ten percent of the profit. I came back and told him, and he said, "Really?" I said, "Yes, $55,000 and ten percent of the profits." Well, I own a third of a thing and I hate to tell you how much the government got out of it, not I. You know, they take all of it away from you. Believe me, [Gann] has made a lot of money on it.

So that's the way the thing was started. It's a real, honest story, just full of enthusiasm. And Tracy read it and thought it was lousy, wouldn't do it. So Wayne had to do it, and Wayne still thinks that he wasn't good in it. I said, "What the hell—you mean to tell me you don't think you were good in that?" He said, "Well, he never had any love story." "He had the greatest love story that had ever been written. No one ever saw your wife, no one ever saw your kids. All they saw was that half-burned-up old little bear that was taken out of the fire and you're a lonesome, attractive, wonderful man. You couldn't ask for anything better. Everybody visualized a beautiful woman and a lovely kid and a wonderful guy that could love but one woman and there are damn few of them like you." Oh, we used to argue like hell. I said, "You stupid bastard, what is your favorite role?" He said, "*She Wore a Yellow Ribbon*." I said, "Well, she *should* wear a yellow ribbon." And he still thinks it's lousy and I think he's crazy.

Now, on *The High and the Mighty* we go ahead a little. We were working on the script, Ernie and I. And I always was a stickler—if I bought a story or a book and I loved it, I wanted to do the book. That's what the big fights I had with a lot of the producers were about. Thought that they wrote better than the writers. Well, they didn't, you know? Have you ever read Zanuck's book? He wrote one book once. Get it and read it.

Anyway, I wanted to stick to the thing, but Ernie kept wanting to change it because he said, "I can improve on it." He had written the story as a novel and it was very successful, and I said, "Look, Ernie, let's just stick to the book. That's all I want." And we almost had a fist fight about it on one occasion. Now, the only change that I wanted—which he agreed on—I wanted to put a kid in there, a four-year-old kid, so that he can go through the whole thing, come out with that Mae West around him, you know, and he's had nothing but a wonderful experience—it has been something he'll never forget. It gave me something to play against, you know. I sold Ernie on it, and he said, "That's great—I should have put it in the book." I said, "Well, it's too late now. Let's put it in the picture." So I said, "We'll use my kid," who he loved—Mike, four years old.

Mike is the greatest actor I have ever used in my whole life. Now, I don't want to say that because he is my son. He had a part where he had four lines at the very end. He was asleep through most of the thing in the foreground with the principals, sometimes in the background, and when we'd come in in the morning, I'd say, "All right, Mike, you go into your spot now and you go to sleep." He said, "Well, you want me to go to sleep or do you just want me to play go to sleep?" I said, "No, really go to sleep." So he would go to sleep and then I'd shoot all around him and lunchtime would come and I'd awaken him. He'd come up and he'd have lunch and play and have a lot of fun. And then we would go right back and he would go right to sleep again. He was beautiful. And then towards the end of the picture his big scene came up and he had four very important lines. So he was asleep in the room right up above us and I went in to say good night to him and I said, "Mike, let's rehearse the lines that you've got to do tomorrow. They are very important." He said, "No, Daddy. I know them. I'll be all right. I'll do okay." So I kissed him good night, and the next morning we got ready and we took the scene and he did his four lines and they were beautiful. He did it just like a pro. And I've often said that if some of the actors had a little more of Mike in them, you know, they'd be much better. He slept when I wanted him to. We woke him up when we wanted to. He did the thing and there was no trouble at all. Gorgeous performance. He was wonderful. Well, that's the story of my Mike. He's twenty-four now.

TRACK OF THE CAT

Track of the Cat is a picture that I wish to God I'd never made. I'll tell you why. And I can tell it very quickly. For seven years, if I remember correctly, I'd looked for a story that I could do—and this sounds silly—in black and white in color. And I found it in *Track of the Cat*. The cattle were either black or black and white. The snow was white, the house was sort of a white, off-white. If I shot a scene with the fir trees, I'd shoot the shadowy side so they were black. The only color in the whole picture was the red hunting coat that Mitchum had and a yellow scarf that one of the girls had—I've forgotten which one it was. That was all the color.

Now, I didn't tell it to anybody. I didn't tell it to my wife. I told it to Bill Clothier, who was my cameraman, who wouldn't give it up —you know, he would die for me. I said, "Bill, don't you tell your wife. And make this the god-damnest picture that has ever been made in color." And we did it. Never said a word. Never said a word to the man that was the head of the lab. And he never spotted it and I said, "Never mind. When it gets all through and we show it to Warner, they'll rave—he and all that gang that comes in with him."

Bill Clothier and I saw it first. Bill looks less like a cameraman than anyone I've ever known. More like a pug. He is a rough, tough, wonderful guy and a great artist. And Bill and I went in to see the thing. And when it was all over, we both cried. You know, you would have thought we were a couple of crying drunks—really, truly. It was so beautiful and so unusual. Warner saw it—the whole gang. They never noticed it. It went out. It was released. Nobody saw it. No one paid any attention to it. It was just a dream that went up like a bubble had burst. Really and truly. It just broke my heart. I said, "For seven years I've been looking for a thing like this, Bill." And Bill did a great job on it—got no mention as a photographer, nothing. And it is absolutely beautiful. It still is, but I missed on that thing, you know.

I began to get a little screwy, too. Mitchum should have been torn to pieces by that black panther, but I had the idea that no, I'm going to play ball with the audiences. They know so much more than we do. And let them imagine. But the audience's imagination didn't imagine and you never saw it. You're supposed to have heard it, you know. And it fell flat on its nose, as far as I was concerned. And it didn't make any money. It was a big flop, Wellmanly and every other way, I think.

. . . AND IN CONCLUSION

You go on location and the townspeople, you know, the tough guys would get together [and try to pick a fight]. We'd kick the hell out of them. You stuck together—the electricians, the grips. I had one man who worked with me on *Wings* who was on my last picture. On *Wings* he did something and I think he was a grip on the last picture. He was an old man. He'd been with me on every picture I'd ever made. Most of the time I had a continuous crew, unless they were working and couldn't get out of it. And the relationship. I never had any trouble with my crew. Never. I had a little property man named Scotty on one picture. He got loaded one night after work and he said something about Mr. Warner that wasn't very complimentary. (I said a lot of things about him that weren't complimentary.) And they fired him. The next morning I said, "Where's Scotty?" And they said, "Well, he got fired last night." And I said, "Okay, why?" They told me, and I told my assistant, "Call up Warner's office and tell them I won't work until Scotty is on the set." And they called down and said, "Look, we can't call Mr. Warner, he's asleep." I said, "Okay, then we'll wait until he wakes up." So they woke him up and told him and he said, "All right, put him back." And I meant it—I wouldn't have worked. The hell with them. And that's the kind of feeling we had, but you can't have it now. They don't have it now because studios aren't making sixty-five pictures a year. These guys now, if they had been working for a big studio, they'd be working every week of the year. They'd go from picture to picture to picture. And that's the way it was. So I don't think it is fair to criticize them, because they don't have the chance. Someone told me how few pictures were made last year. I couldn't believe it. Good God, they tell me there are thousands in the Actors' Guild that haven't had a job, and that if they do, they get around $2000 a year. It's kind of silly. So the whole thing has gone completely. And I don't think it will ever, ever change.

You had stock companies that were absolutely fantastic. And you had a choice of stories, and people went to see pictures then. I wanted to make every type of picture that was ever made and I have. I've made a musical, I've made kids' pictures, and you go through the whole list and you'll find that I've made every different kind of comedy, *Nothing Sacred* as against *Roxie Hart*. And westerns—*Buffalo Bill* as against *The Ox-Bow Incident*. All these different types. This was what I wanted to do. And when I quit I wanted to be sure that I'd done it. And I had to be a studio director to do that. And that's what I was. 'Cause then you'd get your chance.

Now, Frank Capra can take a project and start working on it, get a good writer and work on the script, get everything all ready, do the casting, make the picture and almost a year's gone by. I couldn't do it. I'd be so damned bored. One time when Frank was making a picture, I made six pictures. Four pictures contractually and two other pictures because I had this place but another house was here and we had so many kids, and they were coming all the time, that we had to tear the house down and we built this. And I built this making two extra pictures, never took a dime out of the bank.

Then it was difficult, you know. They had wonderful story departments. They knew who the directors were. They knew what would fit Wellman, what would fit Lloyd Bacon and so on. I never had a publicity agent, a publicity man. You can just keep me out of it. All I'm interested in is publicizing the people that I'm photographing—especially if I had a piece of the picture. A director doesn't draw anybody in to [see] a picture. I'm sorry. Maybe in Hollywood or in New York, but nowhere else. Don't tell me that a guy's going to go and see a picture and say, "Look, Jesus, that was beautifully directed." They don't know what a director is. But they do know what John Wayne is up there, or whoever you're photographing. The director's the guy that makes the picture, you bet your life he is, but he isn't the guy that sells tickets. I don't care who he is. Hitchcock maybe, maybe Orson Welles, Erich von Stroheim, because he was both actor and director. But that's as far as I can go. Don't you agree with me?

Vincente Minnelli at home

VINCENTE MINNELLI

N E X T to Sir John Gielgud, Vincente Minnelli is the most difficult person I've ever interviewed. Like Sir John, he is unfailingly polite and totally impenetrable. Unlike Sir John, however, he gives the impression of really trying to help you, which makes the interviewer's frustration more bearable and leaves him with a warm regard for a man he must assume is making a brave effort to overcome his natural shyness and what may be genuine pain over self-exposure.

Minnelli is different from the other directors represented in this book—indeed, from most directors I've met—in that he is not by nature a story-teller. He does not have a very good eye—or memory—for revealing anecdotes. Nor does he have an analytical turn of mind. He seems mainly to feel his way toward the solution of creative problems, clued more by visual ideas (and, of course, musical ones) than by any of the signs one might term "literary."

Indeed, the only telling details I can recall about *him* are that in his study he has an obviously well-used drawing board, which I suspect he employs more than his shaky-legged Directoire desk, and that nearby he keeps a wicker tray into which he tosses clippings—of drawings, paintings, photos—which provide him with the germs of ideas. He says he thumbs through these papers—he has many more in files—when he begins a project or is groping for an idea to solve some problem that has come up when he is in production.

His personal background, about which he talks more coherently than he did about film-making in our interview, accounts for this. Though he came from a theatrical family, his early professional training was in the visual arts—as photographer's assistant, window-dresser, then designer for Radio City Music Hall and Broadway shows before turning first to theatrical, then movie, direction. The only director I know whose background is anything like Minnelli's is Alfred Hitchcock, but the ways they employ their training could not be more divergent. Hitchcock may occasionally sketch out a shot for a writer or cameraman, but he has no interest in design for its own sake—that is, to make a shot or create a setting that is simply beautiful to look at. He is looking sometimes for symbols of order to contrast with the criminal disorder of his stories. Or he is looking for a novel juxtaposition of angles that will either discomfit us or somehow enhance an involvement with his people or plot. Minnelli, on the other hand, takes a straightforward delight in creating theatrical effects that will just simply wow us—previously unimagined dream sequences, for example, or almost unimaginable images of luxury—anything that is unobtainable in ordinary life outside the movie theater.

Hitchcock, if he wishes (and he often does), can give you the rationale for every shot, every angle he's ever chosen. Minnelli will not—and, I suspect, cannot. His wonderfully moving camera (and he ranks with Murnau, Ophuls and Curtiz as a master of exquisite camera movement) seems to be animated by a seemingly natural curiosity to explore and exploit the artificial wonders Minnelli (and his designers and choreographers) has created. He can be pretentious—as in the huge ballet that is the famous climax of *An American in Paris*—but more often than not an essential innocence, a delight that matches (and of course cues) our delight in these wonders, saves him.

I have never thought that the question of "good taste" should be raised in connection with his work. It can be impeccable—as in his superb evocation of the spirit of turn-of-the-century middle-class American life in *Meet Me in St. Louis*. More often it is crazily daring, even outrageous. For which one can only be grateful, since he has taken movies in directions no one else imagined they might go, exploiting the resources for the deliberately artificial that were inherent in the studio system, but which were rarely used with his kind of brio because of film's built-in bias toward realism.

Minnelli was not properly appreciated at the height of his career in the late 1940s and the 1950s. The literary mind, which at that time dominated movie reviewing, tended to dismiss musicals because their plots were silly or their characters somewhat lacking in dimension. Reviewers missed the sheer movieness of what he did, the fact that the screen musical, like the stage musical, was among the most American of forms, never duplicable, for some reason, by other cultures. While screening *The Pirate*, I began to realize fully the individuality of Minnelli's work. Deft, witty, exciting, it brilliantly exploits Judy Garland's temperament, Gene Kelly's egotism and their oddly matched talents for song and dance. To miss it is to miss one of the authentic glories of our cinema. And if, along with *Meet Me in St. Louis* and, perhaps, *The Band Wagon* (which contains, in "Shine on Your Shoes," Fred Astaire's apogee), it is one of Minnelli's masterpieces, the same spirit animates at least a sequence or two in every Minnelli film—the great waltz in *Madame Bovary*, the shoot-out at the county fair in *Some Came Running*. In these movies this frail, diffident-seeming man masterfully commands huge forces and expands the boundaries of the possible in film.

A THEATRICAL CHILDHOOD

My father and his brother owned a tent show, so I was born into that. We traveled through Ohio and Indiana and places like that. My mother was the star and she'd been on Broadway, but she never liked the theater. We always wanted to settle down. And so eventually we bought a place in a little town called Delaware, Ohio, and I went to school there.

The custom then was to use pirated editions of the Broadway shows so that they wouldn't have to pay royalties. They were dramas, and I played the children's parts whenever there were any to play.

I didn't want much to be in the theater [after that] because I'd had the theater—traveling and actors and so forth—but in winter we would go into stock. My father was a musical director, my mother would act and I played Little Willie in *East Lynne*, as I remember, when I was about five. And my mother tells a wonderful story: I wouldn't rehearse on the stage. It was a bare stage with two chairs for a bed. I would have nothing of that, and they couldn't do anything with me. So she rehearsed me at home, in the hotel. Little Willie is supposed to die, his mother has to leave, the father shows her the door. She comes back when Little Willie is ill and about to die [and takes a job as his nurse], white wig and so forth. I did the whole scene and died beautifully. Then, after that, my mother had a great hysterical scene. She threw off the wig and [said], "Willie, speak to me, tell me that you're not dead!" Well, I sat up and comforted her. I said, "I'm not dead." My father was in the box office and heard this roar of laughter and came running in and of course there was bedlam.

AN ARTISTIC ADOLESCENCE

[After] we settled down in Delaware, Ohio, the movies started to be good and more or less killed the tent-show business. So money was very scarce and we had a rather rough time of it. But I went to school in Delaware. [And] while I was still a kid I used to paint show cards for the different merchants. And sometimes they would send me to Columbus, Ohio, which was only thirty miles away, to a convention and I'd come back with a lot of money.

[Then] I went to the Art Institute in Chicago after I graduated from high school. I was about sixteen and I went to the life classes a couple of times, but couldn't keep it up because I was working very hard. When I first went to Chicago, I got a job right away at Marshall Field's in the window-dressing department and I used to go around sketching the shows that I saw. Paul Stone was a photographer who was also waiting backstage for people [as I was] and he saw [my work] and said, "If you can do that, you can learn to photograph." So I went to work in his photography studio. He photographed all the celebrities of that time, Ina Claire and people like that. But he had a nervous breakdown shortly after I came there, so I had to photograph all these [celebrities and] I was very shy. I stayed behind the camera a great deal.

[After that] I went to the Chicago Theatre and told them if I could learn to photograph, I could learn to design. Frank Cambria there gave me a job, because the Chicago Theatre used to do presentations—about an hour or so with the films. Very elaborate.* And in time they sent me to New York because they amalgamated with Paramount Publix. Their units traveled fifty-two weeks a year. They had different directors and different designers. I couldn't design them all, so I would do about one in three.

DIRECTORIAL BEGINNINGS

While I was still at Paramount, I designed settings and costumes for other shows—*Dubarry* with Grace Moore and all that. And then eventually they asked me to come to Radio City Music Hall as art director. I was there for about three and a half years, and then went on to do my own shows for Lee Shubert with Beatrice Lillie and people like that. But I started to direct at the Radio City Music Hall. Mr. Van Schmus, who was the Rockefeller representative—kind of a New England banker type, you know, with white hair—had the idea that I should do every fourth show. At that time Radio City played one picture a week and they never held a picture over. I think in the three and a half years I was there they held over two pictures for the second week. But it was a great schooling because I had to light the shows and design them—work with the design for the turntables and the interlocking revolving stages and all that sort of thing.

I've always been in a position where I've had to work under pressure and make quick decisions. And there is no room for shyness, you know.

---

* These apparently were themed spectacles, something on the order of the stage shows at Radio City Music Hall and the Roxy.

You have to develop an outer shell to cope with that, but I'm basically rather shy, socially.

FIRST TRIP TO HOLLYWOOD

[Eventually] I had three shows running on Broadway and I didn't want to come to Hollywood, but everyone said you have to. And I got into a kind of an agents' war and the agent that I finally chose took the best offer, which was Paramount's. They paid me a large salary and brought out my staff. But they were only making Bing Crosby pictures and *The Big Broadcast* and that sort of thing. I prepared a screenplay with a writer, but nothing happened. So I spent most of the time trying to get out of the contract. They weren't doing the kind of musicals that I wanted to do. I was very interested in pictures, [but] I wanted to do things in a certain way and use my Broadway experience. And so I went back to Broadway and did the Ed Wynn show *Hooray for What* and [a] Jerome Kern show, and then Arthur Freed* came to my studio in New York and offered me what I thought was the best way to come out, which was anonymously [with] no title or anything, just to work with him and to be available for other producers. All the people I'd known in New York were out there. Dorothy Parker and Lillian Hellman, S. J. Perelman—people like that. And any producer could call on me and ask me to read a script and give ideas and so forth—it was a marvelous time. And at the end of that year Freed bought *Cabin in the Sky* and I directed that.

FIRST FILM

Cabin in the Sky was a realistic film and a drama, but it had fantasy in it too. Little Joe almost dies and the Devil comes in and the Angel of the Lord and they fight for his soul, and so it has surrealistic tendencies, but I had done the first surrealistic ballets in shows in New York with

* The M-G-M producer, who specialized in musicals.

Balanchine. In all my shows I had ballets. In those early days [in the movies] I did *Yolanda and the Thief*, which had a surrealistic ballet with Fred Astaire. And yes, there were spots in various pictures that had surrealistic tendencies. Also in *Ziegfeld Follies*.

Somebody—some reviewer, some person interested in me—said that [there has never been anything like those sequences before in films], but I said, "No, that's not true." Because there was one film that I loved that [Rouben] Mamoulian did, with Rodgers-and-Hart music that was beautifully integrated and a stunning performance by Chevalier, called *Love Me Tonight*. I've always thought that was a wonderful picture. And it still doesn't date, even today. But the things I did then were more or less imaginative because they were required to be. There were dream sequences and things like that.

[The opposition came] mostly from the art department, because they had been used to doing things a certain way and they didn't understand—and, language being what it is, it is very difficult to explain what's in your mind. But they came to understand that I wasn't asking for something just to be asking. It would play an important part in what I was doing. Eventually they were educated up to it, but at the beginning it was pretty difficult.

It's true that the sky is the limit in movies. Because you can do anything, and for that reason you have to have great discipline in what you do. You have to refer completely to the subject at hand. Depending on the subject and depending on the style of the thing that you are doing.

FIRST DRAMATIC PICTURE

They shot for a couple of weeks on *The Clock** with another director and had decided to scrap it. It was a beautiful script by Robert Nathan. It read beautifully, but it didn't play. It was about two people going around New York saying bromidic things to each other, just getting acquainted, and each time you saw them it seemed like a different picture.**

---

* The film was made in 1945.
** It is about a soldier on a pass, played by Robert Walker, who picks up a girl, Judy Garland, and how they lose and find each other in the harsh city before they finally decide to marry despite their brief acquaintance.

And so Judy came to see me and we had lunch together and she asked me if I would take it over and do it. So I saw the stuff that they had shot and read the script, and I decided that the only thing [to do] was to make New York one of the characters—the third character. Everything I could remember about New York [went into it]. A great deal of improvisation [was needed in order to keep] all of the things that were relevant in the Robert Nathan script which were beautifully written. And it was one of my best experiences because, [although] there was a great deal of improvisation, nobody bothered us, they were so happy to have it done finally, you know. For instance, the scene with Keenan Wynn as the drunk. And there was a big scene at the end after Judy and Robert Walker had gotten married and they had spent the night together. It was very noble and had about three and a half, four pages of dialogue. They asked me what I intended to do with that and I didn't know. But when we got to it that morning, I decided to do it all in pantomime, because I thought that was all that was necessary to show that it was a good marriage, deserved to endure. He was going away to war and I gave his speech to Judy because it was more fitting to come from the girl—more gallant, you know. And then the last scene at the station. So it was a marvelous experience.

I've always had enough freedom. The studio never interfered really with what I wanted to do, but this was unique. *The Clock* was unique.

THE PIRATE

The Pirate was ahead of its time. It was sophisticated, you know, taken from a play for Alfred Lunt and Lynn Fontanne, written by S. N. Behrman, and was very exotic, but it had wonderful ideas. I always wanted to do it as a movie. It was the first picture that Judy and I did after we were married. It was full of wonderful numbers. Gene Kelly did fantastic numbers and so did Judy. "Be a Clown" is in it, and "Nina" and "The Fire Dance"—which is again in imagination, a dream, but it is hot and exotic and the way the West Indies would look, you know.

A WORD ABOUT JUDY GARLAND

She was a great artist and a fantastic performer. And a big star by the time I met her [when] we did *Meet Me in St. Louis* together. She was an extraordinary talent. Very unique in pictures. And I remember that when she was ready to go into a scene the makeup people would be fussing over her, fixing her up and so forth. You might tell her twenty things to change in this performance. And God knows she had enough on her mind, and you didn't know whether you were getting through to her or not. But everything would be perfect. She would remember everything. She was fantastic. She knew that there were [many] different ways of playing a scene, and I love working with that kind of person.

The Pirate was the first picture that we did when we came back from our honeymoon in New York (we were there for three months and sublet an apartment). She was pregnant with Liza and so I had to shoot three numbers that she did, long before the picture was done. They had to fit them in [later], but that was necessary because she was getting bigger everyday.

SECOND DRAMATIC FILM— *MADAME BOVARY*

The waltz in *Madame Bovary* is terribly important because that's the biggest scene in the book. The waltz itself is her one moment of gratification. Things are the way she expects them to be. She has a beautiful gown, the men are all mad about her. She looks into this big oval mirror and sees herself as she wants to be, surrounded by men, looking beautiful. And her husband, of course, is out of place and goes into the billiard room and gets drunk, and it ends up a shambles. But in the meantime this waltz—which was very new in Paris then, had just started to come in [fashion]—goes on and on and becomes almost intolerable. Miklos Rozsa, who conducted the music, composed this rather neurotic waltz. It was very much like "La Valse" of Ravel. And I shot completely to that music. It grew and grew and got faster and faster until she was breathless and ready to faint. [And Louis Jourdan] told the host and the host ordered the windows to be broken and so on. And then her husband makes a spectacle of himself on the floor, [he's] drunk and wants to dance with his wife and she runs out and he follows her and you see them going home in the carriage—her driving and her husband asleep.

Flaubert was tried for corrupting morals with this book *Madame Bovary* and James Mason played that part, explaining the character of Madame Bovary as he went along. And he also became the narrator of the film. I thought at the time—and I still think—it is a dramatic way to frame the picture, because then he explains how she was raised on the romanticism of that time—Chateaubriand and things like that. She had her walls covered with pictures of swooning ladies and people at graves and so forth. It was typical of the literature of that time and had a great deal to do with her development, I feel.

The two pictures that I worked on that [have] the most contradictory characters—and I think that those are the best kind to do—are *Madame Bovary* and *Lust for Life*. Flaubert's novel was analyzed by every major literary talent. They all wrote about Emma Bovary, from Freud to Somerset Maugham, and no two agreed about it. She is elusive and you wonder—you ascribe different things to her to explain her. But my point of view is that she wanted everything to be as beautiful as possible, [yet] everything in life that touched her was ugliness. But she never lost her [desire] to have beauty around her. [And then] she got into the hands of LaRue, the moneylender, and [was] ruined and finally took arsenic. Van Gogh [in *Lust for Life*] was a very contradictory type also. There are five or six volumes of his letters to his brother Theo and in all of them he is so eloquent. He writes so beautifully. And at length. He'll write about the affirmative aspect of a thing so brilliantly and so convincingly and then, often in the same letter, turn right around and take the opposite point of view. So it is awfully hard to pin him down. He was too much for anybody. Nobody could live with him (including his brother) for more than a couple of weeks without going mad. Because he gave too much. He wanted too much. And this is the kind of character that is inconsistent and therefore I think brilliant to work out. I remember reading in Maugham's *The Summing Up* that he was often accused of being

Robert Walker, on leave, courting Judy Garland in a race against The Clock (*1945*)

Judy Garland about to bust an incorrigible Gene Kelly in The Pirate (*1948*)

Papa (Leon Ames) lays down the law to his wife (Mary Astor, seated) and his daughters (Lucille Bremer and Judy Garland) in Meet Me in St. Louis (*1944*).

inconsistent and he said, "Well, life is inconsistent." And I agree with that. Often people that you've known, that you think you know terribly well, will do unexpected things.

I suppose [my concern with] the inconsistency of people is reflected in the dream material, because there is no better way to show the inconsistency of people than in dreams.

DRAMA AND MUSIC INTEGRATED

It's practically intuitive, you know. If you are going to do a musical in the right way, and have it linger with people a while, then I think you have to put just as much thought in, and sweat and intelligence, as you do in the dramatic picture. In, say, *Meet Me in St. Louis*, the "Trolley Song" was just a song, you know, that they sang on the trolley. But by putting it into a situation where Esther was looking for the boy and the boy didn't show up and they had to leave without him and she was downhearted and then you saw him running for [the trolley] and then she changed [mood] completely and was very gay and high about the thing and sang the song—that more or less made the number. It fitted into a [dramatic] situation. And so that is a slight example. In *The Band Wagon* you have to do a show that is bad, you know, that Fred Astaire takes over and re-does it and makes it into a hit. Well, you can't do a really bad show, but it has to be pretentious. So you make the director pretentious and with all the fire and the brimstone and the stuff that he is doing you understand, in an entertainment way, why it is bad, and it is funny. And then when Fred Astaire has the show, it has to have some kind of sophistication or the other man [the original director] wouldn't stay with the show.

In the *American in Paris* ballet, [Gene Kelly] plays an artist. He's loved the people that painted Paris, he loves Paris and he loves this girl. And you have to say that when he loses the girl, Paris will lose its flavor, it will become a cold city, it will become an unfriendly city. At times there will be euphoria and happiness and at times there will be the realization that it's—it's ashes, you know.

It opens in the Place de la Concorde and Paris is a colorful city, but it is strange and odd and he is treated like a stranger. Then he's menaced by the furies, there is a change of lights and it becomes almost night-marish and he sees the girl jump onto the fountain and he pursues her and when he gets there she is gone. He sees her in the flower market, which is in the style of Renoir, and dances an adagio with her and [then] she is gone again, elusive. Then the music changes. Deems Taylor in his analysis of the *American in Paris* music said that this was his homesickness and his longing for America. Well, that is typified by the servicemen and they come in and they go into this jolly dance and he forgets completely about the girl. Then he meets her in a setting by Rousseau—the zoological gardens. And they dance very gaily and the Parisians become Americans and then it goes into the adagio again on the fountain, which is a love scene. And that changes into the Place de l'Opéra, where they are all gay and everything. Paris belongs to him. And to her. And then they encounter this sandwich man with the Toulouse-Lautrec drawings and he goes into the Toulouse-Lautrec number, and at the end of that it becomes still again. Paris is empty, he's alone. So the thing always has those emotions going and [though he tries] to keep up the gaiety, the realization that she is gone always is there and [always] gets him down.

Now, when we started the picture, Irene Sharaff had made a few sketches and so on, but we hadn't really gotten the story [for the ballet]. And then Nina Foch, who was playing an important part in the picture, got sick. She had chickenpox. So for three days we couldn't shoot anything. Well, it was a life-saver for us. Because Gene Kelly and Irene Sharaff [and I] locked [ourselves] up in my office and in three days we knocked off the whole idea of the ballet. And Gene kept saying, "You have to have a story." I was determined that this would have to be a story of emotions rather than an actual story, you know. And so it evolved that way. [But, finally,] it all came in a flash; it was very clear.

[The staging is] more or less intuitive. You think about both things at once—what's effective in the way of action in dance and what the camera movement is and how you dramatize [the action] and how you express it. And I can't explain that process because it all happens simultaneously—while you are planning the whole thing. While the costumes are being done and the setting is designed and the music is being done and the choreographers are rehearsing. All that time is taken in planning it.

I remember when Irving Berlin was visiting and the sets were being built and so forth. Arthur Freed and Gene Kelly and myself went with Berlin and showed him all the sets and described what would happen. And finally he said, "Do I understand that you boys are planning on ending this picture with a ballet, twenty minutes? No dialogue after that?" And we said yes. And he said, "Well, I hope you know what you are doing." Well, that's all we needed—our hearts were in our mouths. It was very daring in those days to do it.

COLOR AND DESIGN

Designers, especially in New York, always frequent the print room of the public library and [then, too, they] accumulate an enormous amount of things themselves—articles and so on. And so I found it a great shortcut to have boxes and boxes of clippings—twenty boxes or so. I go through them all before I do a picture, and give them to the art directors and the costume designers to explain what I mean. It is a shortcut. And I find it works very well.

SOME TYPICAL CASES—DESIGN

"Limehouse Blues"* was done in Chinoiserie style—not Chinese, but the French idea of Chinese, and with the light effects and so on. It had to have a prologue and epilogue. Well, just to show you the kind of thing that you don't tell people, but the thinking that has to go on, "Limehouse Blues" came into being because of the Griffith picture *Broken Blossoms*. That inspired the song in England of "Limehouse Blues" and it was done in *Charlot's Revue* by Gertie Lawrence as a Chinese girl. Well, it always involved a melodramatic plot. Somebody was always killed. So you had to keep all those things in mind—at least I did, because I wanted to be true to the period. And I found a set standing. It was from *The Picture of Dorian Grey*, and it served all purposes because it had a side street

* In *Ziegfeld Follies* (1946).

and the waterfront and so on. I only had to build a little Chinese store in the foreground. I then got all the books I could from the library, put in a call for extras of a different kind—Chinese and Arabians and coster women with the shiny pearl buttons. By filling the stage with fog and lighting it with a yellow light and restricting the colors to black, white and yellow, it had the feeling of an English mezzotint, which I felt it needed. It had the feeling of silent pictures.

[In *An American in Paris*] the artists' ball, which was a masquerade, troubled me greatly because they usually look awful. They're just different kinds of colorful costumes. And the ballet was going to follow, which was to be full of color. So I got the idea of making it a black-and-white ball. I called Arthur Freed immediately and told him I was very happy about it. Because, number one, it could be dazzling in itself, you see—all the stripes and checks and swirls and so forth in black and white. There was no color in the set except for the skin. And, number two, it rested the eyes for a long time before the ballet, in which you used great color. It was very fortunate.

[For *Meet Me in St. Louis*] I remembered everything I could of the small town where I was brought up. My aunt used to wear this red tam-o'-shanter [like the one] the maid uses in the winter scene, you know, with the big tassel on top. It is full of things like that, things I could remember. But it was set in an earlier period, with American Gothic architecture and so on. So I spent a great deal of time on research and finding the right things for it. Because I feel that a picture that stays with you is made up of a hundred or more hidden things. They're things that the audience is not conscious of, but that accumulate. They add to the reality of the characters and to the film itself.

In the first picture, *Cabin in the Sky*, it was all [set] in the South, with a black cast, and you had to show the way those people lived. They were rather poor, but they were very happy and so on. So I tried to keep all the symbols—in keeping with what they had in these shacks, these cabins. The fantasy was introduced by a homey object, just a coal-oil lamp. And when Ethel Waters is praying over Little Joe, she blows out the lamp and goes into the kitchen and then you cut to the lamp and it starts to glow by itself and throws the shadow of the Devil on the walls. So you go into the fantasy in the style in which you set the picture, you see. And when Lena Horne visits Little Joe, she isn't wearing a hat, but she stops outside the cabin [where there's] a magnolia tree and takes one of these enormous blossoms and puts that on instead of a hat and it is a very smart-looking hat. But it is a homey object, you see. Something that you could really see and feel.

The Pirate was adapted by [Ludwig] Bemelmans. He writes beautifully and he draws wonderfully in color, but his colors are crimson and green and blue—bright, prism colors, like a child's paintbox. So I tried to keep it in that particular style. Even the ballet has touches of that, though the rest is Spanish Baroque because it happens to be in a very rich country in South America.

Some Came Running [on the other hand, was set] in a small town in Indiana—gamblers and bars and neon signs and all that sort of thing. Especially the carnival at the end with all the lights and the concessions and the Ferris wheels and so forth. I said it should be like the inside of a jukebox. I think it is an apt phrase for it.

DREAM SEQUENCES

It just seemed right in musicals—dream sequences and things like that— to do them in the form of ballet. Even in dramatic pictures there are dream sequences—*Father of the Bride*, for instance, with Spencer Tracy, where he has this awful vision of himself not being able to walk up the aisle. I can't remember the different things that led me into the dream sequences. You can't force them in, but if it seems right, you do it.

Nowadays it is very popular to think of reality and fantasy in conjunction with each other. What is reality and what is fantasy? It's what novelists have always used. And I've always leaned toward that. And I've wanted to do it more than they allowed me to. I often wanted to do things that explained the action and so forth, which nowadays they are doing. I saw it in *The Pawnbroker*, for instance. I believe that was the first [recent] picture I saw it in, [and] I gave a whoop of joy because it was the kind of thing I've always wanted to do. But [earlier] they wouldn't let you. They felt that it would confuse the audience, and things had to be made very clear.

ON HANDLING ACTORS

When Margaret O'Brien was very tiny and very young, her aunt and her mother used to prepare her for scenes. I never could find out what they said, but they would talk in her ear and whisper to her and she would listen with her eyes out on sticks and then she would go in and cry and get hysterical and do the scene. She specialized in things like that: In *Journey for Margaret* she was a troubled child in the war. And it was difficult to get her to act as a child would. But at times you needed that hysteria. One night when we were out on the back lot doing the scene [in *Meet Me in St. Louis*] in the backyard where she hysterically breaks up all the snowmen and cries and yells and screams and so forth, her mother came over to me and said, "Margaret and I have had a disagreement and she won't speak to me. And she wants *you* to prepare her." And I said, "My God, how do you do that?" She said, "Well, she has a little dog that she adores and you tell her that somebody is going to kidnap that dog and kill it." Well, I had to go over because she was waiting. It was very cold and she was waiting with a blanket around her shoulders and I said, "Margaret, I hate to tell you this, but somebody is going to kidnap your little dog and shoot it, you know." And she said, "Will there be lots of blood?" And I went on and elaborated—and finally I said "Turn 'em" and jerked the blanket off her and she went out there and did this hysterical scene all in one. But I went home feeling like a dog. I never want to go through that again.

All actors are different. You have to approach each one in a different way. They all need reassurance and I don't care how blatantly confident they may seem on the surface, they're rather troubled people. There are some people that you can suggest things to and you analyze the part and talk about it. There are others—very few others—who must imitate you, because that is about the only way [they] can do it. But there are as many ways of treating actors as there are actors. Sometimes they will convince you and sometimes you'll convince them. And you'll do it their way or they'll do it your way. But it's got to make sense. And sometimes it *is* a compromise.

You have to use your own intelligence in spite of all the tension on the set. You have to make decisions. You have to feel that it is right yourself. Because if you show that you are in a panic, then the panic spreads all over. So you have to sound as though you're completely self-assured, as though everything is beautiful, everything is going in a beautiful way, even when there is absolute panic.

[Fred Astaire] lacks confidence to the most enormous degree of all the people in the world. He will not even go to see his rushes. He'll stay out in the alley and pace up and down and worry and collar you when you come out and say, "How was so and so?" and keep you there for forty-five minutes. It would be much simpler if he would go and look at them himself, you know. But he always thinks that he is no good. And he is fantastic. He's the most marvelous performer, but lacking in confidence and needs reassurance so much.

As far, certainly, as his dance routines go, he has to polish them to the nth degree. If he does anything wrong, even though it seems right to you, he'll have to do it again. He is a perfectionist.

Gene Kelly is more of an intellectual. He is just as much a perfectionist as Astaire, in his own way. In that he is very much like Astaire, although he is much more confident. But Gene Kelly is more earthy and more romantic. And in all of the things that Gene does, he has the same sense of reality that never leaves.

When Pan Berman and I started to do *Father of the Bride*, we always had in mind Spencer Tracy. It was a book by a man who had gone through the whole thing of marrying off his daughter. There is much reality in the book, and no one else seemed to be right for it. With Tracy it would be a major project, a memorable film, but with someone else, no. We went to one of the executives who had charge of the casting, and he said, "Forget about Spencer, because he doesn't want to do it. He's gone to New York. He's rather insulted that you should ask him to do anything as trivial as this." So we went back and thought in terms of other actors. But nothing was right. And we came back and said, "It's got to be Spencer Tracy or no one." And he said, "Well, then it is no one because he will not do it." So I said to this executive, "Is there any reason why I can't go over and ask him myself?" And he said, "Oh no, of course not." He said, "If you want to go over as a private person and tell him about the project, we can't stop you." So I called Katie Hepburn and she arranged to have him up for dinner—just the three of us. And I said, "Spence, I will be absolutely blunt about this. With you in the cast it would be a memorable picture. Without you, it is nothing."

Well, he blossomed like a rose. He simply wanted to be wanted. He had heard that we were testing people and had other people in mind and he was just one of the boys, and that hurt his ego, you know. And he simply wanted to be wanted, and loved the project and agreed to do it. It was as simple as that.

THE BAD AND THE BEAUTIFUL

John Houseman had just come to the studio and he asked me to read that script. It was called at that time *Tribute to a Bad Man*. The studio wanted me to do *Lili*, and I didn't want to do that because I'd just done *American in Paris* and it was the same kind of thing—Leslie Caron, and it was French, and it had a ballet in it. So Dore Schary asked me if there was anything else I would like and I told him *The Bad and the Beautiful*. He said, "Well, really, you want to do that? It's the story of an out-and-out heel." And I said, "No, I don't think so. I think that anybody who has the charm to get people to work for him and get involved with him must have the charm of the world, you know." So we got Kirk Douglas for it and his strength works so beautifully for that because he played against his strength. He played for charm completely. You knew the strength was there. He didn't have to dredge it up. And then Lana Turner wanted to do it and I'd been told she wasn't a good actress. Well, she was marvelous, just wonderful. I was delighted with her. And I'd always been intrigued by the old Hollywood. And, as you know, the central character is a composite of people—David Selznick and so on, an awful lot of people, the legends of Hollywood. And the form was marvelous, done in three parts with three different narrators. I loved doing the film.

THE BAND WAGON

It began [because] Arthur Freed wanted to do a picture with the music of Dietz and Schwartz and using the title *The Band Wagon*, which was originally [the title of] a revue on Broadway. Comden and Green wrote the script for it. We all pitched in and it all came together wonderfully. Fred was sporting enough to play a dancer who was out of luck in Hollywood and went to New York—time had passed him by, you know. But it [also] involved [as the show's director] a composite of Orson Welles and several people who [had once been] very fashionable. Orson Welles did the *Macbeth* in Harlem, you know, as though it were laid in Haiti, with a black cast. And for that somebody suggested Jack Buchanan, who was absolutely marvelous. Better than I'd hoped. And the whole thing was great fun.

GIGI

Freed and I had wanted to do the Colette story about Gigi for a long time, and finally he cornered Alan Lerner and Alan agreed to do the script and do the score with Fritz Lowe. This was after *My Fair Lady*. And so we went to Paris and a lot of it was written there while I searched for locations and things. Cecil Beaton designed the clothes. But I based it all on the caricatures of Sem because Colette had written about real people who had actually existed and Sem had drawn these people, all of them—and there were hundreds of drawings of them in their natural habitat, in the Bois and in Maxim's and places like that. So it was easy to set the style. For the beach, for instance, I tried to imitate Boudin —the chairs and the sunshades—and also transfer it to 1900. Doing it was a great joy.

Oh, we loved the story. You know, basically, it is awfully good. She wrote it as a kind of throwaway. She never considered it one of her major works, like *Chéri*. But it's the one that has endured. It was done as a black-and-white French movie years and years ago, and was done on the stage in an adaptation that was not very good. But we went right back to the story. And Alan has the faculty of writing lyrics in the style of whoever he is [adapting]. In the case of *My Fair Lady* the lyrics might have been written by Shaw. And in this case they could have been written by Colette.

BRIGADOON

I think that the form of *Brigadoon* is more of an operetta. It involves a lot of melodies and ballads and so forth. It's exciting in itself in certain places—the chase and that sort of thing. We did that all on one enormous sound stage and I had the art department try to get the spirit of Scotland, because you couldn't shoot in Scotland, the weather there is so horrible. We tried to do it so that in every place you looked, there was a different aspect—a cavern or a river, a bridge or hills. And I got as good a replica of Scotland as we could get. It was a very versatile set. And we did it all mostly in that set. It's very difficult to do, with so many ballads and long explanations and long speeches. But, again, you do it the very best you can. That's all you can do.

THE DECLINE OF THE MUSICAL

There are many reasons for that, I suppose. First of all, there haven't been any male star dancers like Kelly and Astaire. Secondly, it took a different form when Alan Lerner wrote *My Fair Lady* and *Gigi*. The lyrics were almost like dialogue. They involved the plot, they explained the plot, and [if] you didn't understand the lyrics the plot didn't exist. Well, that's very difficult to translate into foreign languages, because it's hard enough to make a lyric that rhymes and makes sense and keep it like dialogue.* Is almost impossible, you know. The screen musical, which used to be a dancing-singing form, is now mostly a singing form. I think things go in cycles. One of these days somebody will do a marvelous musical and start it all over again. Or a new personality will come along.

I don't like redoing what I've done before. As in the case of *American in Paris* and *Lili*.** I love doing things that are completely different from each other. Anything that is excellent in the way of a story attracts me. I don't care what it is. I'll find a style for it. There's always a style.

* This, of course, cut into foreign revenues, which are normally around fifty percent of a movie's gross.
** Which Minnelli was offered and which he rejected.

THE COBWEB

It was written by William Gibson, whose wife was a psychoanalyst [in an institution] and [it was] written while she was there. But the thing that attracted me was that it isn't about the inmates, although the inmates happen to be strange. Mostly it was about the doctors and the foul-ups in their lives. And it had Lillian Gish and a great cast. Oscar Levant was in it. Originally in the story his character was a homosexual, but at that time you couldn't do homosexuals and Oscar had called me and wanted to be in the picture, so I patterned the character after Oscar himself— same kind of hangups that he had, you know. And he was awfully good in that.

LUST FOR LIFE

One time I was in Dore Schary's office—he was the head of production then [at M-G-M]—and he asked me if there were anything that they had on the lot that I liked and I said, "Yes. You have one thing that you've had an option on for ten years. And the option is about to come to an end. And that's *Lust for Life*." He said, "Well, we've had two or three scripts on that and there is no story there." And I said, "I don't agree. I think there is a very good story. It has a marvelous character." I told him how I felt, and he got excited and put a writer on it. And then I had to do a picture called *Kismet*, which I didn't want to do because I wanted to work on this other picture. It ended up by my having to more or less treat [*Lust for Life*] as a stepchild. When I finished *Kismet* I had to get on the plane and go to France, where they were keeping a wheatfield alive chemically, long after it was due to die, and shoot the suicide at the end of the picture. A lot of it had to be rewritten. Fortunately, John Houseman, who was the producer, is a very good writer. We shot it all over—the places that Van Gogh actually lived in, Arles and Saint-Remy and the insane asylum where he was incarcerated, and in Paris, and in Holland and in the same mine that he worked in. And all those things lent a reality to it. The part of the story that involves Gauguin was dreadful. They treated Van Gogh and Gauguin like hallroom boys, you know, full of love and—well, that isn't the way it was. Because they couldn't get on, you know. And it ends up with his slashing off his ear. So that was all redone. And Tony Quinn, I think, got an Academy Award for that. Kirk was also up for that—he should have won.

Incidentally that was one of the early Cinemascope pictures and at that time Fox had arranged for Cinemascope so that it was in blatant colors—candy-box colors. This had to be very subtle yellows and misty and all that sort of thing. So they set up a special laboratory for Ansco, which was the nearest thing to Technicolor, and the original print was very beautiful. And the pictures of Van Gogh were exactly as he painted them.

DESIGNING WOMAN

I think that you have to be very strong to adapt to all forms. The only thing I ask of a comedy is that it be played completely naturally. Actors shouldn't go into comedy as though they were slumming. A lot of people playing comedy say, "Oh, this is comedy, so we have to be funny," and dig their elbows into the audience's ribs and say, "Watch out, this is going to be very funny." Well, that sort of thing never is funny to me. Because [comedy] has to be played for blood, you know. I saw the Elaine May picture recently [*The Heartbreak Kid*] and it was so beautiful. I was so glad that they treated it as though each thing were terribly important. Beautifully done. [But *Designing Woman*] was great fun because Betty [Lauren] Bacall and Gregory Peck were wonderful to work with, as were Rex Harrison and his wife, Kay [Kendall], in *The Reluctant Debutante*. Marvelous. That was an English comedy which was done in Paris, of all places, because they [the Harrisons] couldn't work anywhere else and save any money because of taxes. It was from the play about the debutante season in England and was terribly funny.

Designing Woman was written from an idea by Helen Rose, who was the principal costume designer at Metro at that time. And the script was written by George Wells and touched all bases. [A] sportswriter [was] played by Gregory Peck and Betty Bacall played a designer of women's clothes. And it touched the theater and [there were] fights and jealousies and everything.

HOME FROM THE HILL

I loved that script. It was written by the Ravetches [Irving Ravetch and Harriet Frank, Jr.], who I think are fantastic writers. They wrote *Hud* and *The Long Hot Summer*. They are specialists in regional dialogue— it is so marvelous, so full of images. The book itself was rather arty, but they made a magnificent script out of it. In fact, the part that George Peppard plays, the bastard son, was not in the book at all, and he is a very important character in the script. We went to Paris, Texas, where the story was laid, in the sulphur bottoms and quicksands and all that. This is mostly a story about hunting, you know, and I loved working on it, because Robert Mitchum was so strong and it was one of the first pictures for two people—George Hamilton and George Peppard—and it is almost a Greek tragedy. It's a very strong melodramatic plot. I love all kinds of things. I would love to do, for instance, *The Lower Depths*, because I think there is beauty in that kind of squalor. There is beauty in more things than people know.

STUDIO AND INDUSTRY

The word "industry" doesn't mean much to me because even when I worked at Metro I was always involved with the producer I was working with and the cast and the different people connected with it, so it was almost like making an independent picture. I never became involved with the executives.

The great [thing about] a studio [is that] things are there, you know. Things were always there. There was a stock company to choose from and there were great technicians and great cameramen. Nowadays you work independently and that means that you are like a producer. You have to get the book and get the writer and get the stars together and make a package. Well, that takes an awful lot of time and sometimes it comes through and sometimes it doesn't.

Nearly every studio was running full blast and there were many stars there and people that you knew, and many places to go to, like Mocambo and so forth. But Hollywood is a peculiar town. Most of the entertaining is done in homes. It isn't like New York. New York you can decide at seven o'clock where you want to go and have dinner, what theater you want to see, and you can usually get in. But here there's nothing much to do except go to those few nightclubs and entertain in people's homes or entertain yourself. People work very hard here. And they had to get up very early and there wasn't much free time. So you had to fit in your social life somehow with your working life. I know that I couldn't carry on a social life except on weekends, when I was working. At that time you did two pictures a year, and sometimes three. You worked for six days a week. You worked on Saturday also and you had to get up very early and [you would] come home at night so dead tired that you didn't dare go out. And so you lived more or less like a hermit for that particular time while you were making a picture. When you were free, there was a camaraderie. Social life was quite marvelous at times.

THEORIES OF DIRECTING: AUTEUR VS. ''LOST COW''

I think in some cases the auteur theory is right. It certainly works in the case of people like Hitchcock and Fritz Lang and Kubrick. There are a great many whose work you can tell at a glance. But not for the run-of-the-mill movies.

I think that once you've accepted a subject, you have to get involved with that subject to the point of saturation and do the very best you can under great pressure. But I always say that being a director is like the story of the farmer who lost his cow in a country of great hills and ravines and tortuous cliffs. No one had ever found a cow that strayed away, but, lo and behold, he came home that night leading the cow. The neighbor said, "How did you ever find it?" And he said, "Well, I thought to myself, 'Where would I go if I were a cow?' and I did and he had." So I think you have to learn to be a cow.

THE SEARCH FOR BEAUTY

I think that the reason [a] picture haunts you a little is that it has completely involved you. There are all kinds of beauty, you know. *The Pirate,* for instance, is very exotic-looking because it is laid in a free port in the West Indies in the 1830s. At that time it was cosmopolitan and filled with Chinese, Spanish, Italians, all the mixtures of races that eventually went to New Orleans and became Creoles. But there is a beauty of its kind in *Some Came Running.* I feel that the surroundings of people are very important. You don't see people isolated. You see them with their surroundings. And the environment and the look that the surroundings have is very important to me. I think it shows character.

The search in films, what you try to create, is a little magic. And if that depends on the turning of a leaf, then fine, so be it. But the main search is for a little magic in our lives. Every once in a while a great film comes along. I think *The Conformist* is a marvelous film. And Bergman's *Cries and Whispers,* I think, has magic. And even, in its way, *The Godfather,* which I like very much. If you get involved and if the picture haunts you a little bit afterwards, then you have created a little magic.

There are so many movies on so many different levels nowadays. It is almost—you have to change your whole personality to go in and see a movie, to be able to accept it. I pity the poor movie critics.

But I'm a very good audience. If a picture is rather bad, but has one or two marvelous sequences in it, I think of it as worthwhile.

A picture requiring no explanation

ALFRED HITCHCOCK

ALFRED HITCHCOCK's fears and anxieties dominate his imagination and the conduct of his daily life, just as, more lightly and artfully expressed, they dominate his films. Now seventy-five years old, and active as ever professionally, he continues to arrange his existence so that nothing untoward—the sort of mischance that so often propels his protagonists into danger—will happen to him. As he has often said, he has never learned to drive a car in order to obviate the possibility of receiving a traffic ticket. Indeed, unless he is shooting a picture or is out promoting one, he rarely ventures away from home or office, which is a bungalow at Universal City studios in the San Fernando Valley. A chauffeured car deposits him there in the morning, he nips quickly through a side door and does not emerge again until quitting time. The studio commissary is not a hundred yards away, but lunch is brought in and served in a spacious dining-*cum*-conference room a few steps from his desk. (Lunch, incidentally, is extremely modest considering his girth and his reputation as a gourmet—lean steak or broiled sole, salad and coffee; no bread, potatoes or dessert.) Once a week, when they're both in town, Lew Wasserman, head of mighty MCA—of which Universal is the major subsidiary—takes lunch with Hitchcock and he, like the rest of the world, beats a path to the director's door.

Behind that door one finds a well-ordered world. The director's office is dominated by an extraordinarily large desk with a tooled-leather top. It is extremely neat, with a few trimly stacked papers and perhaps some books of film criticism and theory on it—along with a well-thumbed European railway timetable, which he employs to plan imaginary journeys to exotic places. When he does travel, it is rarely to unfamiliar locales. New York, London, Paris—these are on his beat, but when he goes to them he always stays in the same room in a hotel he has frequented for years and, once ensconced, encourages people to visit him in the hotel so he does not have to chance the streets more than is absolutely necessary. As for the rest of his office furnishings, they combine to give the impression of being modeled on the library of an English country home, or perhaps the writing room of a London club. There is a profusion of leather-covered sofas and easy chairs, breakfront bookcases containing, among other items, the books on which he has based some of his films as well as other mystery and suspense tales he has obviously considered. Across from his desk is a comic painting of Mount Rushmore—site of the famous climax in *North by Northwest*—with Hitchcock's face worked in among the American presidential visages there. Elsewhere in the bungalow are offices—empty when we shot our interview—where writers, production managers and other functionaries can establish themselves when Hitchcock is preparing or shooting a film. The draperies are closed against the California sun, the air-conditioner thrums steadily, and in the world capital of casual attire, the director wears a funereal black suit, a white shirt whose starched collar inevitably starts to curl up by day's end and a conservative narrow tie.

In short, he has gone to every effort to create a serene, stable, *traditional* atmosphere around him. He has done so because, even though he is one of the few film directors who are truly household names, even though he has more control over his career than almost any other director (absolutely free choice over projects, final cut of the finished film), even though he is wealthy, he remains prey to the phobias and fantasies of his childhood. Indeed, it is because he is so closely in touch with them, and because they are to greater or lesser degree common to so many of us, that his films have through the years exercised such consistent mass appeal. Acrophobia, agoraphobia, claustrophobia—these have been recurring motifs in his films from the beginning. And, of course, there is his overriding preoccupation, which is a form of paranoia: Hitchcock has time and again returned to the "wrong man" theme, in which an innocent individual is wrongly accused of some crime and is nightmarishly pursued by the police or some other agency of the state which normally we would turn to in search of peace if not justice, and also by the true miscreants trying to silence him. What makes that preoccupation so compelling to the rest of us is the implication that the protagonist, though he may not be guilty of the crime he has been accused of, is indeed guilty of something. That may not be an indictable offense, it may be (as it is with Tippi Hedren in *The Birds*) only the crime of indifference. Or insensitivity. Or nothing more than membership in the human race, for Hitchcock was raised a Catholic and there is no question that he believes we are all tainted by something like Original Sin. And though he never comments directly on the matter, one can speculate that he believes he is as guilty as the next man of some vague imperfection for which he deserves punishment.

Hence his cautious life-style. Hence the careful way he covers his tracks in his movies, making sure his tormented heroes and heroines are bright and witty and handsome, so that the heavy—not to say tragic—themes of his best work don't spoil our identification with them or interfere with the entertainment values of the pictures. Hence the dazzling yet subtle technique which so entrances sophisticated viewers, who might otherwise speculate more deeply on his meanings. Hence—and this is perhaps the most interesting revelation one gains by spending some time with him—the almost entirely fictional persona he has created for himself: the jolly fat man with the macabre, punning sense of humor.

He put that one over on us when he was host of the *Alfred Hitchcock Presents* television series in the 1950s. An appealing characterization, it served to hide from the public the fact that he is a serious artist who has a craving (constantly checked) to be taken seriously. The problem was, I think, that he calculated that this desire (a perfectly reasonable one, after all) might interfere with the popularity of that art; if people saw that he did not create it in an entirely larkish spirit, they might start to probe a little more deeply and thus find themselves discomfited by films they had taught themselves (with a little help from the master) to take lightly. Certainly, few in the general public—and not many critics outside the film quarterlies—perceived the general darkening of tone in his films once he had left behind the genial little English comedy thrillers and passed through the overdressed, perhaps excessively psychoanalytic, certainly more romantic Selznick phase. However, such great works of the 1950s and 1960s as *Strangers on a Train, Rear Window, The Wrong Man, Vertigo, North by Northwest* and, climactically, *Psycho* and *The Birds* were much more ambiguous, pessimistic and richer in meaning than most of what had gone before. (*Shadow of a Doubt*, which Hitchcock has said is his favorite film, would be the one film of his earlier career that I would rank with these in complexity and ambition.)

Be that as it may, Hitchcock has favored most interviewers from the popular media with nothing more than re-runs of his television personality. On the other hand, he has been exhaustive, and entirely sober, about technique with François Truffaut as well as with scholarly and well-prepared interviewers from the more serious film journals, from whose writing has grown—especially among younger critics and filmmakers—an increasing regard for him as a film artist in recent years. It would appear that he is attending to his "image" with the journalists, his posterity with the students. Happily, he chose to put me and my film crew with the latter group—doubtless because we were representing public television—and so we came away with an interview of considerable duration (thirteen camera rolls) in which he spoke earnestly about technique and, to the limited extent that he chooses to, about his view of the world.

BEGINNINGS

I think it would be interesting to talk about fear and how it first came to one. Psychiatrists will tell you if you have certain sort of psychological problems [and] you can trace them back to, say, your childhood, all will be released. And, of course, I don't believe this to be true at all. If you go back and trace the origins of when you were first scared as a child, I suppose the earliest thing I can think of is when my father, who was a wholesale and retail fruit and greengrocer at the time, sent me with a note to the local chief of police, who glanced at the little piece of paper and then led me along a corridor and I was locked in a cell for five minutes. Then he let me out and said, "That's what we do to naughty boys." I always think it was the clang of the door which was the potent thing— the sound and the solidity of that closing cell door and the bolt. But it hasn't altered the fact, even though I can trace that episode so many years ago, that I'm still scared of policemen. In fact, I don't drive a car on the simple fact that if you don't drive a car you can't get a ticket. I mean, the getting of a ticket, to me, is a rather suspenseful matter.

I think somebody once said to me: "What's your idea of happiness?" And I said, "A clear horizon, no clouds, no shadows. Nothing." But being given a ticket is a cloud on one's personal horizon, and this was brought home very, very forcibly to me when I was at college,* a Jesuit college called St. Ignatius. It may be that I was probably born with a sense of drama because I tend to dramatize things, and at college the method of punishment was rather a dramatic thing. If one had not done one's prep, the form master would say, "Go for three." Well, going for three, that was a sentence, and it was a sentence as though it were spoken by a judge. And the sentence then would be carried out by another element, which would mean a special priest in a special room, with the help of a rather old-fashioned sort of strop for sharpening razor blades, only it was made of gutta-percha, which is a soft black rubber. And the awful part about this to, say, a little boy of ten was that, having been sentenced, it was up to him when he should take it. He could take it at the first morning break, lunchtime, mid-afternoon or the end of the day. And always it was deferred until the end of the day. And then you'd go into this room and the priest would enter your name in a book and then grab the hand that was to be punished and lay this thing in. Never more than three on one hand because the hand became numb and it was no good putting four on the hand because a fourth one you'd never feel it. So then they started on the other hand. And if, by chance, the crime was

* Hitchcock means a prep school, not a university.

so great that you were sent for twelve, I mean, that would be for a terrible crime of some kind, you could have only six a day and then the
other six the following day. Well, this was like going to the gallows. And
the other interesting thing—and one almost compares it with the crowds
that used to watch public executions—was that if one went into this particular room, outside the door a number of the boys would gather and
listen for these loud thwacks and then wait and look to see what kind of
expression the culprit had on his face as he emerged. Yes, they were
voyeurs. But I don't think that when one emerged you were aware of
them, really. That was the least important factor. The most important
factor was this making up your mind when to go, when to have your
head removed, shall we say. I think it's a most horrible kind of suspense.

DEGRADATION AS PUNISHMENT

The degradation really occurs when the persons being charged with an
offense are, for the first time in their lives, removed into a world to which
they've been totally unaccustomed. As I showed in *The Paradine Case*,
the most degrading moment, but it was a true moment, was when the
wardress, the woman guard, went through Alida Valli's hair and put her
fingers through the hair and let it down. This beautifully coiffed head,
you see, already was degraded and reduced. You know, it's like the
medieval sort of stories when a woman is going to have her head chopped
off and the scissors [are] going through the hair to lay bare the neck;
[that] is another degrading moment.

If I may digress while we're on the subject of head removing I read
some long time ago a fascinating story about a Chinese executioner who
was able to wield a sword so skillfully that there was an occasion when a
victim mounted the steps onto a platform and the executioner was
slightly behind him. And the victim said, "Mr. Executioner, please don't
keep me standing here in agony. Why don't you do your work?" And
the executioner said, "My dear sir, please nod your head slightly."

But going back to the degradation thing—I once saw a picture of the
head of the New York Stock Exchange going to jail handcuffed to a
criminal, and by contrasting their clothes and general demeanor it was a
weird thing to see a man of such eminence as this going off to jail.

I've always thought that the handcuff thing was almost a kind of a fetish. If you notice, any press photographer around a courthouse will try and get the picture of the man in handcuffs. There's some strange appeal that it has, and just in the same way the man who is hand-cuffed tries to cover them up. He'll even take his topcoat and hang it over his hands. It's almost a symbol of reduction, as it were, to the lowest form. It's like a chain on a dog, you know? And it's always been, and that's why in *The 39 Steps,* used in a different context as a comedy thing, it nevertheless had a fascinating effect on audiences—the fact that the man and woman were handcuffed together. And it sort of brought out all kinds of thoughts in their minds; for example, how do they go to the toilet was one natural, obvious question. And the linking together is a kind of—I think it relates more to sex than to anything else.

EVIL AS DISORDER, DISORDER AS EVIL

If you take your bourgeois family and then the element of the bizarre comes into it, like one of the members of the family gets into trouble, you can pretty well say that that family—if it all comes out that either the daughter or son is a murderer—that family's life is ruined for good and all. When I was working in the city of London, they had a social club and as part of the activities of the club we were given the oppor-tunity to learn to dance—waltzing or what have you. I suppose I was about eighteen or nineteen at the time, and a middle-aged gentleman taught me to waltz. Three or four years later his daughter [Edith Thompson] was not only arrested as a murderess but was hanged as well. Now the whole family—the mother, the father, the sister—they were practically isolated from society. There's no question that one is very definitely fascinated by this [kind of material] because if one does stories, we'll say, about policemen or about criminals, they're profes-sionals, so there's no—how shall we say?—dramatic counterpoint. Or there is one, but it's not good enough for me. The color contrast is not [the same as] where you have the laymen suddenly placed in a bizarre situation, whether it's people being hijacked in a plane or being in some disaster like the *Titanic.* When I first came to America the film I was going to do was the story of the *Titanic*. And they changed it to *Rebecca*. But I can remember researching the whole of the *Titanic* thing and as I researched it I wanted to epitomize visually what the sinking of this great big ship meant to ordinary passengers and I thought of one idea which might express the whole thing. That would be to show, after you've shown the iceberg rip away under the water—three-hundred-feet-long gash, I think it took—go to the smoke room, you see, because it was about eleven at night, eleven forty it occurred, where men are playing cards. And all I wanted to do was to do a closeup of a glass of Scotch and soda, but the level of the liquid in the glass was slowly changing. And that to me said all I wanted to say: Here are ordinary people playing cards, unaware of what's really happening. How long will it be before they realize? Will a man glance at that glass and see that the level of the liquid is changing? So that really is the prime example of taking the complete bizarre and putting it among the ordinary people.

But this is [another] point. These situations are so familiar that you have to put into them unfamiliar pieces of activity so that it makes the whole of the activity fresh. You can't take [an ordinary] street. That's not enough. But the Statue of Liberty, Mount Rushmore, the Washington Memorial . . . Or, if you like, a chase through the House of Representatives—you see, jumping across the Speaker's desk. I mean, these are the symbols [of order].

Imagine. Imagine the Queen reading the government speech, which she does when she formally opens Parliament in England. She goes to the House of Lords and stands before a throne and she reads a speech written by the Prime Minister of the day. Well, this is all terribly formal. [But] the Members of Parliament, you see, are called to the bar of the House of Lords, they have no seats, they all stand. Well, imagine the Queen reading [and] a voice from the back shouting: "Liar!" It's a dreadful thought; it's lèse majesté, of course. I don't know what the penalty for shouting at the Queen might be, but these [ideas] occur for one because you take symbols of complete order and throw into it the element of disorder.

Evil is complete disorder, although common in practice. I don't think you can say that evil is bizarre, because there are so many gradations of evil. Whether it's filching a small coin, thievery as such, or saying bad things about somebody which are not true. Evil is a pretty, pretty broad spectrum, really.

There was a thing on TV the other day—an interview with two condemned men—they'd murdered six people. There the element of evil was exemplified by their attitudes—the complete lack of remorse, they didn't even apologize. They were almost giggling over it. And that struck me as being the epitome of evil.

But going back—we talked about the House of Representatives and the man jumping up and running around. If you take an average courtroom which is dealing with evil, examining it, processing it, the interesting thing, the contrapuntal thing, is the remark of the usher, and he says, "Order in court." You see. As though it was a special thing, that in court they only had disorder. And I must, to give an example of this, tell you a story that Ben Hecht once told me. He was a famous reporter at the time in Chicago and he was in court and the accused got up and jumped on the bench and stabbed the judge. Well, there was certainly disorder in that court immediately. And the interesting thing was it was such an unusual thing, this piece of evil coming out in the court itself, that everybody was petrified. All the reporters stopped. But Ben Hecht noticed one reporter was scribbling away. No one else had written a thing. And he saw the man call for a messenger and he gave the messenger his copy. And Hecht stole it. And he looked to see what the man had written, with the idea of copying that himself. "The judge has been stabbed. The judge has been stabbed. The judge has been stabbed." It was a repetition of the one sentence. It was a fascinating example of the bizarre.

THE OMNIPRESENCE OF EVIL

There's that scene outside the church in *Shadow of a Doubt** that really at the time gave an indication that the sheltered life in the town of Santa Rosa, where this young girl lived, may have been her world but it wasn't *the* world. Outside there, there were many other things happening. And of course unfortunately, you see, today to a great extent evil *has* spread,

---

* In which Macdonald Carey, as a policeman who has tried to warn Teresa Wright that her uncle, played by Joseph Cotten, may be a psychopathic murderer, attempts to explain to her that the world is more dangerous than she believes.

every little town has had its share of evil. It's like the town near where we live in northern California, Santa Cruz. You would have felt that this was a [quiet] little seaside resort town and yet they had the most bizarre murder. I don't think the man has been sentenced yet, he may have been—killed five people and tied them up and threw their bodies into a pool. Then you go further north in California and there's this man who killed twenty-five farm workers. So we can't say there is somewhere to hide. I would say, you know, if we take a period [around] the turn of the century, before World War I, the world was very placid in many ways. And if one country had a conflict with another, they didn't immediately go to war. They sent a gunboat. And all the gunboat did was to go and anchor off the other country's coast, but not do anything. I think they had a word for it. It was called "gunboat diplomacy." Well, that today would be looked upon as ridiculous because you don't just wag a finger any more and say, "Be careful, other country, or else."

MURDER AND THE ENGLISH

One is often asked, "Why do you have a predilection for crime?" and my answer has always been that that is typically an English thing. The English for some reason seem to have more bizarre murders than any other country, and in consequence literature used to treat crime fiction on a very high level—unlike America, where crime literature is second-class literature. If you go back to Conan Doyle, Chesterton—they were all interested in crime as a source of literature. And I think the British more than anyone else are interested in themselves in this, right up to Agatha Christie. I know that one used to read in the English newspapers of a famous trial in progress at the Old Bailey and among the spectators was Sir George Somebody, a famous actor or a novelist was there. And it's like the moors murders. They had a case where a young boy and a girl kidnapped little children and put them to death and turned on a tape recorder so that the cries of anguish from these children were recorded and they used to play them back. Well, when the trial came on, the famous actor Emlyn Williams was noted to be present at the trial, and another playwright, a woman, Mary Hayley Bell, was noted to be present, and eventually, of course, Emlyn Williams came out with a book called *Beyond Belief.*

There does exist in London today a group called Our Society and they meet every few months above a famous restaurant, in a private room. They have dinner and then go over a previous cause célèbre. And you know who these men are? They are the lawyers in the particular case— both prosecution and defense. Now, they're not satisfied with having practiced the trial in open court and disposed of it, they want to go over it again, they're so interested. Of course, the judge isn't present and it is mainly for the benefit of writers, playwrights and all those sort of people who are their guests for the evening as they rehash the case. They have all the exhibits, photographs and everything. And that strikes me as being, well, so far into the subject that how can you go further except to do a murder yourself?

ON THE CHARACTER OF VILLAINS

One of the main essentials in constructing a story is to make sure that your bad man or your villain doesn't behave like one or even look one. Otherwise, you see, you've taken the line of least resistance, and in reality he can't practice his evil wearing a cap with the word EVIL on it, anymore than a man can be a spy with s-p-y on the front of his cap. You don't know. It's true of me. A lot of people think I'm a monster. They really do. I've been told that they don't care to be associated with me because of the nature of the work one does. And afterwards I've found women say, "Oh, you're nothing like I thought you were." I'd say, "What did you expect?" They'd say, "Well, we thought you'd be very unpleasant and this and that." It happened more than once. I'm talking not about actresses, but responsible women. And with a complete misconception due to the fact that I deal in crime and that kind of thing, while I'm just the opposite. I'm more scared than they are of things in real life.

Most people don't realize that if you have a man like the Joseph Cotten character [in *Shadow of a Doubt*] who's murdered three or four women for their money or jewelry or what have you, he has to be an attractive man. He's not a murderer in the sense of a fiction murderer where the tendency would be to make him look sinister and you'd be scared of him. Not a bit. He has to be charming, attractive. If he weren't, he'd never get near one of his victims. There was a very famous man in England called Haig, known as the Acid Bath Murderer. He murdered about four people and was a dapper, very presentable-looking little man; he could never have committed these murders without being accepted.

Here [in *Shadow of a Doubt*] Uncle Charlie comes to visit the family and his favorite niece, whose name is Charlotte, even called Charlie by the family, and only by terribly slow degrees does the young girl begin to suspect that beloved Uncle Charlie has something strange about him. Why does he cut pieces from the newspaper? And gradually, and almost imperceptibly, it's brought to a climax where they are so close together that she finally goes to the library and sees the item in the paper that he had cut out and this brings it home to her. Then he makes a plea to her when she challenges him. And he nearly wins her over, and the young man—the young detective—in the story, of course, is the direct antagonist to Uncle Charlie. But she can't betray Uncle Charlie because there's the mother to think of, her family must never, never know. So she has to keep this secret to herself and even forbids the young detective to do anything about it until Uncle Charlie makes two attempts on her life and loses his own on the third attempt, after she has really finally persuaded him that he's got to go.

ON ADAPTATION

There are two schools of thought there. One producer I worked for insisted that a novel be followed meticulously, especially if it was a bestseller, because then the public, having read the scene, would want to see it come to life on the screen. And I felt, myself, that when you consider the vast world audience, a best-seller—I don't care how big it is—doesn't reach anything like the same number of people or meet the same conditions as a film. For example, if you take your, say, Japanese market, it's very possible that the novel hasn't reached a Japanese audience. So my instincts are to go first with the visual and not follow the words of the novel. Follow the story line if you like, but retell it in cinematic form. So that you would read the novel, you get a concept of the story and characters and how you'd start to retell it.

That's what makes me often wonder when I read that X, who has written a novel, has been engaged to write a screenplay of his own novel. Now, that's done again and again, and the reason for it is he can get more money that way in selling his book because he or his agent makes it a condition. Now, in truth you're asking a man to be two things—a screenplay writer with a visual sense and a man who is conscious only of words and descriptions. I mean, a man can take a page to describe, we'll say, a scene of the Hawaiian Islands and what they look like at a certain time of the day and so forth. Where he takes a page to do it, the visualist, if we can coin a new word, sees it immediately. It's a photograph, that's what it is. It's rather like certain styles of reproductive painting. A man spends ages painting this picture—faithfully, accurately —and you say, "Why don't you take a color photograph? It's quicker, and you'll get the same result."

So, one reads a book, and, providing all the story elements are there and the characters are there, it's best then to lay the book aside and start with scene one in cinema terms. The rectangular screen in a movie house has got to be filled with a succession of images. And the public aren't aware of what we call montage or, in other words, the cutting of one image to another. It goes by so rapidly that they [the public] are absorbed by the content on the screen. But such content is created on the screen and not necessarily in a single shot.

For example, devising, in a picture like *Psycho*, the murdering and the stabbing of a girl in a bath—in a shower in a bathroom: this scene is forty-five seconds long, but was made up out of seventy-eight pieces of film going through the projector and coming onto the screen in great rapidity. In fact, in the scene itself, the knife stabbing at the camera never touched the flesh of the woman at any time. You went to her face, you went to her feet, you went to the assailant in quick, rapid shots. But the overall impression given the audience is one of an alarming, devastating murder scene.

I would prefer to write all this down, however tiny and however short the pieces of film are—they should be written down in just the same way a composer writes down those little black dots from which we get beautiful sound. So I usually start with the writer long before dialogue comes into it, and I get on paper a description of what comes on that screen. It is as though you ran a film on the screen and turned off all the sound so you would see the images filling the screen one after the other.

These have to be described. If I'm describing the opening, say, of a film like *Frenzy*, it starts this way: The camera is high above the city of London. In the righthand corner is a heraldic arms device with the word LONDON on it. The camera descends lower and lower until it approaches Tower Bridge and the arms of the roadway have opened. The camera proceeds to go through the opening and is lost in a cloud of smoke from a passing tugboat. When the smoke clears, the camera is now approaching the terrace of what is known as County Hall. As it gets near we see a speaker addressing a group of people. Another angle shows that he is being photographed by press people and he is talking about the pollution of the river and how it has all been cleaned up. We then go to a scene of people leaning over the parapet, turning from the speaker and looking down. From their viewpoint, we see a body floating. There are immediate cries, and from another angle we see the whole listening crowd turn from the speaker and all rush to the parapet to look at this floating body.

Now, you see the way I've described it—I've described what takes place. Of course, interspersed with it later will be the speech of the speaker about pollution and there will be cries of the crowd: "Look, it's a body!" Another voice: "A woman!" Another voice: "She's been strangled! There's a tie." Then another voice: "A necktie murder again!" So these are the things that fill out later. But the early description is literally of the action and the picture.

In a sense, I'm bringing the writer into the direction of the picture, letting him know how I'm going to direct it. So we end up with possibly seventy to a hundred pages of description of the film. I have a very strong visual sense, and while I'm going through this process I am absorbing all the visual side of the film. So what happens? By the time that the script is finished and the dialogue has been added, I know every shot and every angle by heart. So when I'm shooting the picture, I very rarely look at the script because I've now by this time learned the dialogue myself. I have to say I am equivalent to, though maybe not so good as, a conductor conducting an orchestra without a score.

I could almost say I wish I didn't have to go on the stage and shoot that film because from a creative point of view one has gone through that process. That's why, you see, I never look through the camera. People say, "You don't look through the camera?" I say, "Why should I? I'm looking at a screen." When we've been putting this thing down on paper, my mind and my eye are on a motion-picture screen. The only reason one would look through a camera is that, having made a request to the cameraman for a shot, he takes it into his head to do something different. In other words, you're checking up to see whether he's lying or not. And it actually happened to me once. In the first version of a picture called *The Man Who Knew Too Much,* I had a German cameraman and I was a most astonished individual when I went to see the dailies or the rushes—the work of the previous day—and found out he'd used different lenses. Applying his own opinions didn't exactly meet the story requirements. So in a light but halting German, I said a few things.

P O V

I'm what they call a purist in terms of cinema, as much as I can be. I'm inclined to go for the subjective. That is, the point of view of an individual, so that visually you do a closeup of him, then you show what he's looking at, then you cut back to the closeup and you see his reaction. The other way is what we call the objective. That's setting the audience to look at the whole action in one. There are a lot of people who believe in that. I use it too. But the picture where pure cinema in the subjective sense was used was *Rear Window.* Here you have a man in one position in one room, looking out. You do a closeup of him—Mr. Stewart —show what he sees. Now you come back to his face and he's reacting. Well, of course, by this process he uncovers a murder situation. This couldn't have been done in any other medium. Certainly not in the theater. It might have been done in a novel, but it would have been a much longer process and without the economy. I did illustrate the power of this kind of treatment when I did the production section for the *Encyclopaedia Britannica.* I said, if you take the man looking, you do his closeup—say it's Mr. Stewart. He looks. And now you cut to what he sees. And you show a woman holding a baby in her arms. Then you cut back to him and he smiles. Now take away the middle piece of film, have his closeup and, instead of cutting to a woman with a baby, cut to a girl in a very risqué bikini. Now you use the same smile, but you've changed him from the benevolent gentleman to a dirty old man only by changing one piece of film. And that is the power of montage.

I haven't done it myself, but I've heard of young directors saying, "I'm going to make the camera be another person," so the camera goes up to the mirror and at the bottom of the screen there's a hand putting on a bow. And you see the face of the man in the mirror. Then the camera moves away and goes all around the room and talks to people, but that's a trick, the camera being a person. You must show the closeup of the person first, then what he sees and how he reacts—that's a subjective treatment. And you can use it in many, many, many ways. I mean, you can do, we'll say, a man falling into the sea. You could do his closeup shooting up and he can be falling. Then you reverse the camera and show what he sees and there's the approaching ocean below. Then back to his face in horror and then you go right into the splash.

It [has always] seemed natural for me to put the audience in the mind of the particular character. You can't do it continually because sometimes the characters get so close together that you'd be looking at a nose. You know, like you go cross-eyed when you are too close to a person. Then you've got to go to the objective. I'll give you an example. In *Frenzy*, when the murder takes place, you see the woman sitting at the desk powdering her nose. She looks up. Now I put the camera where she was sitting and the other man—the murderer—comes in the door, closes the door and wanders around the room. And the camera follows him around, but you intercut that with the girl—the wife in the story— watching him and talking to him. And she's in one position doing that. So the intercut is her head turning and he going until he drops into a chair there. But eventually they do come face to face against the wall. Then I have to go to the objective. I have to detach myself from the woman and look at them both at the same time. Well, she eventually tries to get away, falls on the floor and he throws her into a chair. Now we're back to the subjective again because she in the chair looks up and finds him leering over her. Then you go back to her face again.

DIALOGUE

Obviously, the only thing wrong with the silent film was the fact that people opened their mouths and no sound came out. So when the talking picture came into being, of course, everybody went for talk. And for a time the visual was forgotten. That's why all of a sudden we found that stage plays were being taken from the theater and put into the studio. So dialogue, in a way, took over. The idea—it's almost an impossible thing to achieve—would be to have the dialogue counterpoint to the visual. By that I mean, if you show a girl's face and she's smiling, the dialogue shouldn't be "I am feeling happy," because the words are making the same statement as the girl's face. I achieved [that] once years ago in a film of *Ashenden*—the famous spy of Somerset Maugham. I had the girl, Madeleine Carroll, in a quarrel and tears were streaming down her face. And the man was trying to placate her and she turned to him and she said, "Oh, don't make me laugh!" You see, the words were directly counterpoint to her expression, but unfortunately I think [normally] it would take any writer about three years to work out every line to be in contrast to the visual.

Dialogue carries you along with the scene. But it has to be, in a cinematic film, properly interspersed or overlaid. For example, in *Rear Window* you probably have Stewart looking across through a telescopic lens and making a remark which has some bearing on the activity he's looking at, but you don't see his lips and you don't use his face when he says those words. You lay them over in the scene. Now, I did some other things in *Frenzy* which I've never done before, and this was to use sound dramatically. The absence of it in two cases and making it excessive. For example, when the murderer takes the barmaid up and you know he's going to kill her, I retreat the camera out of the house, across the street and you see the upper windows where the murder is obviously going to take place.

When I say that I'm not interested in content, it's the same as a painter [not] worrying about the apples that he's painting—whether they're sweet or sour. Who cares? It's his style, his manner of painting them—that's where the emotion comes from, same as in sculpture. Any art form is there for the artist to interpret it in his own way and thus create an emotion. Literature can do it by the way the language is used or the words are put together. But sometimes you find that a film is looked at solely for its content without any regard to the style or manner in which the story is told and, after all, that basically is the art of the cinema. And I would like to add that this does not relate to being artistic as such and therefore having an appeal to a very limited, appreciative audience. The whole art of the cinema, it seems to me, is its ability to appeal to a world audience in any language. Therefore, the stress on the pictorial enables you to reach the widest possible audience, whether they be Japanese, Germans, Peruvians, you name it. This always was the power of the cinema.

Now, back in the silent-film days, instead of dialogue, which we couldn't use, we had titles. And the great aim of the silent-picture makers was to be able to tell their story with the minimum of titles. And if [possible] without any at all. So that the whole film from beginning to end was a series of pictorial images. It was achieved in a big picture once only in the history of the cinema, and that was Murnau's *Last Laugh* starring Emil Jannings. That film was about the reverence the Germans had for uniforms and the poor old doorkeeper got too old and was relegated to the men's room. [But] he couldn't go home without the uniform, so he stole it and put it away in a checkroom in a railroad station and wore it home every night. The whole story was done without a single title, without anything. That was the great aim—to reach a complete world audience. I believe that in that film they even invented an imaginary sort of Esperanto language for the advertisements in the street.

THE MACGUFFIN

That really almost is a sidelight on the importance of content. When I made the film *Notorious*, the story was that Ingrid Bergman had to go down, accompanied by Cary Grant, an FBI man, to find out what some Germans were up to in Rio. Among the Germans was an old friend of her father's. Her father had just been sent up for treason. So the question arose, in designing the story for the film, what were the Germans up to down in Rio, what were they doing there? And I thought of the idea they were collecting samples of uranium 235 from which the future atom bomb would be made. So the producer said, "Oh, that's a bit far-fetched—what atom bomb?" I said, "Well, both sides are looking for it." We read of the Germans experimenting with heavy water. Of course they were on the atom bomb. I said, "Look, if you don't like uranium 235, let's make it industrial diamonds. But it makes no difference, it's what we call the 'macguffin.' " What's that? The macguffin is the thing that the spies are after, but the audience *doesn't* care. It could be the plans of a fort, the secret plans of an airplane engine. It's called a macguffin because, as the story goes, two men are in an English train and one says across to the other, "Excuse me, sir, what is that strange-looking package above your head?"

"Oh, that's a macguffin."

"What's that for?"

"That's for trapping lions in the Scottish highlands."

"But there are no lions in the Scottish highlands."

"Then that's no macguffin."

And macguffin doesn't matter at all. You have to have it because the spies must be after something. And I reduced it to its minimum in *North by Northwest* when Cary Grant says to the CIA man, "What is this man after?" The heavy, James Mason.

"Oh," says the CIA man, "let's say he's an importer or an exporter."

"What of?"

"Um, government secrets."

And that's all we have to say about it. We didn't have to show anything. But every spy story must have its macguffin, whether it's microfilm or whether it's hidden in the heel of the shoe of a woman.

Anyway, this story was sent around to several producers. And the film cost $2,000,000 and grossed $8,000,000 and that was in 1945. These two or three producers who had read the script all turned it down because of the uranium. And I met one of them coming back on the *Queen Elizabeth* after the war and he said to me, "By the way, how did you get on to that atom-bomb thing a year before Hiroshima?" I said, "Well, it's self-evident. I mean, there was something going on." So he said, "Well, when we read the script we thought it was the god-damnedest thing on which to base a picture." I said, "There you are, you lost yourself probably $2,000,000."

ATMOSPHERE IN THE CHASE

In chase films what you do get the opportunity to show is a variety of backgrounds; characters on the run and moving are likely to dodge in a doorway. For example, in *The 39 Steps*, Robert Donat, the hero, is arrested in a police station and he flings himself out through the window into the street and it so happens that the Salvation Army band is going by. So he joins the Salvation Army and marches with them until he reaches an alleyway and he dodges down the alleyway and there's an open door and an elderly lady says, "Ah, at last you're here. Come on, this way." And before he knows where he is, he's on a platform at a political meeting and is forced to make a speech. This is what your chase film should be. You got it in De Sica's film *Bicycle Thief*. There the man searching for his bicycle got into a seance, he got into an old persons' home, he got into a crowd outside a football stadium and a tremendous variety of settings.

People have said to me, "What would you like to make as a picture?" I said I'd like to do twenty-four hours in the city, starting at dawn and ending the following morning. And think of the varieties of backgrounds you'd go through, say, in New York or London. Why, you get yourself in the Stock Exchange, you get yourself a couturière's, backstage, boxing matches. In the afternoon you get out to Aqueduct, you have racing in it. You have the food markets in the morning. You probably end with the scows going out to the harbor and emptying their rubbish into the sea and polluting everything. You see, in your chase story, your man is on the run, but each stopping-off point becomes a menace to him. As when Cary Grant in *North by Northwest* goes into an auction room. He's trapped. He can't get out. He only gets out one way and that's by bidding in a crazy way. You know, many is the time we've seen a man on the run dodge into a church, and you get that at the end of John Galsworthy's play *Escape*. He's a convict. The whole theme of the play is whether people will hide him or whether they won't. And he gets into a church and hides in a cupboard and the police get there and they say to the parson, "Is there a man here?" And the parson doesn't know what to say. And the guard says, "Parson, Reverend, on your honor, do you have a man in here or not?" And, of course, the parson is saved by the

The grim silhouette of Tony Perkins in Psycho (*1960*)

Joseph Cotten drowsily scheming in Shadow of a Doubt (*1943*)

Pinned in the wreckage of a carousel, psychotic villain Robert Walker dies as Farley Granger looks on in Strangers on a Train (*1951*).

wanted man stepping out. When you devise picaresque films of this nature, you've got to be pretty original each time you stop off or drive your central character into a setting. It could be, you know, into a hospital, into a girls' school. I mean, there are innumerable places he can go. You get that at the end of *Strangers on a Train*. Chasing after a man into a midway on a fairground. The man gets onto a merry-go-round and then there's a fight on the merry-go-round. And you get all the excitement using your artifacts of the midway.

Imagine if part of the escape or the chase got onto a freight train. Now you begin to examine—what does a freight train carry? Cattle? Can you imagine the two poor people—a boy and a girl who are on the run—getting into a van [and being] nearly crushed to death by cattle climbing over their backs and so forth? Or it might be carrying a load of automobiles. So what will they do there? They get up and they make love in an automobile high up while it's being carried by the train. There are tremendous possibilities if you examine all these things. If you take ordinary things, you see, you get into things like the beginning of *Topaz*. You have a whole scene at the Royal Copenhagen works—delicate china which is interesting to look at. And what I do there is to show the process of how they paint the flowers on the china and so forth. And yet there are overtones—unspoken overtones—of the sinister going all through it. You could do it in a bakery. It's the event rather than the setting, the situation, which carries for the audience the contrast [between the] normality of the setting and the situation in which you put it. This is far removed, as you can see, from what I call the creaking-door type of film or what the novelists call the Gothic. You know, you go upstairs and the old latch is undone and—well, you're back to *Frankenstein* then. The nearest I [have come to that, I] would say, is the girl's walk around the house in *Psycho*. Not because the house itself is essentially so Gothic. Actually, it was a very accurate house. There are hundreds of these houses in northern California. We call them California Gingerbread. It's the added fact that somewhere in this Victorian-looking house is a menacing figure with a knife. The audience know it, but they don't know where she's going to pop out. You can do it in a modern house, providing—providing—that the audience know that in this innocent-looking house death may appear at any minute.

The California Gingerbread type of house helps the atmosphere—a rather cheesy motel. But what do we have? We have a girl who has stolen $40,000, all of a sudden, out of the blue, attacked in a shower by a woman with a knife. Now, this is such a shock because we have been leading the audience along the lines of $40,000 stolen. But suddenly the twist and the shock is this thing in the shower. From that point on the audience's mind is full of apprehensions, but as the film went on, you got less and less violence on the screen.

There was one quick murder after the shower, but no more in the rest of the picture. But because there were no more, the audience got itself worked up to expect more. To sum it up, you are transferring the menace from the screen into the mind of the audience. And it increased to a point where, with the girl going around the house, it became unbearable to them, until you reach your climax.

SUSPENSE VS. MYSTERY

All suspense, you see, or audience preoccupation is based on knowledge. The word "mystery" often creeps into [descriptions of my movies, but] they're not mysteries. The essential fact is, to get real suspense, you must let the audience have information. Now, let's take the old-fashioned bomb [plot]. You and I are sitting talking, we'll say, about baseball. We're talking for five minutes. Suddenly a bomb goes off and the audience have a ten-second terrible shock. Now. Let's take the same situation. Tell the audience at the beginning that under the table—and show it to them—there's a bomb and it's going to go off in five minutes. Now we talk baseball. What are the audience doing? They're saying, "Don't talk about baseball! There's a bomb under there! Get rid of it!" But they're helpless. They can't jump out of their seats up onto the screen and grab hold of the bomb and throw it out. But one important factor: if you work the audience up to this degree, that bomb must never go off and kill anyone. Otherwise, they will be extremely angry with you.

I made a mistake in an early film by having a long bomb-suspense thing and I let the bomb go off and kill a little boy. I remember I was at the press show and a very sophisticated press woman came at me with raised fists and said, "How dare you do that? I've got a five-year-old boy at home." And she was furious with me. What must happen is that a foot must touch it and they say, "My God, it's a bomb! Pick it up and throw it out of the window." The moment it's out of the window, off it goes. But we inside are all safe and sound.

Sometimes the audience have no feeling for the victim, but they want [the thief] not to be caught. You see, it's the eleventh commandment—thou shalt not be found out. For example, supposing there's a burglar in a bedroom stealing jewelry from a woman. The woman has gone out, but suddenly she comes back and comes in the front door. What does the audience say? "Quick, burglar—get out, get out. You'll get caught."

In *Frenzy* you have the man in the potato truck. You see, you build up all the suspense—will he get the tie pin out of the girl's hand in time before he's caught? So we show the truck stopped a couple of times, he hides, and eventually he achieves it. But we're rooting for him all the time to get that tie pin back.

WHY DON'T THEY
CALL THE POLICE?

Cary Grant on the run in *North by Northwest* is an innocent victim. But in the United Nations he pulls a knife out of a man's back. He holds it and looks at it and everybody in the room points to him. Now, the very thing he ought to do, he can't do—go to the police. Because the police are after him [because of the U.N. incident]. We had that in *39 Steps*. Exactly the same situation. So, you see, really, going to the police would end the picture and then it would be a piece of logic which would be very dull. So the story is devised in such a way that he can't go to the police.

[One] situation [like that] would be a spy behind enemy lines—he doesn't know where he can go. I once had a thought that might be an interesting situation—to have a spy, with all papers perfect in every way, parachuted down into Russia. Speaks Russian fluently, everything impeccable. As the door opens for him to parachute out, the little uniformed sergeant with him falls as well, and when the spy lands with the parachute in the Russian countryside, he's got with him a man who cannot speak Russian, wearing a uniform. What is he to do, kill him? So there you have a real dilemma. It's not enough merely to have every hand against him—he's got an encumbrance now. Incidentally, I've never solved that one.

You pigeonhole certain ideas, you know. It's like the one I tried to get into *North by Northwest:* to get into Detroit and have two men walk along an assembly line and the camera goes with them. But in the background is just the frame and you actually see a car go together. And when it gets to the end of the line, all batteries are in, gasoline is in, everything's dried and they drive it off. And one of these two men goes off and opens the door of this newly assembled car and a dead body falls out. And yet we've been watching this thing go together to a detail—but I haven't worked that one out yet. Mount Rushmore was in the pigeonhole for fifteen years before I ever used it [in *North by Northwest*]. The Statue of Liberty* is, you know, to me an obvious one. I've often thought to have a scene behind the clock face of Big Ben and that famous bell toll while the men are in there. Then, suddenly, somebody looks up and sees the hands changing the time or something.

I AM AN AMERICAN

I'm actually American-trained because the first job I ever got inside a studio was in London, when Paramount were opening studios in different parts of the world. They opened one in London, I think one in Paris and even one in India. Well, I got a job in the editorial department of the London studio—and they imported everyone from Hollywood. When you went in that door, you might as well just be in Hollywood, because everyone—cameramen, directors, actors and actresses—were all from Hollywood. And being in the editorial department or the script department, that's where I learned to write scripts—from American writers.

I always admired the technical superiority of the American film. As a

* Used as the setting for the climax of the chase in *Saboteur.*

matter of fact, it was interesting when I made my first film—that was in Munich, Germany, in 1925—the producer came over from London and ran the film. And he came out and he said, "Well, it doesn't look like a Continental film. It looks like an American film." I said, "What did you expect it to look like?" He said, "Well, you know, typical Continental." And I remember the first film I worked on as a writer—not [as] the director, but [as] writer and art director—was reviewed by a leading London paper and the headline was "Best American Film Made in England." And, of course, the influence wasn't the director, it was me designing the sets and writing the script that way, because the director had never been to America.

Basically, the design of [my] early English pictures was almost instinctive. There was less calculation in terms of an audience. It's when I came to America that I became more aware of audiences. And then as one went on, the question came up of (a) avoiding the cliché in my type of material and (b) trying to avoid the repetition of the same situations. And the only way to avoid it is through character: you can have a murder story as a murder story, but by whom? I mean, whom do you choose as a character to participate? And that's where the difference comes.

SHADOW IN A SMALL TOWN

Shadow of a Doubt was one of those rare occasions when a film was to be laid in a small town, so the writer, Thornton Wilder, and I went and stayed in the town, lived in it, got to know the people, got to know the rent of the house where they were living, and came back and wrote the script based on the people and nature and character of the town itself. I always remember, we had a scene with Teresa Wright where she ran across the street and had to speak to a policeman. She ran in front of traffic and the policeman admonished her for it. Of course we had to have an actor for that. So we stood the actor in the middle of the intersection, but the real policeman on the site said, "Look, the traffic's piling up. Tell your actor to let some of the stuff through." He did and then the real policeman says, "All right. Tell him to stop and let some pedestrians across." And he did. A pedestrian—a woman—went up to the policeman and said, "Could you tell me the way to so-and-so?" and she mentioned the street. The actor said, "I'm sorry, I'm a stranger here myself."

The leading character, the heavy, Joseph Cotten, gets killed in front of a train. And we staged his funeral right in the main square of the town at that intersection. It was fascinating to see the whole cortege slowly moving around the main square, then down the side street. We were photographing it with two cameras. And we had a few extras, not many, but all the town's people, who never saw the cameras [because] they were concealed, solemnly took their hats off as the empty coffin went by.

THE BIRDS

What you have in *The Birds* is a kind of overall sketchy theme of everyone taking nature for granted. Everyone took the birds for granted until the birds one day turned on them. The birds had been shot at, eaten, put in cages—they'd suffered everything from the humans and it was time they turned on them. Now there was no repulse. The hero was helpless against them, because they were a collective army. That's why we had an opening which was very lightweight, frivolous, expressing the thought that everybody too easily takes life for granted. The girl's a cocktail-party-going girl with not much upstairs—she's frivolous, well-to-do, and suddenly she gets a dose of nature which pulls her up and everyone else as well. I would say the theme of *The Birds* is don't mess about or tamper with nature. Look, man's fooled around with uranium 235 out of the ground and look where it's brought us. And he's just taken uranium 235 for granted, it's a nothing. But it's plenty. Now, who knows?—it's feasible in the year 3000 or 4000 for all the animals to have taken over. After all, we've had the clearest example of the prehistoric animals who have become extinct. Who knows that man may not end up the same way? He'll be regimented. I mean, brains will be controlled—that's inevitable. Who knows? The brains of the birds may improve. I know that in making *The Birds* we had some extremely clever ravens—answered to their names, pick up cigarettes and matches, do any-thing we wanted, no problem.

A PSYCHOLOGICAL MACGUFFIN

Marnie is about a fetish. A man wanted to go to bed with a thief. There was a case—horrible case—in England, I think it was about seven or eight years ago, where a one-armed woman sued a woman with one leg for the alienation of her husband's affections. This went before the English law-courts. And of course, to everyone's astonishment, it turned out that the husband was the real culprit. He had a penchant for maimed women. And the case was thrown out of the courts.

So *Marnie* is about a man who wanted to marry—or marriage came afterward, but he wanted to go to *bed* with a woman whom he knew to be a notorious thief. She tries to uncover the secret [of why she steals compulsively], but I don't think that does much good. I'm sure that even though they went off to get married, she'd probably steal his nightshirt on their wedding night.

There were script problems. It wasn't the opportunity for the comedy I would have liked, because the worst scenes were the girl going to the psychiatrist, [though] they were quite comic in their way.*

ON THE FUNCTION OF HUMOR

Irony usually takes the form of a joke. You know, it's like the opening of *Frenzy*. Here's a man talking about the purity of the water, of the Thames River, no pollution, and along comes a body floating. Well, there's a complete irony there, but it's comic irony. At the same time, it's making a plot point: there are necktie murders going on in London.

I think in suspense an audience wants to have a little relief and change of pace and a lark if necessary. But, you see, again in *Frenzy*, you get

---

* These scenes did not survive the final cut and were never shown to the public.

the wife of the inspector talking over the plot with her cooking and his problems of having to stomach her cooking. But, really, the audience are being nursed along. Petted and worried about so that they laugh while pieces of plot are being thrust into their minds. But we deal with them gently. And in understatement. Understatement.

Let's go back to my early days at school when I feared physical punishment. Lo and behold, I go into the room one day—I know it sounds [as if] I was always going in for punishment. That isn't true. But on one occasion I went in and, of course, there was my favorite priest, my friend. And he shook his head and said, "This isn't nice, is it?" I said, "No, Father." And he took the hand and he let the instrument just drop on it. Very touching, of course. But—oh, all understatement. I'm all for understatement. The stronger the situation, it becomes stronger by the understatement. You see, the world today is full of brutality, but, more than that, [it has kind of] developed into brutality with a smile. It's worse than brutality. You know, it's coming in, pointing a gun at a man and saying, "I'm sorry, but I'm afraid I'm going to have to take your money. I hate doing this because my father always said one shouldn't steal." BANG! He shoots. 'Course that's a horrible situation because he's talking in reasonable terms. Not "Stick 'em up." That's not it. [For example,] the killing of the German in a farmhouse [in *Torn Curtain*]. I wanted to show that without a gun and without a knife it's a very difficult thing to kill. The woman stabbed the man and the blade broke. She couldn't fire the gun because there was a taxi driver outside. She tried hitting his knees with a spade, and eventually, of course, she thought of the gas oven. And having got him on the ground, [there was] this terribly slow process of putting the German's head into the gas oven and holding it there. And one couldn't help think that here we are back at Auschwitz again and the gas ovens. But the main purport of the scene —I remember I was in Paris and I was listening to the BBC and I heard a film man say, "You know, it's only lately I realized what Hitchcock was after. He was trying to show us how difficult it was to kill a man. I thought it was just intended to be a brutal scene." It was awkward and clumsy, but difficult, you see.

HEROINES

I've often been asked why I choose what people seem to call "cool blondes." I think the blonde, really, stems from the tradition of the cinema, whose first heroine was a curly-headed blonde named Mary Pickford. And thereafter she became a symbol of the heroine. I personally object to the blondes who wear their sex round their neck and it hangs in front of them like oversized jewelry. And I've always felt that you should try and discover in the course of your story whether the woman is sexy or not. For example, in the film *To Catch a Thief* I kept cutting to Grace Kelly in profile, very still and not much expression until Cary Grant sees her up to her room. And suddenly, in the doorway, she turns and plunges her lips onto his. Bowls him over completely. The cool blonde does give you somewhat of a surprise if she does turn out to be very sexy. In the main, I would say that the sexiness in women is somewhat geographical. I feel the Scandinavian women are more sexy than the southern European women. I would say that the Englishwoman is more sexy. The southern Europeans, the Italians, the French women, you know, they wear black on Sunday. You mustn't mistake gaieté parisienne for sexy girls doing the can-can. I think if you look at the Swedish-type or the Norwegian-type women in Swedish films they're fairly, I won't say plain, but they're not what you call glamorous girls. And yet they betray on the screen an acute, sharp sense of sex. I sometimes feel that a lot of American women are rather like the southern European women. They talk sex. The magazines advertise sex. And they seem to make a lot of it. And yet, if a man approaches one, it's possible she'll run screaming for Mother.

MAN'S INHUMANITY TO MAN

You're deliberately making things difficult because you demonstrate to an audience that you can be trapped in a crowd and turn to your neighbor and say, "Look, there's a man coming after me!" and nobody in the crowd would believe you. It's the same old thing—people don't want to be getting tangled with others in trouble. We have it in *Frenzy*—here are two people who could give the man an alibi, but not they, they're too human. They want to get out of it, not be involved. And it's the same if you were to rush up to anybody in the street and say, "Quick, quick, where's a policeman? A thief is chasing after me." The people look around and they say, "I'm sorry," and they walk away, they don't want to get involved.

What was the old saw by Robert Burns? "Man's inhumanity to man makes countless thousands mourn." He must have had some reason for saying that. It's a dogfight. I think money has a lot to do with it. It's a dogfight all the time. In my career, I run up against political situations time and time again. I became a director entirely because a particular cameraman had curried favor with the director and the director said he didn't want me on his next picture. It was then I was asked would I like to be a director, which hadn't occurred to me. I was maneuvered deliberately away from my job and I knew who it was and how it was done. It happens in our business all the time. I used to say, "Well, one thing they can't take away from me is my talent." You see, I have a very strong objection to hatred. I feel that hatred is a wasted energy. There's nothing good can come out of it. And I think one of the silliest phrases you can ever hear is to hear somebody say, "I'm going to give him a piece of my mind." Now what good does that do? All you've done is to make an additional enemy. The hardest thing to get anyone to say is, "I'm sorry, it was my mistake." People don't do that. They get mad and they say, "I'm going to get that so-and-so if it's the last thing I do." But the admission of error is a hard thing to come by. And that's why I say I don't hate anybody, I really don't. Maybe if somebody does me wrong, I just turn my back on them. And that may even be crueler, I'm not sure. I'm pretty well a loner. I don't get involved with conflicts. I don't see the point of it. Not even to the point of getting a ticket for parking.

SUMMING UP

Generally speaking, I would say that first of all, possibly from the age of fifteen, I was a devotee of film. I mean, I didn't read fan magazines at the age of fifteen or sixteen, I read trade papers. So I used to be aware of the making of films and was determined to get into them eventually. I didn't want to get in as a director. It didn't occur to me that I would be a director of films. I just wanted to be a part of it. And the earliest days I was in the editorial department and then did assistant-director work on the stage on "crowd days," as they called them then.

This, coupled with one's reading habits, which veered toward the adventurous. I don't mean Robert Louis Stevenson, but—say, Sherlock Holmes and then, of course, John Buchan, who wrote *The 39 Steps*, *Greenmantle* and many famous English [spy] books. They were very elegant, and of course they were very, very descriptively written. And the hero was inevitably the adventurer—preferably, the gentleman adventurer. I think Buchan's work was a tremendous influence on me. Then, in another direction there was a famous woman writer, Mrs. Belloc Lowndes. It was her story *The Lodger* which became my first English-made picture.

I remember there was a period when I was learning to write scripts— I fought terribly hard, [but] I could not understand how the various cuts went together. It seemed almost like a blank wall to me. Then one day, all of a sudden, I discovered it. And then I learned cutting. And out of that, of course, learned the pure cinema.

Having started to write, I became involved with the German film industry, which in its day was the greatest—even greater, from an artistic standpoint, than Hollywood. I mean, they were making films like *Siegfried* and the *Ring* operas and all of [Emil] Jannings' films. And I became tremendously influenced by them.

My style was influenced [by] the German—angles of photography, the visual ideas. And it was the visual ideas that began to come to one very, very instinctively. There was no sound in those days. And in the film *The Lodger*, which was about Jack the Ripper, I even show him going out at night, shot from above a big staircase with a continuing handrail. And all you saw was a white hand going down. This, I would say, is almost oblique. And I suppose it's part of one's mentality that one is driven toward the oblique. Not to do the obvious. To avoid the cliché. And gradually—I suppose it's the religious training—the general theme became the triumph of good over evil. And that maintains itself even to this day, actually.

And so it goes on, and so the next film, obviously, will have to be a crime film, not necessarily a murder film. It will have to have humor. But, most of all, it's got to have some fresh background. And where that will be I don't know. It may be in the kitchen of a hotel, it may be on the assembly line in Seattle where Boeing are building 747s. Think how nice it would be: the interior would be the young lady and her lover seated in two unfinished seats, with aluminum walls and an empty background, making love.

INDEX

Richard Schickel was the movie critic at LIFE *from 1965 until its demise in 1972. He currently reviews films, television and other matters for* TIME. *Mr. Schickel produced the television series* THE MEN WHO MADE THE MOVIES *in 1973; it was named one of the year's outstanding television programs by* THE NEW YORK TIMES *and nominated for an Emmy. He is the author or coauthor of thirteen books, among them the highly acclaimed* THE DISNEY VERSION, HIS PICTURE IN THE PAPERS *and* THE STARS. *Mr. Schickel has written extensively for many periodicals, and has been a lecturer in the history of art at Yale University. He also has held a Guggenheim Fellowship. He lives in Manhattan with his wife, Julia Whedon, the novelist, and their two children, Erika and Jessica.*